Cloud Cost Optimization Handbook for AWS

Collection of ideas and best practices for saving on cost in AWS

Copyright © 2019 by Qinlin Luo and Ernesto Ruy Sanchez

All rights reserved. No part of this publication may be reproduced, distributed, or transmitted in any form or by any means, including photocopying, recording, or other electronic or mechanical methods, without the prior written permission of the publisher, except in the case of brief quotations embodied in critical reviews and certain other noncommercial uses permitted by copyright law. For permission requests, please visit:

https://CloudCostOptimizationHandbook.com

eBook:

    ISBN-13: 978-0-578-52995-0

    ISBN-10: 0-578-52995-5

paperback:

    ISBN-13: 978-0-578-52996-7

    ISBN-10: 0-578-52996-3

Table of Contents

Chapter 1. Get Started with AWS Account Setup 14
   1.1 Introduction 15
   1.2 AWS Account Structure Considerations 15
   1.3 AWS Account Initial Configuration Checklist 17
   1.4 Summary 18

Chapter 2. Measure, Analyze, and Control AWS Cloud Cost 19
   2.1 The Cloud Economics 21
      2.1.1 Introduction 21
      2.1.2 Total Cost of Ownership 22
      2.1.3 Summary 25
   2.2 Understanding AWS Pricing 26
      2.2.1 Introduction 26
      2.2.2 Estimate the Cost of Amazon EC2 27
      2.2.3 Estimate the Cost of Amazon S3 27
      2.2.4 Estimate the Cost of AWS Lambda 28
      2.2.5 Estimate the Cost of Amazon EBS 28
      2.2.6 Estimate the Cost of Amazon RDS 28
      2.2.7 Estimate the Cost of Amazon DynamoDB 29
      2.2.8 Estimate the Cost of Amazon CloudFront 29
   2.3 Overall Cost Optimization Strategies 30
      2.3.1 Introduction 30
      2.3.2 Start Early 30
      2.3.3 Start with AWS Trusted Advisor 32
      2.3.4 Promote a Culture of Cost Transparency, Ownership and Accountability 35

- 2.3.5 Start with the Largest Expenditure Categories 37
  - 2.3.5.1 Get to Know AWS Bills 38
  - 2.3.5.2 Compute 39
  - 2.3.5.3 Storage Costs 40
  - 2.3.5.4 Databases 41
  - 2.3.5.5 Optimize EBS Volumes and EBS Snapshots with DLM 42
  - 2.3.5.6 Identify Big Expenditure with Cost Explorer 43
  - 2.3.5.7 Export Billing Data to Excel 43
  - 2.3.5.8 Analyze and Control the Biggest Expenditure Items 44
- 2.3.6 Follow AWS Well-Architected Framework - Cost Optimization Pillar 44

2.4 Measure AWS Cloud Costs 46
- 2.4.1 Introduction 46
- 2.4.2 Establish a Cost Baseline and Measure the Change 46
- 2.4.3 Select What to Measure: by Tags, Teams, or Business Units 47
- 2.4.4 Link Costs to Business Outcomes - Revenues, Goods, and so on 47
- 2.4.5 Measure Costs by the Progress Made 47
- 2.4.6 Measure Efficiency 48
- 2.4.7 Summary 48

2.5 Analyze AWS Cloud Costs 49
- 2.5.1 Introduction 49
- 2.5.2 Analyze Costs with AWS Cost Explorer 50
- 2.5.3 Analyze AWS S3 Inventory Data 58
- 2.5.4 Top Five S3 Inventory Reports for AWS S3 Cost Optimization 59
  - 2.5.4.1 Report #1: Summary Reports of All Buckets 59

    2.5.4.2   Report #2: Top Ten Top-Level Prefixes by Size 59

    2.5.4.3   Report #3: Top Ten File Types by Size 60

    2.5.4.4   Report #4: Six-Month-Old Objects Summary Report 61

    2.5.4.5   Report #5: Twelve-Month-Old Objects Summary Report . 61

  2.5.5   Summary 62

2.6   Control AWS Cloud Costs 62

  2.6.1   Introduction 62

  2.6.2   Create a Plan 63

    2.6.2.1   Set a Target 63

    2.6.2.2   Define the Approaches 64

    2.6.2.3   Define Roles and Responsibilities 68

    2.6.2.4   Define the Milestones 68

    2.6.2.5   Evaluate the Risks 69

    2.6.2.6   Communicate Adequately 70

    2.6.2.7   Celebrate Each Achievement 71

  2.6.3   Iterate and Develop the Feedback Loop 71

  2.6.4   Create Policies for Using AWS Resources 72

  2.6.5   Summary 73

Chapter 3.   Optimize the Cloud Cost Multipliers 75

3.1   Introduction 76

3.2   Cloud Cost Multipliers 77

3.3   Time Multiplier 80

  3.3.1   Optimize the Time Multiplier 81

    3.3.1.1   Hours to Consider 83

    3.3.1.2   Days to Consider 83

    3.3.1.3   Months to Consider 84

  3.3.2   Questions to Ask to Optimize the Time Multiplier 85

- 3.3.3 Things to Consider to Optimize the Time Multiplier 86
- 3.3.4 The Checklist to Optimize the Time Multiplier 88
- 3.3.5 Summary 89
- 3.4 Environment Multiplier 89
  - 3.4.1 Introduction 89
  - 3.4.2 Things to Consider to Optimize the Environment Multiplier 90
- 3.5 Capacity Multiplier 91
  - 3.5.1 Introduction 91
  - 3.5.2 Things to Consider to Optimize the Capacity Multiplier 92
- 3.6 Chapter Summary: Cloud Cost Multipliers 92

Chapter 4. Optimize Baseline Costs 94
- 4.1 Introduction 95
- 4.2 Optimize EC2 Baseline Costs 96
  - 4.2.1 Introduction 96
    - 4.2.1.1 Dedicated Hosts and Instances 97
    - 4.2.1.2 On-Demand Instances 97
    - 4.2.1.3 Spot Instances 97
    - 4.2.1.4 Reserved Instances 98
    - 4.2.1.5 Standard Reserved Instance 98
    - 4.2.1.6 Convertible Reserved Instance 99
  - 4.2.2 Choose the Right Type and Size 99
  - 4.2.3 On-Demand Instances or Spot Instances 100
    - 4.2.3.1 What Workload Is Appropriate to Run on Spot Instances? 102
    - 4.2.3.2 Architect Applications to Run on Spot Instances 102
    - 4.2.3.3 How to Maximize the Utilization of Spot Instances 103
  - 4.2.4 Reserved Instances 105

- 4.2.4.1 Introduction 105
- 4.2.4.2 Defining RIs 106
- 4.2.4.3 The Instance Attributes Related to RIs 106
- 4.2.4.4 Consolidated Billing and RIs 107
- 4.2.4.5 Standard RIs 107
- 4.2.4.6 Convertible RIs 108
- 4.2.4.7 Scheduled RIs 109
- 4.2.4.8 Things to Consider When Purchasing RIs 109
- 4.2.4.9 How to Maximize RI Utilization 113
- 4.2.4.10 Effect of RIs 114
- 4.3 Use Serverless Architecture or Managed Services 114
  - 4.3.1 AWS Managed Services 115
  - 4.3.2 Serverless Architecture 116
- 4.4 Choose a Free OS Platform 118
- 4.5 Choose a Free Database Software 119
- 4.6 Leverage Nonstandard S3 Storage Classes 121
  - 4.6.1 Four Main Classes of S3 Storage 121
  - 4.6.2 Cost Savings over Standard Storage Class 122
  - 4.6.3 Identify Candidate Objects for Standard IA and One Zone IA 123
  - 4.6.4 Standard Vs. Standard IA - the Optimization Model 124
  - 4.6.5 Save Data Transfer Costs with AWS Snowball 129
- 4.7 Avoid Creating Multiple Copies of the Same Objects 129
- 4.8 Use AWS Select 132
- 4.9 Consider Business or Enterprise Support Contract 134
- 4.10 Chapter Summary 135

Chapter 5.   Optimize Cloud Costs with 10 Step-by-Step Implementations 137

    5.1   Introduction 139

    5.2   Implementation #1: How to Estimate the Monthly AWS Cost, Save It and Share It.. 140

        5.2.1   Introduction 140

        5.2.2   Instructions 140

        5.2.3   Summary 149

    5.3   Implementation #2: How to Set Up AWS Budget Alerts.............. 150

        5.3.1   Introduction 150

        5.3.2   Give Teams Permissions to Create Budgets........................ 151

        5.3.3   Create a Budget and an Alert to Monitor EC2 Costs by Project 152

        5.3.4   Create a Usage Budget to Monitor S3 GET Object Requests 163

        5.3.5   Create a Reservation Budget and an Alert for RI Utilization of a Project 170

        5.3.6   Summary 176

    5.4   Implementation #3: How to Implement a Schedule to Start and Stop an EC2 or RDS Instance 177

        5.4.1   Introduction 177

        5.4.2   Auto Start and Auto Stop Using Tags 177

        5.4.3   Auto Start and Auto Stop Using AWS Instance Scheduler .. 178

        5.4.4   Things to Consider When Implementing Auto-Start and Auto-Stop Schedules 179

        5.4.5   Summary 181

    5.5   Implementation #4: How to Implement S3 Lifecycle Policies for AWS Cost Optimization 182

        5.5.1   Introduction 182

5.5.2	Lifecycle Policies and Cost Optimization	182
5.5.3	A note on Multipart Upload:	183
5.5.4	Lifecycle Policies Implementation	184
5.5.4.1	Move Objects from Standard to Standard IA after 30 Days.	184
5.5.4.2	Archive Objects to Glacier After Sixty Days	190
5.5.4.3	Delete Objects and Their Versions After Ninety Days	191
5.5.4.4	Archive Objects to Another Region Using CRR	193
5.5.5	Things to Consider When Adding Lifecycle Rules	202
5.5.6	Summary	202
5.6	Implementation #5: How to Implement Data Lifecycle Management	204
5.6.1	Introduction	204
5.6.2	Create a Snapshot Lifecycle Policy	205
5.6.3	Things to Consider When Implementing DLM	215
5.6.4	Summary	216
5.7	Implementation #6: How to Tag AWS Resources for Cost Optimization	218
5.7.1	Introduction	218
5.7.2	The Benefits of Tagging in Cost Optimization	219
5.7.3	Cost Allocation with Tags	219
5.7.4	How to Tag AWS Resources	222
5.7.5	Get Billing Data by Tags Using AWS Cost Explorer	228
5.7.6	Get Data Using AWS Cost Explorer API	236
5.7.7	Summary	236
5.8	Implementation #7: How to Monitor RI Utilization and RI Coverage	237
5.8.1	Introduction	237

5.8.2	RI Coverage	238
5.8.3	RI Utilization	240
5.8.4	Reservation Summary	242
5.8.5	Reserved Instance Recommendation	244
5.8.6	Summary	245

5.9 Implementation #8: How to Set Up and Use AWS Athena for Cost Optimization 246

5.9.1	Introduction	246
5.9.2	Data Gathering and Data Analysis with AWS Athena	247
5.9.3	AWS Athena as a Managed Service	252
5.9.4	Collect Billing Data in S3 Bucket	252
5.9.4.1	Create S3 Bucket to Store the AWS Billing Report Data	253
5.9.4.2	Create an AWS Billing Report to Send Billing Data to an S3 Bucket.	255
5.9.4.3	Get to Know the Billing Data in the S3 Bucket	262
5.9.4.4	Set Up for Athena Query	264
5.9.4.5	Use Athena to Analyze Billing Data	265
5.9.5	Identify Cost-Saving Opportunities with AWS Athena	269
5.9.6	Areas of Improvement	270
5.9.7	Summary	272

5.10 Implementation #9: How to Set Up and Use AWS S3 Inventory for AWS Cost Optimization 273

5.10.1	Introduction	273
5.10.2	AWS S3 Inventory and Cost Optimization	274
5.10.3	Set Up S3 Inventory for an S3 Bucket	275
5.10.4	Grant Permissions	276
5.10.5	Configure S3 Inventory	277

5.10.6 Use Athena to Query S3 Inventory Data 282

    5.10.6.1 Obtain Permissions to Run Athena Queries on S3 Inventory Data.. 282

    5.10.6.2 Create S3 Inventory Reports Using Athena Queries ... 284

    5.10.6.3 Verify Athena Output Data with AWS S3 Metrics 289

5.10.7 Archive Inventory Data 291

5.10.8 Summary 296

5.11 Implementation #10: How to Set Up and Use AWS S3 Server Access Logging for AWS Cost Optimization 298

    5.11.1 Introduction 298

    5.11.2 Enable S3 Server Access Logging 299

        5.11.2.1 Create a Bucket to Store S3 Access Logs 299

        5.11.2.2 Enable Server Access Logging 303

        5.11.2.3 Content of the Access Log File 307

    5.11.3 Use Athena to Query Data in the Server Access Logs 308

        5.11.3.1 Obtain Permission to Run Athena Queries on S3 Access Logs 308

        5.11.3.2 Create S3 Access Reports Using Athena Queries 310

    5.11.4 Summary 316

5.12 Chapter Summary 318

Preface

Purpose

The purpose of this handbook is to share our experiences and knowledge acquired while implementing different cost-saving strategies and tactics to optimize and control AWS (Amazon Web Services) Cloud expenses on an enterprise at scale.

Use this handbook as a quick reference guide for best practices and considerations for using AWS resources in a cost-effective way.

Audience

The intended audiences for this handbook are:

- AWS users
- AWS billing managers

Limitations

This handbook is not a one-size-fits-all guide or general check list for saving on cost. Each organization has its unique business needs and technical challenges that need to be considered.

The information in this handbook is limited to our conclusion and opinions based on research and learning experiences acquired during our careers as of the date of publication, which is subject to change, and may evolve over time.

Chapter 1. Get Started with AWS Account Setup

1.1 Introduction

This chapter explains what to consider when building a structure to manage multiple AWS accounts using AWS Organizations.

There are several AWS Cloud-specific concepts that you need to be familiar with for this chapter to be effective for your organization:

- AWS Billing
  - Cost Explorer
  - AWS Budgets
  - AWS Cost and Usage Reports
    - EC2 Instance Usage Report
    - EC2 Reserved Instance Utilization Report
    - AWS Usage Report
  - AWS Cost Allocation Tags
  - Consolidated Billing
  - AWS Organizations
  - Preferences
  - Credits
- AWS Organizations
  - AWS Child Account
  - Service Control Policy (SCP)

For purposes of this chapter, we will assume that you have already registered and created at least your primary AWS account.

1.2 AWS Account Structure Considerations

To be able to organize your AWS accounts, you need to know the answers to these questions:

- Who are the users of AWS, and what are their Cloud resource needs?
- How do I want to control access to Cloud resources?
- How do I want to visualize my AWS costs?
- How do I organize by service / resource type / account (using AWS Cost Explorer)?
- How do I organize by company department / project (using cost allocation tags)?

If you intend to allow access to AWS resources to a diverse user base with different needs, you can consider departments or projects: either keep everyone on the same account, or create a child account per department or project.

If you create a primary AWS account and child AWS accounts using AWS Organizations, you will have the ability to apply Service Control Policies (SCPs) to control the services to which child accounts have access.

If you enable Consolidated Billing on your primary AWS account, this account becomes the payee account for all child accounts, which means you will still receive individual detailed billing information per account, but AWS will issue only one invoice on the main account.

Don't forget that although you get the service control flexibility and detailed billing information per account, there are some considerations.

For example, if you create multiple AWS accounts, user management and access control can become complex; thus, we recommend considering cross-account access.

If you intend to use the VPC service with private subnets on your child accounts, you have to think about the number of NAT instances you have since you will have to pay for each one; behind the scenes they are just managed EC2 instances. You may also end up having to peer your VPC across different accounts if you want to access services privately between accounts. To save costs on peering and NAT instances on more complex networking architectures review the AWS Transit Gateway service.

1.3 AWS Account Initial Configuration Checklist

This is an opinionated check list to review your initial AWS account configuration to ensure that it is set up properly. This information will allow you the ability to analyze and control your AWS billing information:

1. Make sure you activate the IAM user and role access to billing information. This can be found in the "My Account" section, accessible in the top right corner under your AWS account name. This is only available when you are logged in as the account owner or root and not as an IAM user.

2. Make sure you have created an AWS budget with billing alarms to receive alerts when current or forecasted expenditures meet certain criteria.

    LINK: Implementation #2: How to Set Up AWS Budget Alerts

3. Make sure you add the cost allocation tags that you decided you want to use to group AWS resources and calculate expenditures.

    LINK: Cost Allocation with Tags

4. Make sure to update your billing preferences. You should at least enable "Receive PDF Invoice by Email" and "Receive Billing Reports on an S3 bucket". Check your desired granularity. This will help further analyze the bill.

5. Create an S3 bucket to store detailed billing information for Analysis.

    LINK: Collect Billing Data in S3 Bucket

6. Create an AWS Cost and Usage Report for QuickSight or Athena.

    LINK: Use Athena to Analyze Billing Data

1.4 Summary

The outcome of this chapter should be a well-defined AWS accounts structure using AWS Organizations.

Chapter 2. Measure, Analyze, and Control AWS Cloud Cost

This chapter explains Cloud economics, and the TCO (Total Cost of Ownership) of using AWS Cloud. This chapter also covers cost optimization strategies. Finally, you will learn how to measure, analyze, and control AWS Cloud costs.

2.1 The Cloud Economics

2.1.1 Introduction

The AWS Cloud offers high capacity, flexibility, and ease of deployment. The AWS Cloud also offers tremendous opportunities for faster execution, lower total cost of ownership, and increased agility.

Faster execution:

> AWS provides on-demand infrastructure to run your business applications without operating your own data center. You acquire infrastructure very quickly. For a startup, this means faster-to-market for your product development. As an enterprise, you innovate more, expand faster, and gain competitive advantages for your products and services.

Lower total cost of ownership:

> In addition to the time savings, AWS also saves you money since it is pay-as-you-go. Pay-as-you-go lowers the barrier to trying new ideas for a startup or for an enterprise.

Automation and agility:

> As Cloud adoption continues to accelerate, Cloud infrastructure management tools emerge every day. With Docker it becomes easy to create, deploy, and run applications by using containers. With Kubernetes, containers are orchestrated to run clusters of nodes at scale in a more efficient manner.
>
> There are also Continuous Integration / Continuous Deployment (CI/CD) tools such as Jenkins, Teamcity or Bamboo that fully automate the deployment process. Ansible,

Chef, or Puppet helps you manage configurations. Boto3 is the AWS SDK for Python.

The new trend in micro-services, such as AWS Lambda, requires no server infrastructure. The cost of AWS services is thus further reduced.

These tools, most of which are open source and free, integrate your development and operations (DevOps) seamlessly. The Cloud infrastructure saves you time and money. It may be the only option for some of the new generation of software and applications.

AWS Cloud offers so many benefits. The usage of AWS Cloud resources and services may increase quickly inside an organization. The seemingly cheap resources and services become expensive without proper management and control.

Some organizations create a cross-functional team, such as Cloud Center of Excellence, to manage and optimize Cloud infrastructure.

2.1.2 Total Cost of Ownership

The AWS TCO (Total Cost of Ownership) calculator tells you the total cost of the infrastructure, and compares it to on-premises or colocation costs to determine the cost savings.

https://awstcocalculator.com/

For example, you have twenty VMs for websites and web applications, six VMs for SQL Server Standard, plus 500 TB of HDD storage. Enter these parameters into the following screen:

Select Currency					United States Dollar			
What type of environment are you comparing against?					● On-Premises	○ Colocation		
Which AWS region is ideal for your geo requirements?					US East (N. Virginia)			

Servers

Are you comparing physical servers or virtual machines?   ○ Physical Servers   ● Virtual Machines

Provide your configuration details:

Server Type	App. Name	Number of VMs	CPU Cores	Memory(GB)	Hypervisor	Guest OS	DB Engine
Non DB	Website	20	4	64	VMware	Linux	
DB	backend	6	8	32	VMware		SQL Server Sta

Total no.of VMs: 26

Storage

Provide your storage footprint details

Storage Type	Raw Storage Capacity		% Accessed Infrequently	Disk Type
SAN	500	TB		HDD

Figure 2.1: AWS Total Cost of Ownership - TCO Calculator - Inputs

Next is the TCO comparison of AWS and on-premises:

Figure 2.2 AWS TCO Calculator - Results

The following figure details the cost breakdown:

Figure 2.3 AWS TCO Calculator - Results - Cost Breakdown

2.1.3 Summary

Getting the TCO and ROI (Return On Investments) is one of the first steps to planning a migration to the Cloud. The AWS TCO Calculator makes it easy for you. However, it is a very rough calculator. When you evaluate whether a project or service should be in the Cloud or on-premises, you should get more information on what you need; then calculate the TCO and ROI.

2.2 Understanding AWS Pricing

2.2.1 Introduction

AWS pricing is different for every service and changes over time. This is what makes it complex and challenging.

There is an entire white paper dedicated to this subject, which is updated from time to time:

https://aws.amazon.com/whitepapers/how-aws-pricing-works/

If you are getting started with AWS, check out the details of their AWS Free Tier to determine which services you can use for free. Keep in mind that some services will expire in twelve months, at which time you will be charged for them.

Besides time, there are three main components that will drive your AWS bill:

- compute
- storage
- outbound data transfer

Each of these three main components consists of one or more AWS services.

Although each AWS service is priced differently, we provide the cost estimation considerations for some of the most important AWS services.

Please note that this is just a quick overview of the cost components of each service. We will provide the details later when we discuss the cost optimization strategies and execution.

LINK: Implementation #1: How to Estimate the Monthly AWS Cost, Save It and Share It

2.2.2 Estimate the Cost of Amazon EC2

According to the AWS white paper, you have to consider the following when you estimate the cost for EC2:

- clock hours of server time
- instance type
- pricing model
- number of instances
- load balancing
- detailed monitoring
- auto scaling
- elastic IP addresses
- operating system and software

2.2.3 Estimate the Cost of Amazon S3

Understanding the different storage classes and lifecycle policies to automate moving data from one storage type to another over time is the key to optimizing costs. Consider the following to estimate the cost of S3 service:

- storage object count and size
- storage class

- requests
- data transfer

To estimate costs on Amazon Glacier, you need to understand:

- data access time
- data retrieval cost per GB
- retrieval request cost

LINK: Leverage Nonstandard S3 Storage Classes

2.2.4 Estimate the Cost of AWS Lambda

The AWS Lambda cost estimation is based on the number of requests and the time the function takes to run.

2.2.5 Estimate the Cost of Amazon EBS

To estimate the cost of EBS volumes, consider the following:

- volume size
- snapshots
- data transfer

2.2.6 Estimate the Cost of Amazon RDS

Review the following items to estimate the cost of your RDS resources:

- clock hours of server time
- database characteristics
- database purchase type
- number of database instances
- provisioned storage
- additional storage
- requests
- deployment type
- data transfer

2.2.7 Estimate the Cost of Amazon DynamoDB

Consider the following to estimate the cost of DynamoDB tables:

- provisioned throughput (write)
- provisioned throughput (read)
- indexed data storage
- data transfer
- global tables

2.2.8 Estimate the Cost of Amazon CloudFront

To estimate the cost of CloudFront services, consider the following:

- traffic distribution
- requests
- data transfer out

2.3 Overall Cost Optimization Strategies

2.3.1 Introduction

There is no silver bullet for saving cost on AWS. The strategies that will work for you depend on the stage of your company and the workloads you run on the Cloud. What is for sure is for the Cloud Cost Optimization efforts to work it requires discipline, consistency, and use of tools.

2.3.2 Start Early

Starting early is one of the most important practices when optimizing AWS Cloud costs. When you utilize best practices early in the process, whether for a new project or a new organization, your journey to minimize costs will be easier.

This is why we positioned the chapter of "Get Started with AWS Account Setup" at the beginning of the book.

Starting early helps you establish the correct processes and behaviors very early on. Some mistakes are bound to happen, but the earlier they occur, the less costly they become.

Account setup:

> LINK: AWS Account Structure Considerations
>
> LINK: AWS Account Initial Configuration Checklist
>
> You can set up multiple accounts for an organization. For example, you can have a "master" account as the primary account for the

general audience, a "dev" account for software developers, a "prod" account for the production environment, or a "vendor" account for vendor-related AWS resources.

Multiple accounts allow you to isolate resources and group resources for administrative controls.

Multiple accounts allow the most visibility of costs by business units or functional teams.

Multiple accounts allow the consolidation of billing and maximize volume discounts.

Building a team:

Create a cross-functional team with members of the Finance team with knowledge of the budget and experience in procurement, and with members of the Cloud Operations teams in charge of provisioning and maintaining the AWS Cloud resources.

Project kickoff meeting:

Include the best practices of using AWS resources in your project kickoff plans.

Create cost awareness by presenting the best practices to engineers or anyone who might launch or use AWS resources.

Tell each member of the team what to do and what not to do during the project to keep the costs down.

New employee orientation:

Create a course or presentation and make it part of your employee on boarding process. Create the culture of frugality. Instruct new employees to be cost conscious when it comes to using the AWS Cloud.

LINK: Promote a Culture of Cost Transparency, Ownership and Accountability

Provide each new employee with the corporate policy on using AWS resources if you have one.

Share the lessons learned in AWS cost overrun.

Architecting for cost:

When an application has been deployed, cost optimization after the fact could be very challenging. It may be too late to optimize the cost, or the payoff of the optimization may not be economical.

Teams should be empowered to architect for cost as early as possible.

For example, some applications, if architected correctly, can be run on Spot Instances instead of the much more expensive On-Demand Instances.

2.3.3 Start with AWS Trusted Advisor

If you just get started with AWS Cloud cost optimization, you will likely be able to decrease your AWS bill quickly and easily. These easy cost-saving opportunities may easily be identified with AWS Trusted Advisor.

AWS Trusted Advisor checks under-utilized AWS EC2 instances, unattached EBS volumes, unassociated elastic IP addresses, idle load balancers, and so on.

When you launch the AWS Trusted Advisor, the first item on the dashboard is "Cost Optimization." This item tells you three things: the number of problems detected, the number of investigations recommended, and the number of actions recommended.

Figure 2.4: AWS Trusted Advisor Dashboard

When you click on the "Cost Optimization" icon above, you will see "Cost Optimization Checks." Now you can explore all the checks.

▶	**Low Utilization Amazon EC2 Instances**
	Checks the Amazon Elastic Compute Cloud (Amazon EC2) instances that were running at any time during the last 14 days and alerts you if the daily CPU utilization was 10% or less and network I/O was 5 MB or less on 4 or more days.
▶	**Idle Load Balancers**
	Checks your Elastic Load Balancing configuration for load balancers that are not actively used.
▶	**Underutilized Amazon EBS Volumes**
	Checks Amazon Elastic Block Store (Amazon EBS) volume configurations and warns when volumes appear to be underused.
▶	**Unassociated Elastic IP Addresses**
	Checks for Elastic IP addresses (EIPs) that are not associated with a running Amazon Elastic Compute Cloud (Amazon EC2) instance.
▶	**Amazon RDS Idle DB Instances**
	Checks the configuration of your Amazon Relational Database Service (Amazon RDS) for any DB instances that appear to be idle.
▶	**Amazon Route 53 Latency Resource Record Sets**
	Checks for Amazon Route 53 latency record sets that are configured inefficiently.
▶	**Amazon EC2 Reserved Instances Optimization**
	Checks your Amazon Elastic Compute Cloud (Amazon EC2) computing consumption history and calculates an optimal number of Partial Upfront Reserved Instances.

Figure 2.5: AWS Trusted Advisor - Checklist and recommendations

Cautions:

> Before you clean up the idle, unused or underutilized resources, be sure to talk to the owner of those resources.
>
> There may be legitimate reasons to keep the idle resources running. For example, an idle load balancer may be idle temporarily for quick deployment next time. A detached EBS volume is kept so that when it is needed, it can be quickly re-attached to an EC2.

Note that you can monitor Trusted Advisor check results with Amazon CloudWatch events to detect and react to changes in the status of Trusted Advisor checks. CloudWatch Events can be used to invoke one or more target actions when a check status changes to the value you specify in a rule you create.

For details, please check:

https://docs.aws.amazon.com/awssupport/latest/user/cloudwatch-events-ta.html

Another opportunity for cost optimization is to check the AWS resources on the development environment.

Such resources may be stopped at nights and on weekends. Please check more details:

LINK: Time Multiplier

LINK: Implementation #3: How to Implement a Schedule to Start and Stop an EC2 or RDS Instance

2.3.4 Promote a Culture of Cost Transparency, Ownership and Accountability

Unlike the traditional IT operations which are centralized in cost and decision-making, the Cloud environment is quite decentralized. Many teams are allowed to launch AWS resources at any time.

Here are some ways to promote a culture of ownership and accountabilities.

<u>Create cost visibility for teams:</u>

When teams know how much they are spending, or how much they are expected to spend, they are more cost conscious. When they are cost conscious, they tend to consider the cost implications of their decisions.

Teams are often surprised at how much they spend when they look at their AWS bills. Therefore, grant teams access to AWS Cost Explorer. If this is not possible, send the AWS billing reports to teams at least once a month.

Teams can also use AWS Budgets to get alerts on incurred and forecasted costs.

Create AWS Budgets per tag to alert a team when they are over their forecasted budget.

LINK: Implementation #2: How to Set Up AWS Budget Alerts

LINK: Implementation #1: How to Estimate the Monthly AWS Cost, Save It and Share It

Promote the value of efficiency and frugality:

As illustrated in the "Cloud Cost Multipliers" section, an insignificant $0.85 per hour is equivalent to $7,445 per year.

When an AWS resource in the development environment is not needed on the weekend, shut it down for the weekend.

Encourage teams to save.

Establish a baseline for an application or a team.

Set a target for savings. Celebrate the achievement of hitting the target.

Discourage any unnecessary spending, such as keeping AWS resources running when they are no longer needed.

Train teams in cost optimization:

Empower individuals and teams with the knowledge and tools they need to optimize the costs.

Train individuals and teams to tag their own resources properly.

Cost optimization is everyone's responsibility.

Remove or lower the barriers to the change process:

Change process requires some time to review and approve the changes.

Time is a big cost multiplier. If a change takes too much work or takes too long to implement, the cost-saving potential will not be fully realized. It may not even be possible at all when teams become discouraged or frustrated by the change process.

Tag AWS resources:

Tagging the AWS resources makes teams accountable for managing their own resources. The cost can be allocated by tags. Cost reporting can be grouped by tags.

LINK: Implementation #6: How to Tag AWS Resources for Cost Optimization

2.3.5 Start with the Largest Expenditure Categories

AWS provides over one hundred products in twenty service areas. The list keeps growing. The starting point of your cost optimization efforts is to review the top spending categories on your AWS bill.

2.3.5.1   Get to Know AWS Bills

AWS bills under "Billing & Cost Management" give you the estimated cost for the current billing cycle and the actual billing amount for the previous billing cycles after the AWS bills are finalized.

On the Web Console, you can view your AWS billing details by service or by account.

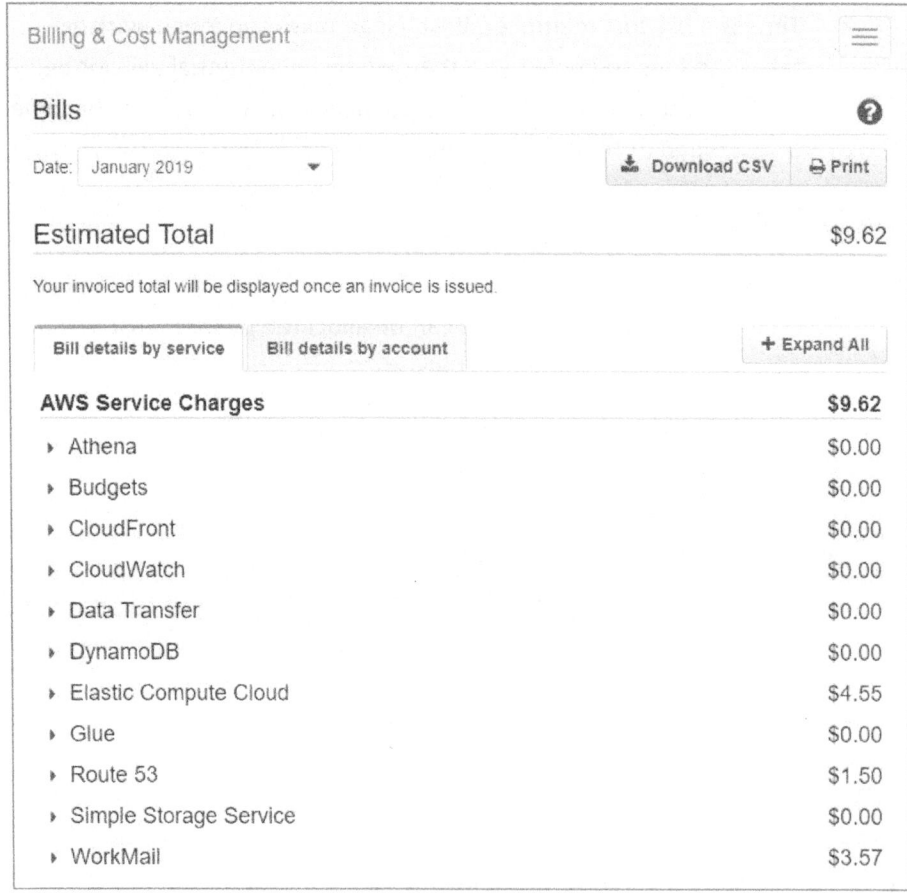

Figure 2.6 AWS bill details by service

With AWS bill details by service, you can see the cost of each service.

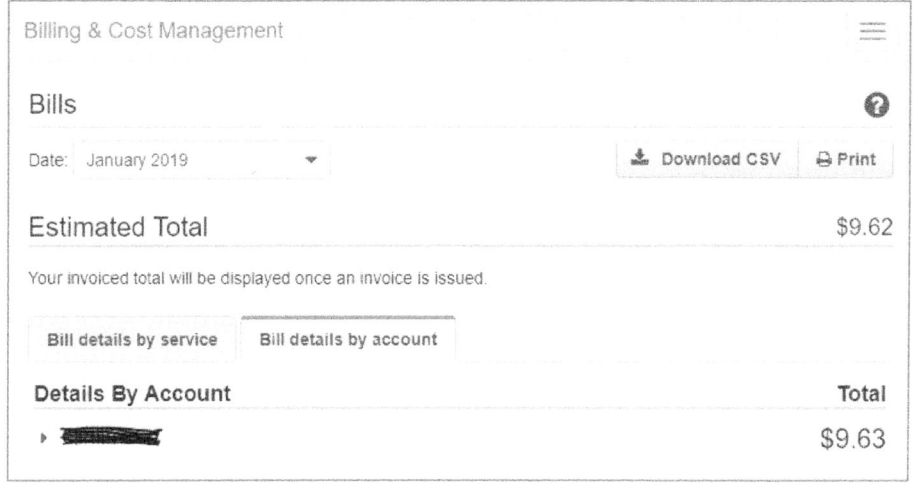

Figure 2.7 AWS bill details by account

With AWS bill details by account, you can see the costs of all accounts. Then you can click on each account to see the details by service for that account.

In many organizations, the biggest expenditure items are compute, storage and data transfer.

2.3.5.2   Compute

Compute costs are mostly listed under "Elastic Compute Cloud" on your AWS bill. Compute costs are the usage of EC2 instances, EBS storage, networking and data transfers, and so on.

▸ DynamoDB		$0.00
▾ Elastic Compute Cloud		$4.55
▾ **US West (Oregon)**		**$4.55**
Amazon Elastic Compute Cloud running Linux/UNIX		$3.84
$0.0058 per On Demand Linux t2.nano Instance Hour	662 Hrs	$3.84
EBS		$0.71
$0.10 per GB-month of General Purpose SSD (gp2) provisioned storage - US West (Oregon)	7.118 GB-Mo	$0.71
▸ Glue		$0.00
▸ Route 53		$1.50

Figure 2.8 AWS bill details by service - EC2

2.3.5.3 Storage Costs

Storage costs are generally listed under "Simple Storage Service" on your AWS bill. Storage costs are the cost of S3 storage and the cost of data transfers.

▼ Simple Storage Service		$0.00
▼ US East (N. Virginia)		$0.00
Amazon Simple Storage Service Requests-Tier1		$0.00
$0.005 per 1,000 PUT, COPY, POST, or LIST requests	4 Requests	$0.00
Amazon Simple Storage Service Requests-Tier2		$0.00
$0.004 per 10,000 GET and all other requests	1,252 Requests	$0.00
Amazon Simple Storage Service TimedStorage-ByteHrs		$0.00
$0.023 per GB - first 50 TB / month of storage used	0.016 GB-Mo	$0.00
▼ US West (Oregon)		$0.00
Amazon Simple Storage Service USW2-Inventory-ObjectsListed		$0.00
$0.0025 per 1 million objects listed in S3 Inventory	9 Objects	$0.00
Amazon Simple Storage Service USW2-Requests-Tier1		$0.00
$0.005 per 1,000 PUT, COPY, POST, or LIST requests	288 Requests	$0.00
Amazon Simple Storage Service USW2-Requests-Tier2		$0.00
$0.004 per 10,000 GET and all other requests	102 Requests	$0.00
Amazon Simple Storage Service USW2-TimedStorage-ByteHrs		$0.00
$0.023 per GB - first 50 TB / month of storage used	0.038 GB-Mo	$0.00

Figure 2.9 AWS bill details by service - S3

2.3.5.4 Databases

Database costs are generally listed under "RDS Service," "SimpleDB" and "DynamoDB" on your AWS bill. Databases are centered on RDS instances and the AWS managed services, such as DynamoDB. The Relational Data Services include RDS for MySQL, PostgreSQL, SQL Server, Oracle, and Aurora (with MySQL or PostgreSQL).

▾ DynamoDB		$0.00
▸ US East (N. Virginia)		$0.00
▾ US West (Oregon)		$0.00
Amazon DynamoDB		$0.00
$0.00 per hour for 25 units of read capacity for a month (free tier)	6,640 ReadCapacityUnit-Hrs	$0.00
$0.00 per hour for 25 units of write capacity for a month (free tier)	6,640 WriteCapacityUnit-Hrs	$0.00
Amazon DynamoDB USW2-TimedStorage-ByteHrs		$0.00
$0.00 per GB-Month of storage for first 25 free GB-Months	0.000121 GB-Mo	$0.00

Figure 2.10 AWS bill details by service - DynamoDB

2.3.5.5 Optimize EBS Volumes and EBS Snapshots with DLM

EBS costs are usually significant and may be a large part of your cost optimization effort.

DLM (Data Lifecycle Management) automates the snapshot creation with snapshot lifecycle policy.

Please check here to find one way to optimize EBS volumes and EBS snapshots:

LINK: Implementation #5: How to Implement Data Lifecycle Management

2.3.5.6 Identify Big Expenditure with Cost Explorer

AWS Cost Explorer - Explore Cost and Usage is another quick way to identify the biggest expenditure items.

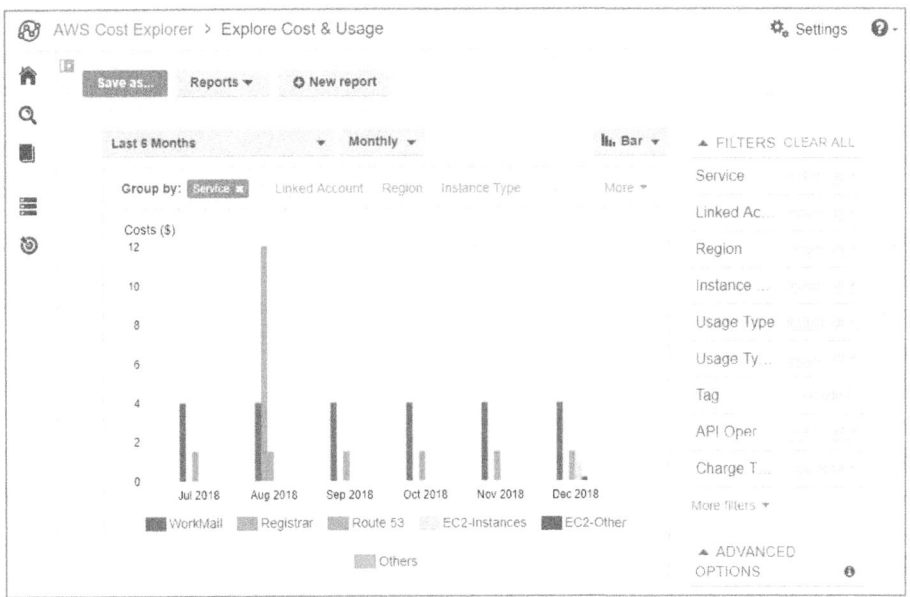

Figure 2.11 AWS Cost Explorer - Exploring Cost and Usage

This graph illustrates the service with the greatest cost. You can drill down further using the filter on the right. You will see how to use Cost Explorer in other sections of this book.

2.3.5.7 Export Billing Data to Excel

Excel is the best friend of an accounting professional. When he or she dumps all the billing data into Excel, a lot can be done to analyze that data. One approach that has worked every time is sorting all the items by dollar amount in the descending order. Pick anything over perhaps

$500. Send the relatively short list to the owners of the AWS resources.

The owners have a short list of items to focus on. They check the resources, evaluate each item, and come back with a list of opportunities to improve.

2.3.5.8 Analyze and Control the Biggest Expenditure Items

Once you have identified the greatest expenditure items, you can analyze them and identify opportunities to optimize costs in that area.

The rest of this book provides plenty of tools to help you optimize costs.

2.3.6 Follow AWS Well-Architected Framework - Cost Optimization Pillar

AWS Well-Architected Framework provides guidance and best practices on how to architect systems to be run on the Cloud. It is based on five pillars:

1. Operational Excellence
2. Security
3. Reliability
4. Performance Efficiency
5. Cost Optimization

Cost Optimization pillar provides guidance and best practices on how to architect systems that most effectively use AWS services and resources at minimal cost.

This book covers Cost Optimization pillar comprehensively. Not only does the book provide the cost optimization framework but it also provides practical implementation and step-by-step guides for best practices.

One example of architecting for cost optimization is how to architect your application to run on Spot Instances.

LINK: 5.2.2.4 Architect Applications to Run on Spot Instances

LINK: 5.3 Use Serverless Architecture or Managed Services

For more details on AWS Well-Architected Framework, please visit:

https://aws.amazon.com/architecture/well-architected/

2.4 Measure AWS Cloud Costs

2.4.1 Introduction

How will you measure AWS Cloud costs?

How will you know whether you still have room for cost optimization?

What is the next goal for cost savings?

In this section, you will find ways to measure your progress and the success or failure of your outcome.

2.4.2 Establish a Cost Baseline and Measure the Change

It is essential to know how much you have saved in your cost optimization efforts and where you are with regard to your goal.

The baseline could be the cost of your previous month if your use of AWS resources is relatively predictable month to month.

The baseline could be the cost of the previous iteration. For example, if the cost of the previous AI model training is $100,000 for three months, that could be your baseline for the next AI model training.

The baseline could be the average cost per product, per customer, per $1,000 revenue, and so on.

The baseline could be your own KPIs (Key Performance Indicators) and business metrics.

Pick a baseline and stick to it.

2.4.3 Select What to Measure: by Tags, Teams, or Business Units

When you create metrics to measure your cost optimization outcome, ask yourself how much granularity you want.

If you're just getting started with cost optimization, start from the top level, such as teams or departments.

As you progress, create more advanced and granular metrics. This is one of the benefits of tagging every AWS resource with the cost associated with it. If you have consistent and reliable tags, your metric could be quite granular.

2.4.4 Link Costs to Business Outcomes - Revenues, Goods, and so on

If your AWS costs are positively correlated with your revenues or other business outcome, a metric such as "cost per $1,000 revenue" is a good measure of your cost optimization efforts. As your revenues grow, so do your AWS Cloud costs. You can determine whether costs are increasing proportional to revenue growth.

2.4.5 Measure Costs by the Progress Made

When the workload of a project is not evenly distributed across more than one period, you may measure the cost by the progress being made.

You might launch a big data project to analyze the weather data for the last fifty years across the world. This project has a cost of $20,000 for this month and is 20 percent completed.

Using this month as the baseline, we know that the cost of 1 percent of the workload is $1,000.

If we made another 30 percent progress next month, the cost would be expected to be $30,000. Any deviation from this amount represents a savings or over-spending. If the actual cost is $50,000, we know the spending is out of control and merits some explanation.

2.4.6 Measure Efficiency

You may measure cost by efficiency - how much you spend for the same output.

An example is a machine learning with medical images.

Last month, you processed 100,000 medical images for a total of $5,000 in compute costs. The processing cost per medical image is $0.05.

This month you processed 150,000 medical images for a total of $6,000 in compute costs. The processing cost per medical image is $0.04, which is 20 percent less than in the previous month. This is an improvement.

2.4.7 Summary

Each company is different. Each project is different.

Choose the right metrics to measure your cost optimization efforts.

Be consistent in your choices.

The purpose of these metrics is not merely to monitor the cost of AWS resources. Teams are quite motivated by these metrics too.

The ups and downs of your monthly AWS bill may not tell the whole story. Be ready to dive into the details, and choose the right metrics to explain the changes.

2.5 Analyze AWS Cloud Costs

2.5.1 Introduction

AWS billing data tells you where every penny is spent. You might see over ten million line items for a $500,000 monthly invoice.

The billing data is stored in a designated S3 bucket.

This is great for a data engineer who wants to dig deep into the data.

This is not so great for a finance manager who lacks the time and knowledge to query the data.

AWS has created a number of ways to let you visualize and analyze the billing data. Cost Explorer is the most useful and powerful tool.

Then there is AWS QuickSight, an Amazon business intelligence tool. You can use AWS QuickSight to visualize the raw billing data in the S3 bucket.

You can use your company's own Business Intelligence tools, such as Tableau and PowerBI, to analyze the billing data. However, the raw billing data may have to be loaded into a database first. One huge benefit of using Tableau is that a lot of financial managers already know how to use Tableau, rendering it a viable option in an enterprise environment.

If you don't spend a great deal on AWS, Excel is always a very good option. You can export billing data into Excel and analyze the data there.

2.5.2 Analyze Costs with AWS Cost Explorer

The first tool for most of us is AWS Cost Explorer. It is free and it is powerful. You don't need much knowledge to play with the billing data.

Go to AWS Console. In the upper right corner, click on your name, then "My Billing Dashboard."

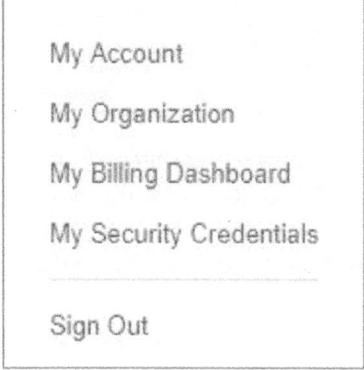

Figure 2.12: Launch "My Billing Dashboard."

If you don't see "My Billing Dashboard," you may not have permission to see the billing data. Please ask your admin to grant you that permission.

Here is an example of such a policy to allow IAM users to access the reports console page:

```
{
  "Version": "2012-10-17",
  "Statement": [
    {
      "Effect": "Allow",
      "Action": [
        "aws-portal:ViewUsage",
        "aws-portal:ViewBilling"
      ],
      "Resource": "*"
    }
```

```
    ]
}
```

Click on "Cost Explorer" on the left, then "Launch Cost Explorer."

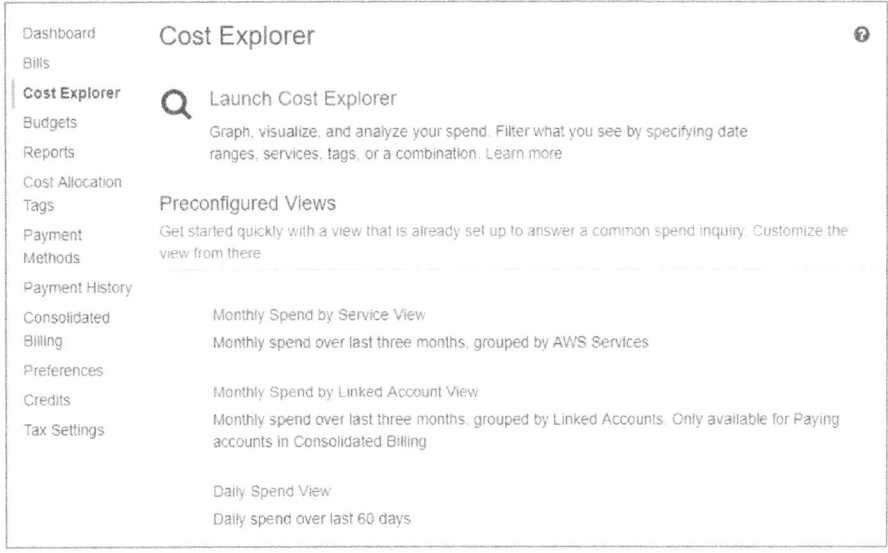

Figure 2.13: Launch Cost Explorer

Now you see the default view of your Cost Explorer, which is "daily unblended costs" with month-to-date costs and the forecasted month-end costs for the current month.

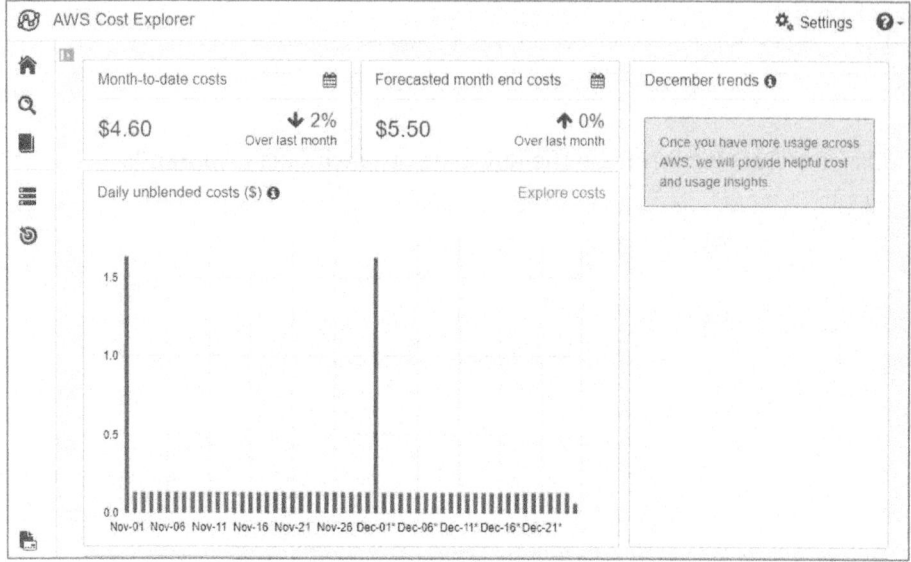

Figure 2.14: AWS Cost Explorer - Main

Click on "Explore costs" it the upper corner of the chart.

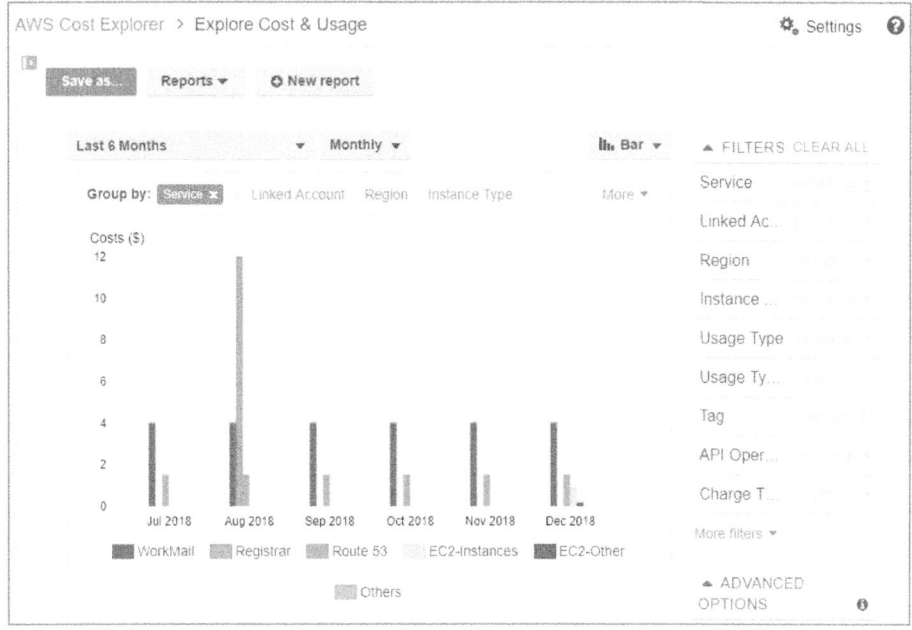

Figure 2.15: AWS Cost Explorer - Explore Cost & Usage

By default, the report shows the monthly spending by services for the last six months.

Now you can add filters on the right. For example, if you only see the cost related to S3 storage, click on "Service" under "FILTERS" on the right, and select "EC2-Instances (Elastic Compute Cloud - Compute)"; then click on "Apply filters."

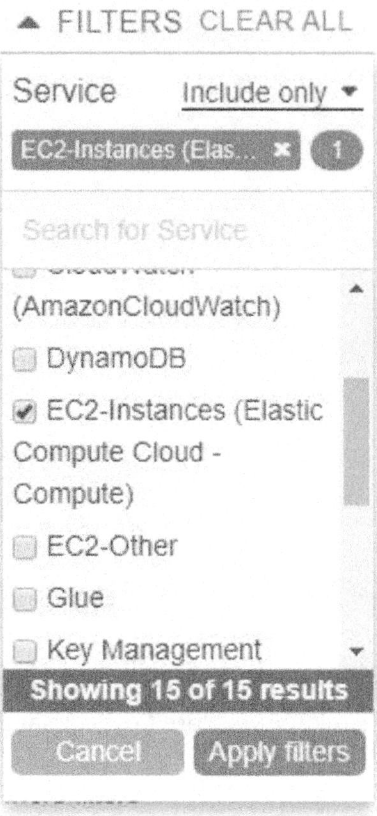

Figure 2.16: AWS Cost Explorer - Filter by Service

Here you see a report on EC2 costs for the previous six months.

Figure 2.17: AWS Cost Explorer - EC2 Cost

You can save this report by clicking the button "Save as..." in the upper left corner. Enter "EC2 Costs in the last 6 months" in the popup screen.

Figure 2.18: AWS Cost Explorer - Save as - report name

Click on "Save Report."

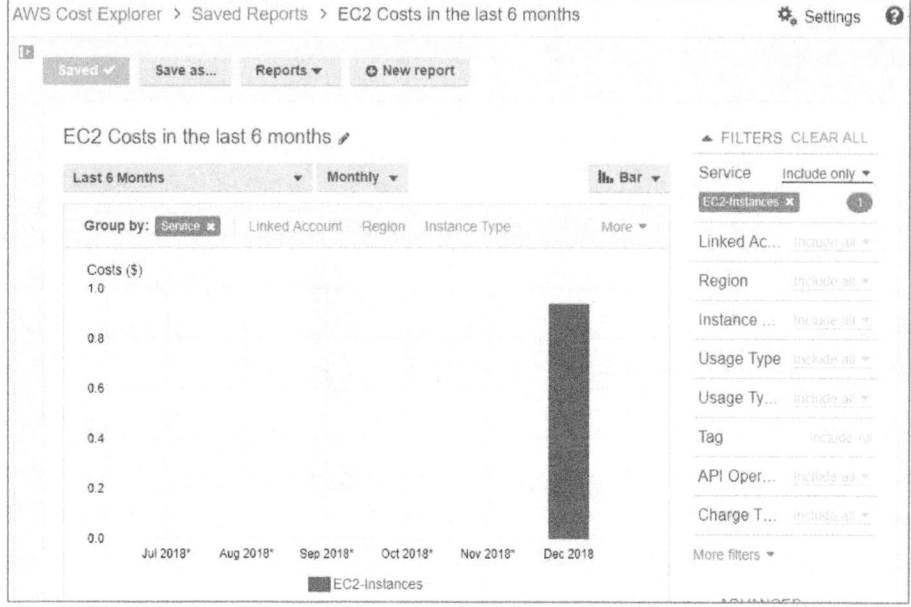

Figure 2.19: AWS Cost Explorer - Saved report

Now you have the saved report "EC2 Costs in the last 6 months" in "Saved Reports."

To see this newly created report, go to "Saved Reports" by clicking on the third icon on the left of the page.

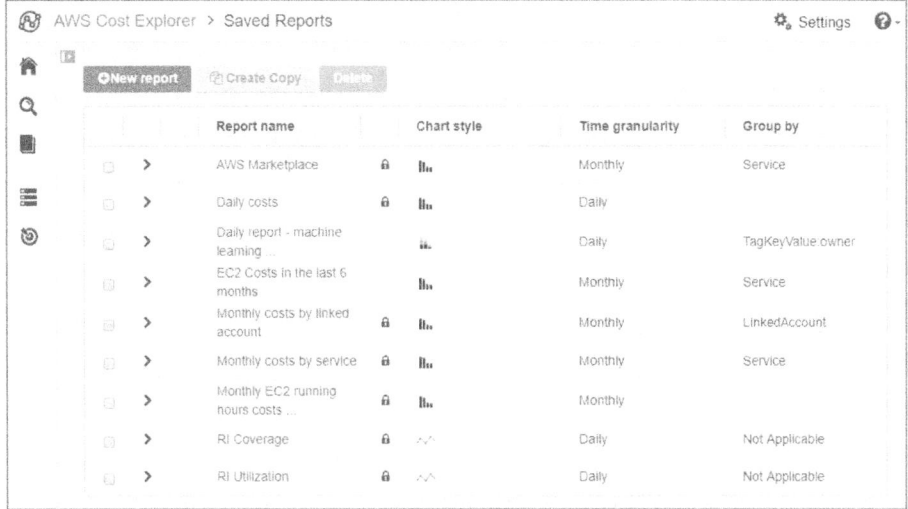

Figure 2.20: AWS Cost Explorer - Saved reports

Repeat the above processes to create reports that track your team's AWS costs.

You can create very granular reports if you have consistent and high quality tags. For more details on drilling down your AWS costs by using tags, please check "Implementation #6: How to Tag AWS Resources for Cost Optimization".

AWS Cost Explorer API:

> You can use the Cost Explorer API to extract billing data. You don't get thousands or millions of items in return, but you can get aggregate data and some granular data.
>
> The end point for the API is: https://ce.us-east-1.amazonaws.com
>
> As you can see from the end point, this API is in the "us-east-1" region. When you use AWS CLI or Boto3, please make sure your current region is "us-east-1". If this is not the region in your profile, you will need to specify the region in your API call parameters.

2.5.3 Analyze AWS S3 Inventory Data

AWS S3 Inventory data are the files with the metadata of the S3 objects. The metadata describe attributes of the objects: bucket name, key, size, last modified date, and storage type.

> Please note that the metadata do not have a last-accessed date. You will have to rely on S3 Server Access Logs.
>
> LINK: Implementation #10: How to Set Up and Use AWS S3 Server Access Logging for AWS Cost Optimization
>
> You can use CloudTrail to analyze a bucket usage: Logging Amazon S3 API Calls by Using AWS CloudTrail. For details, please visit:
>
> https://docs.aws.amazon.com/AmazonS3/latest/dev/cloudtrail-logging.html

You can analyze these files using your own method of consolidating, aggregating and visualizing data.

AWS Athena is a very good tool with which to extract and analyze the billing data if you know how to write database queries.

AWS Cost Explorer can't tell you how many objects are over twelve months old - one of several indicators that these objects might be moved to the cheaper Standard IA or Glacier storage type.

You can identify these objects with AWS Athena and S3 Inventory data.

For more details, please refer to the following:

LINK: Identify Cost-Saving Opportunities with AWS Athena

LINK: Use Athena to Query S3 Inventory Data.

2.5.4 Top Five S3 Inventory Reports for AWS S3 Cost Optimization

With S3 Inventory and Athena, you can create the following five monthly reports, which provide in-depth knowledge with which to make decision on how to optimize your S3 storage costs.

2.5.4.1 Report #1: Summary Reports of All Buckets

Report name: Summary reports of all buckets: storage size group by storage class.

Purpose: To identify the biggest buckets by the size, cost, and storage class.

This report tells the number of objects, the storage size, and the estimated cost of all the buckets. You know how much each bucket costs you. More importantly, you know how much you spend in each storage class, especially those in Standard because having more in Standard could potentially provide greater opportunities to save.

2.5.4.2 Report #2: Top Ten Top-Level Prefixes by Size

Report name: Top ten top-level prefixes by size of each bucket, group by storage class.

Purpose: To identify who spent the most or which top level prefixes cost the most in each bucket when the top-level prefixes are employees, projects, departments, or others.

This report tells you the number of objects, the storage size and the estimated cost of the top-level prefixes for each bucket and for each storage class.

If you have a bucket for the department, the top-level prefixes could be the employee names. This report tells you the estimated storage and cost by employee. In this case, this report is very useful to clean up the space used by an ex-employee.

If you have a bucket for the customers, the top-level prefixes could be the customers' names. This report tells the estimated storage and cost by customer to help estimate how much you spend for a customer.

Please note that this is not an accurate number for the billing purposes. To get the billing amount for a prefix, you need to tag the prefix with, for example, "customer=Mercy Hospital." Then you can create a query on AWS Cost Explorer using the filters: "AWS Resource" with the value of "S3" and "customer" tag with the value of "Mercy Hospital."

2.5.4.3 Report #3: Top Ten File Types by Size

Report name: Top ten file types by size of each bucket, group by storage class.

Purpose: To identify the files in each bucket and how much storage these files use or how much they cost.

This report tells you where your money goes in terms of file types.

The file types can tell you a lot about your business. For example, how much do you spend on medical images? How much do you spend on genetic sequence files? How much do you spend on compressed (.zip, .gzip, etc.) or uncompressed files? Why are only 25 percent of your medical images in Standard IA while you expect 60 percent of them to be in Standard IA? Can you compress some of the uncompressed files to reduce the storage size?

This report can generate numerous questions and you can follow up with many action items.

2.5.4.4 Report #4: Six-Month-Old Objects Summary Report

Report name: Six-month old summary report of each bucket, group by storage class

Purpose: To identify how many files in each bucket are older than six months. Can these files be moved to a lower storage class such as Standard IA or AWS Glacier?

This report tells you the number of objects, the storage size, and the estimated cost of those objects which were created or last modified six months ago.

You could answer the following question based on the numbers in this report:

Can these six-month-old objects in this bucket in Standard storage class be moved to Standard IA?

Please note that the last-modified-date is not the same as the last-accessed-date. For the last-accessed-date, you need to enable the S3 logs and the information from the S3 log files. However, if you present this report to the owners of the bucket, the owners could analyze the objects further and give you further instructions, such as moving them to Standard IA.

2.5.4.5 Report #5: Twelve-Month-Old Objects Summary Report

Report name: Twelve-month-old objects summary report of each bucket, group by storage class.

Purpose: To identify how many files in each bucket are older than twelve months. Can these files be moved to a lower storage class such as Standard IA or AWS Glacier?

Like Report #4, you can use this report to answer this question: Can we move these twelve-month-old objects from Standard to Standard IA, or even to Glacier?

2.5.5 Summary

With all these analytical tools, you can extract a lot of information to produce intelligent decisions. You should choose the tools that you are comfortable with or that you can get help with.

Once you have gathered and analyzed the data, the next step is to present the findings to teams and management.

2.6 Control AWS Cloud Costs

2.6.1 Introduction

You have the metrics to measure the costs and establish the baseline for cost optimization. You have the data and analytics to identify the opportunities of cost optimization.

Now it is time to control your AWS Cloud costs.

Previously, you learned cost optimization strategies.

LINK: Overall Cost Optimization Strategies

In this section, you will learn the processes to optimize costs.

In the next two chapters, you will learn in great details what actions to take. Then you will learn in a laboratory-style setting how to execute those actions.

2.6.2 Create a Plan

Assume cost optimization efforts as a project.

For an enterprise, this is a big project. You may have to create a cross-functional team, assign the roles to each team member, and map out the inter-dependency among the tasks.

For a small company or a team in a company, this may be a small project.

Big or small, create a project plan. Manage the project as you manage other projects. Adopt an Agile approach and use the SCRUM or Kanban method if you can.

2.6.2.1 Set a Target

Your target could be based on your overall AWS spending for the year.

For example, our target is the total AWS spending of this year: $1.2 million.

Your target doesn't have to be the overall AWS spending. Set your own goals using the metrics you define.

LINK: Measure AWS Cloud Cost

For example, you could lower the AWS Cloud cost per customer by 20 percent in six months. You could lower the AWS Cloud cost for each medical image processed by 10 percent within three months.

Once you have the overall target, you can divide and conquer. Collect the billing data, analyze the data, create reports, discuss reports with teams, and establish the target for each team.

You can also set a target for each type of resources (compute, storage, data transfer, etc.).

Should the targets be part of the employee performance review? That is dependent on your business needs.

Please note that if you are overly aggressive in cost cutting, you could hinder innovation or even disrupt your business.

Your approach could be different.

2.6.2.2 Define the Approaches

Armed with the billing data, you could define the strategies as laid out in this book.

Consider the following approaches to execute your strategies.

1. Always attempt the easiest tasks first.

   For example, you could clean up un-used or under-utilized resources such as those used by ex-employees.

2. Attempt the ones with the best returns.

   Sometimes the easiest may not give the best return. Calculate your ROI by estimating how much effort it takes in man hours and how much money will be saved.

3. Divide and conquer.

   Break up big tasks into smaller pieces.

   For example, you could create one task to tackle each type of AWS resource - storage, compute, database, data transfer, and so on.

4. Create transparency and cost awareness for each member of your team.

   For example, you could give each team access to AWS Cost Explorer so that they are aware of their current and projected expenditures.

   Create budgets based on resources, teams, departments, or tags. Set up alerts on estimated or current expenditures.

5. Improve your business processes to cut costs.

   For example, do as much compute off the Cloud as possible before you move data to the Cloud. Not only can you save on compute costs, but you can also save storage costs because your data are cleaner and smaller.

6. Review and change how you implement backup and retention policies.

   Review all the raw data and the data that could be derived or computed from the raw data.

   Does it make sense to just store the raw data without the derivative data? What is the cost of re-computing the derivative data? What is the cost of storing the derivative data? Does it make sense to store both the raw data and derived data?

Ask these questions. You may find a much more cost-effective way to implement backup and retention policies.

7. Review the colocation requirements for your business or applications.

   Colocation is expensive. What is your primary purpose for the colocation: disaster recovery or performance?

   For example, you may want to situate your applications and data as close as to your customers as possible to boost performance.

   How many customers will benefit from this co-location? Can application performance be improved by better architecture? Do you have to colocate both the applications and the databases?

   Ask these questions. You may minimize or even eliminate colocation costs.

8. Modify the software that runs the business to use fewer or less expensive AWS resources.

   For example, you could modify the software to manage the state of the application so that AWS Spot Instances could be used, which would create a huge savings over On-Demand Instances.

   You could modify the software so that it costs much less to run on nonproduction environments with the same CI/CD (Continuous Integration / Continuous Deployment) process.

9. Create corporate policies and standard training modules on using AWS resources.

   For example, you could enforce tagging in your corporate policies. You could incorporate the best practices in your specific business areas into this policy document.

Corporate training could be involved to develop the training materials, deliver them and record the training outcome.

10. Get other departments, such as HR, involved.

    For example, new processes and materials could be added to the new employee on-boarding or employee exiting process.

    AWS best practices could be presented to new engineers.

    Employee-owned AWS resources could be reviewed before or after an employee leaves the company.

11. Use some of the third-party tools to help you manage costs.

    There are many tools on the market to help you control the costs. Get to know them, evaluate them, and deploy them.

    Please note that, these tools help you cut costs reactively on your existing infrastructure.

    Don't forget to manage costs proactively. You could improve business processes, create cost awareness, and drive toward excellence.

12. Use open source tools in the open source communities.

    You can find numerous open source codes on Github contributed by a large community, including Fortune 500 companies and major Cloud spenders.

    Check out how they automate the cost optimization processes. Download their codes, revise them to fit your needs, and build your own programs.

Consider all of these eleven approaches. Include those applicable to your project plan.

2.6.2.3 Define Roles and Responsibilities

If you have a small team using the AWS resources, you may not have to define the formal roles and responsibilities because everyone knows who is supposed to do what.

If you are in an enterprise environment, a cross-functional team is more appropriate to the cost optimization effort, which could be a dedicated project.

Your cross-functional team could have members who represent different teams in the company.

Choose the sponsor of the project and the leader of this cross-functional team. The sponsor could be from finance or a business group that pays the bill. The leader could be DevOps or an engineer who can execute engineering tasks.

Agile could be adopted to run the project. With Agile, each member can be self-motivated and self-managed. A SCRUM master can organize the SCRUM meetings and manage the backlogs using a tool like JIRA. You could have two fifteen-minute standup meetings every week. In each meeting, all attendees go through their own list of tasks on the JIRA Board or the Kanban Board.

Each member of the cross-functional team must be clear about his or her role and responsibilities.

2.6.2.4 Define the Milestones

Once you have established a target, with a team behind it, you can define your milestones.

Break your target up into smaller, achievable milestones. Break the milestones up into smaller tasks and stories. Assign these tasks and stories to members of the team. Put these tasks and stories on each Sprint.

For example, if your target is to save $200,000 this year over last year with only six months left, each expected annualized saving of $50,000 could be a milestone. The milestones do not have to be evenly distributed.

Celebrate each milestone. Recognize significant contributions from members. Have a "lessons learned" session.

2.6.2.5 Evaluate the Risks

Mistakes are bound to happen. There are several risks in cost optimization.

<u>Collaboration risk:</u>

Teams may blame each other when a target is missed.

<u>Innovation risk:</u>

If the cost optimization is overly aggressive, teams will stop innovating simply to meet the cost-saving target.

<u>Compliance risk:</u>

For example, retention policy may be in question if objects are deleted when they should be kept for fifteen years in some industries.

<u>Business risk:</u>

Normal business may be disrupted if the cost optimization is not planned and executed carefully.

For example, an EC2 instance that is terminated by mistake could bring the application on that instance down.

Financial risk:

Cost optimization can incur additional costs.

For example, it costs money to delete millions of objects, especially when you need to check whether they exist in the backup before deletion.

It costs money to develop programs to automate repetitive cleanup tasks.

It costs money to recompute the raw data to generate the derivative data.

If you are considering these risks, you probably know how to mitigate them in your environment. Add these risk mitigations to your project plan.

2.6.2.6 Communicate Adequately

Communication is very important whether you are a small team or an enterprise. Many of the risks mentioned above can be reduced or avoided with adequate communication.

When objects are to be deleted permanently, make sure the owner and stakeholders know which objects will be deleted and when.

If an EC2 instance will be terminated, manually or by automation, the owner should be notified ahead of time.

This is why a SCRUM master helps a lot: it ensures that everyone is on the same page.

This is how a ticketing system such as JIRA Service Desk can help with communication. The task is clear and documented. The workflow, such as the approval process, is built in. Progress can be tracked. Stakeholders are notified as each task is updated.

The fifteen-minute stand up meeting allows everyone to raise blockers, things that prevent moving forward.

In your project plan, list the primary communication tools and channels that the team will be using. Specify how often the team will get updates on progress.

2.6.2.7 Celebrate Each Achievement

Celebrating each milestone is a special kind of communication.

Get together for a lunch. Share the lessons learned. Share the stories during the process.

Everyone makes mistakes. When a mistake happens, take necessary steps to correct the mistake. If the mistake is a bug in a program, fix the bug. If it is lack of communication, enhance the communication. If it is lack of resources, add a resource.

It is important to turn everyone's focus to the big picture. When the milestone is achieved and you are on the way to meet the target, the mistakes can be downplayed.

2.6.3 Iterate and Develop the Feedback Loop

Cost optimization can be an ongoing effort. Things may be chaotic in the beginning. Opportunities may be everywhere, but priorities may be lost. Communication may be missing. Teams may not be collaborating. Mistakes are made.

You may have to iterate the process several times before it becomes smooth. Collect feedback from each iteration. Fix issues so that they don't reappear in the next iteration. Set reasonable expectations.

Help each member become familiar with the tools or programs. Acquire new tools and programs. Bring in outside vendors in if necessary.

Have a "lessons learned" session to reinforce the feedback loop.

For the repetitive tasks such as deleting objects that are no longer needed, it is acceptable in the first or second iteration to complete them less efficiently. You may gradually write a program, such as a Lambda function, and schedule it to run periodically.

When you become serious about cost optimization, you may realize that you are building a software product whose source codes get larger and larger and whose features work better and better over time.

2.6.4 Create Policies for Using AWS Resources

When you have a large AWS Cloud infrastructure and you have a large user base in your organization, it may make sense to elevate your AWS Cloud cost optimization to a higher level: create policies and guidelines for all AWS usage. Like other corporate policies such as your Internet usage policy, your AWS usage policy defines what is allowed and what is not allowed.

Although some behaviors are very popular, they should be avoided. Here is a partial list of such behaviors.

- EC2 instances are launched with the default SDD disk even though SSD disk is not necessary and costs nearly twice as much as the alternative GP2 disk.
- Compute and storage capacity are over provisioned.
- RI instances are not leveraged.

Without a policy on AWS usage, these behaviors may be overlooked.

Like the Internet usage policy, AWS usage rules and guidelines should be presented to new AWS users. When AWS users have questions and doubts, there is a policy document for them to review.

The document should include the best practices that all engineers could learn. There should be a reviewing or approval process before a large compute project is launched.

Each company is different. This book can help you create such a policy.

2.6.5 Summary

Previously you learned how to gather the billing data and analyzed the data. This section explains the process of controlling your AWS Cloud costs:

- create a plan
- set a target
- explore approaches
- assign roles and responsibilities
- define the milestones
- evaluate the risks
- communicate with stakeholders

- celebrate the achievements

Iterate the process, gather feedback, and improve the process in the next iteration.

To elevate your cost optimization effort into a higher level, develop policies and procedures for AWS usage in your organization. At that level, cost optimization becomes a consistent and sustaining business operation, instead of a one-time effort.

Chapter 3. Optimize the Cloud Cost Multipliers

3.1 Introduction

Chapter 1 taught you how to set up your AWS Organizations so that your AWS Cloud costs can be managed at the root level. You have the fundamental structure in place to make costs easier to manage and to optimize AWS Cloud costs.

Chapter 2 taught you how to measure, analyze and control AWS Cloud costs, focusing on concepts, tools and processes.

In this chapter and the next one, we will divide and conquer. We will dissect the AWS Cloud cost components and their sub-components and optimize each one of them.

The on-demand feature of the Cloud means you can typically launch or stop services at any time. You only pay for the time you use the AWS resources. In Cloud economics, the time component is the first thing to look at when you optimize the cost.

The following is the AWS Cloud cost model in its simplest form.

AWS Expenditures = Amount of Resources * Length of Time

Although "Amount of Resources" seems to be the first component you should look at, you need deeper knowledge to optimize this component. You need to understand how AWS pricing works, what types of resources are available, and what the requirements are for your applications and for your business. We will discuss this component in the next chapter.

Let's start with the simpler and easier component, "Length of Time."

3.2 Cloud Cost Multipliers

Let's take one step back to dissect AWS Cloud costs.

Let's dissect the most important AWS resources for most organizations, the compute costs of EC2 instances.

Below is a cost model for EC2 instances:

EC2 Spend = Unit Price (per instance)

* number of instances per environment

* number of environments

* number of hours

* number of days per month

* number of months per year

This model is simplified below:

> AWS Spend = Unit Price * Cloud Cost Multipliers

Let's call "number of instances per environment" the *Capacity Multiplier*.

Let's call "number of environments" the *Environment Multiplier*.

Let's call the three time components the *Time Multiplier*.

Capacity Multiplier:

> The capacity multiplier is the number of units you need.
>
> For example, machine learning model training requires thirty t2.xlarge On-Demand EC2 instances. The capacity multiplier is thirty.
>
> If x is the cost of a single t2.xlarge On-Demand EC2 instance, your total cost in capacity is 30x.

Environment Multiplier:

> You may have dev, test, stage and production environments for your systems.
>
> If you deploy your systems in the same way for each environment, your costs could be multiplied by the number of environments.
>
> If x is the total cost for one environment, your total cost for all environments is 4x if you have dev, test, stage and production environments.

Time Multiplier:

Most of the AWS resources are billed by the hour. Some are even billed by the second.

If the unit price is by the hour, the time multiplier is 24 for a day, 24x7 for a week, 24x(365/12) for a month (approximately), and 24x365 for a year (approximately).

Redundancy Multiplier:

One multiplier that is not included in this model: the *Redundancy Multiplier*.

You probably have built-in redundancy for your systems. You have load balancers, multi-AZ databases, and so on. Your costs could be multiplied by the redundancy.

You could also have co-location infrastructure for disaster recovery, application performance, or data backup and retention. When one region is not available to your customers, another region is.

Not all of your AWS Cloud costs can be multiplied by the redundancy multiplier.

For example, you may have storage for all four environments although you may only have redundancy for production environment. Thus, the redundancy multiplier is not plugged into this model.

Nevertheless, the redundancy multiplier can still be applied to key components of your costs. If you enable Multi-AZ for your RDS databases, your costs may still be multiplied by the number of Availabilities Zones you select.

Thus, optimizing the redundancy multiplier remains significant.

The payoff of optimizing these Cloud cost multipliers is enormous. Potential savings are not 10 percent or 25 percent. Potential savings are the multiplier of 100 percent, or at that magnitude, whenever one of these multipliers can be applied.

3.3 Time Multiplier

All major AWS resources are charged by the time consumed. Compute, storage and databases are all charged by multiplying the number of resources by the amount of time.

For EC2 instances:

> Amount of Resources = Unit Price (per instance) * number of instances per environment * number of environments

> Length of Time = number of hours per day * number of days per month * number of months per year

For S3 storage:

> Amount of Resources = Unit price per GB * number of GB

> Length of Time = number of hours * number of days per month * number of months per year

For Databases (Let's just consider RDS for now):

> Amount of Resources = Unit price (per database) * number of instances per environment * number of environments

> Length of Time = number of hours * number of days per month * number of months per year

The length of time is the time multiplier.

3.3.1 Optimize the Time Multiplier

Is the AWS Cloud cheap or expensive? If you look at the unit price, it is cheap. If you look at your AWS bill, it is expensive. Before applying the time multiplier, it is cheap. After applying the time multiplier, it is expensive.

For example, if you use t3.large Linux On-Demand EC2 instance for a year:

> The unit price is $0.0832 per hour. Yes, that is extremely cheap! What can you buy for less than a dime?

> The time multiplier is 8,760 (=24 hours per day * 365 days). Now it becomes very expensive! Such a multiplier will turn any insignificant dollar value into a significant one: $728.83 per year.

Unfortunately, in an organizational setting, the unit price is the one that is presented to engineers and decision makers when the decision to use it is being made. The decision makers may see the billed amount a month later, or they may never see it if the bill is not available to them, or the billed amount may be buried in details.

That is why the following rule would be helpful across your organization.

AWS Cost Optimization Rule #1: Estimate your monthly spending before you purchase any AWS resources.

Such a rule ensures that you don't make decisions based solely on the unit price. Fortunately, AWS makes it easy for you to estimate the monthly cost.

LINK: Implementation #1: How to Estimate the Monthly AWS Cost, Save It and Share It

> The monthly cost estimates may be included in your project budget or cost estimate. You can save the link to your estimate and share the link with your team members. You can embed the link in your project plan. Your teammates or project managers can click on the link and see the original estimate of the resources you plan to use. These resources could be EC2, S3, RDS, and others combined.

If you are leading a cross-functional team to drive down the AWS costs, emphasize the following again and again in every communication:

Estimate your monthly spending before you purchase any AWS resources.

If you are managing the AWS infrastructure, you can start by building the culture of AWS cost awareness. Develop a culture of Cloud cost awareness in your organization by enforcing this simple rule.

The best part of optimizing the time multiplier is that you don't need much knowledge of the underlying applications or the insight into AWS resources. It will likely not be difficult to implement either.

For example, the RDS database instance x for y application in the development environment can be stopped outside regular working hours between 8:00am and 5:00pm, Monday to Friday.

> Stopping RDS instance x outside of regular working hours saves up to 73 percent.

The best part is that it takes only one call or one email to confirm that this RDS database instance can be stopped outside regular business hours.

Let's break the time component into hours, days, and months.

3.3.1.1 Hours to Consider

If your instance runs 24 hours a day, the hour multiplier is 24. If your instance only runs during the working hours between 8:00 a.m. and 5:00 p.m., the hour multiplier is 9, a savings of 62.5 percent.

Optimizing Tip:

Stop the appropriate instances outside of regular working hours.

Effective October 2, 2018, all Linux instances are charged per second. Windows instances are charged per hour. Thus, for Linux instances, the savings could be even more if you can start and stop the instance more precisely.

3.3.1.2 Days to Consider

AWS resources are not charged by days or months. However, it is still very helpful to estimate the cost by days or months and consider reducing the number of days or months when it is feasible. Several different days should be considered.

Weekends:

> If your instances can be stopped on weekends, that is a savings of 29 percent.

Other days:

> Instances can be stopped on idle days, such as the days before the product launch.
>
> For example, production instances have been deployed in anticipation of an official launch. These instances could be running weeks or even months before the launch date. Stopping these instances could actually save you a lot.
>
> Other days to consider are vacation days, sick days, and holidays. Although these may not save a lot, if you are looking for every opportunity to cut costs, consider these days if they are easy to implement.

3.3.1.3   Months to Consider

Some AWS resources are charged by the month, such as S3 storage, which is charged by per GB per month.

Even though most AWS resources are charged by the second or hour, it is still convenient to estimate costs by the month and by the year. Most organizations develop annual or quarterly budgets that can be translated into months.

Month Multiplier

> If you manage to save $84,000 a month, that is over $1,000,000 a year, or a total of $5,000,000 over the next five years.

The month multiplier is an important concept because the number is usually quite significant. An insignificant amount may turn into a very significant amount after being multiplied by twelve.

If your project has a life of five years, the month multiplier is sixty, which is even more significant.

When you present the total cost of a system, apply the month multiplier. When you demonstrate the potential cost savings, apply the month multiplier. When you plan the budget, apply the month multiplier. Your total cost of ownership, cost savings, and budget reflect the true picture over time after the month multiplier is applied.

The month multiplier is the Cloud cost magnifier. If you manage to save $84,000 a month, that is over $1,000,000 a year, or $5,000,000 in five years!

If you manage to save $250,000 a month, that is $3,000,000 a year, or $15,000,000 in five years.

3.3.2 Questions to Ask to Optimize the Time Multiplier

To optimize the time multiplier, ask the following questions:

- ◆ Does this instance (EC2 or RDS) only need to be up during regular working hours?

For example, an internal HR application for training is only needed during working hours.

- Does this instance (EC2 or RDS) only need to be up during a specific period of the day?

    For example, an instance may be needed for two hours between 2:00 a.m. and 4:00 a.m. every day to run a data aggregation task from multiple applications.

    Don't pay for twenty-four hours when you only use the instance for two hours.

- Is this a development environment?

    More often than not, a development environment does not have to be up for twenty-four hours a day.

3.3.3 Things to Consider to Optimize the Time Multiplier

<u>Time taken to start or stop:</u>

How long does it take to bring up or stop this instance (EC2 or RDS)?

If it takes five minutes to start the instance, you may schedule it at 7:55 a.m. instead of 8:00 a.m.

The Windows instance is charged by the hour. Make sure you don't pay for the whole hour for using only a few minutes.

Consider the extra minutes for starting and stopping the instance.

You are charged for eight hours if the instance is up for seven hours and fifty-five minutes. You are charged with 9 hours if the instance is up for eight hours and five minutes.

The Linux instance charges by the second, so you don't have this issue.

Dependency between AWS resources:

Are there other instances (EC2 or RDS) depending on this instance? For example, if this instance is a host for databases of your web application, you will need to stop the web host EC2 instance first before you stop the database host EC2 instance or the RDS instance. Otherwise, your web host will generate a lot of database connection errors in the logs. Numerous unnecessary alerts may be created because of the failed attempts to connect to the database.

Time Zones:

Where are the affected users? Your schedule should consider the time zones if the affected users are in different time zones or even in different countries.

Production Environment:

Is this a production environment? You should be less aggressive with regard to cost savings for a production environment than for a nonproduction environment.

3.3.4 The Checklist to Optimize the Time Multiplier

Risks:

Don't disrupt your normal business operation. Plan very carefully before execution.

Communications:

Your plan should be communicated well before the implementation, especially to the stakeholders of a production system. Do not shut down the systems or delete the AWS resources without warning.

Documentation:

Your implementation should be clearly documented. For example, starting on January 1, 2018, instance x is scheduled to be stopped at 8:00 p.m. EST and restarted at 7:55 a.m. EST the next day. If necessary, provide a link to the documentation. If you have a built-in approval process, include the link to the request: who approved the schedule and when it was approved.

If you have hundreds or thousands of instances to track, documentation is crucial.

Periodical Review:

Your schedule for the instance should be reviewed periodically.

Some production systems may have been decommissioned. Some development environments may have been promoted to production environments. There may be some new systems. The team who owns the systems may have changed. There may be new data retention policies. Periodic review keeps you up to date on each instance and keeps you up to date on costs.

3.3.5 Summary

The on-demand feature of the Cloud means that when you need it, you can have it. It also means that when you don't need it, you should get rid of it. The latter is often forgotten in an organization. The users may not be the payer. The payer does not know what the users are using. Such disconnection leads to overpaying for resources that are not used or are underutilized.

Time multiplier is one of the first items to optimize. The payoff is often huge.

3.4 Environment Multiplier

3.4.1 Introduction

The environment multiplier is the number of environments you need, such as development, QA, test, stage and production. For a homegrown application, you may need all five environments. For a third-party vendor application, you may just need two of them: test and production. For mission-critical applications, you may need more than one test environment.

The environment multiplier is another Cloud cost multiplier that makes some applications so expensive on the Cloud.

From the perspective of the business owners, the production environment is what they see as having value. However, some nonproduction environments are necessary and they should be accounted for in your budget or in your decision-making.

Yes, production environments typically cost more than nonproduction environments, but nonproduction environments still carry similar cost items, such as software licenses.

When you calculate the Total Cost of Ownership (TCO) and Return On Investment (ROI), the environment multiplier should be applied.

3.4.2 Things to Consider to Optimize the Environment Multiplier

The cost component of the application:

> Which part is the most expensive: databases, applications hosting, licenses, support fees, etc.?
>
> Which component is prohibitive in cost in nonproduction environments?
>
> Do you have to deploy as many resources to a nonproduction environment as to a production environment?

The uptime for a nonproduction environment:

> Can the nonproduction environment be shut down outside regular working hours?
>
> Can other cost multipliers be applied to nonproduction environments? If so, nonproduction environments become expensive to maintain.

The distinction between environments:

> Can the dev environment use t2.small instances even though t2.4xlarge instances are required for the production environment?

Deployment model:

> Can certain environment variables be set in the deployment packages?
>
> It will be very helpful if you have a variable "env." Then you can use this setting as a base to launch different types of resources. For example, if "env=dev," launch t2.small instances. If "env=prod," launch t2.8xlarge instances.

3.5 Capacity Multiplier

3.5.1 Introduction

The capacity multiplier is the number of units you need to reach capacity. For example, a machine-learning model requires 30 t2.xlarge On-Demand EC2 instances for 5 hours. The capacity multiplier is 30.

A third-party vendor application requires a cluster of 8 t2.8xlarge instances. The capacity multiplier is 8.

This capacity multiplier is very important. It is also very tricky to optimize because it is application-specific and requires deep knowledge of the job and the AWS resources.

The capacity multiplier also requires some tried-and-true experiments to determine what the optimal capacity multiplier should be.

3.5.2 Things to Consider to Optimize the Capacity Multiplier

Check the following while you try to optimize the capacity multiplier.

- Make sure the task and the budget have been approved.

- Make sure reasonable efforts have been made to ensure that the estimate of the number of instances needed is the most intelligent guess.

- Make sure that there is a plan with the expected inputs and the expected outcome.

- Make sure that there is a limit cap to the expenditure. You do not want to accidentally launch thousands of nodes using a "for loop" without an exit.

- Diligently watch the cost in progress and be ready to stop the task when something goes wrong.

3.6 Chapter Summary: Cloud Cost Multipliers

AWS Cloud can be very expensive when the Cloud cost multipliers are applied to the unit price. You can identify many opportunities to save when you optimize each of the following 4 Cloud cost multipliers:

- time multiplier
- environment multiplier
- capacity multiplier
- redundancy multiplier

When trying to save a lot, please keep the risks in mind. Do not disrupt normal business operations.

In an enterprise environment, communication and documentation are very important.

To keep the Cloud cost multiplier optimal over time, it may be necessary to create a corporate policy and best practices on how to use AWS resources.

Chapter 4. Optimize Baseline Costs

4.1 Introduction

Let's revisit the simplified optimization model:

> AWS Expenditures = Unit Price * Cloud Cost Multipliers

In the previous chapter, you optimized Cloud cost multipliers. In this chapter, you will learn how to optimize the unit price.

Optimizing your Cloud cost multipliers is your top priority. You could see a reduction in spending in a very short time.

If you do a good job optimizing the Cloud cost multipliers, you may not have to try too hard to optimize the unit price. Even though the unit price is only part of the baseline costs, it is usually the only cost that you can optimize.

For example, the baseline costs for an EC2 instance is the unit cost (hourly rate) plus other costs, such as EBS storage, IP addresses, data transfer, and so on.

As far as optimization is concerned, let's make a simple assumption: unit price = baseline price.

For EC2 instances, the unit price is the hourly price of the instance.

For databases such as RDS, the unit price is the hourly price of the RDS instance.

For S3 storage, the unit price is the storage cost per GB (gigabytes) per month.

Throughout this chapter, we explain the following nine steps to optimize AWS baseline costs. They will be specified as we discuss how to optimize the baseline costs of major AWS resources.

Nine Steps to Optimize AWS Baseline Costs

Step 1: Maximize the utilization of Spot Instances.

Step 2: Cover the On-Demand Instances with RIs.

Step 3: Use managed services or serverless architecture.

Step 4: Choose the free OS Platform for EC2 instances.

Step 5: Choose free database software for RDS instances when possible.

Step 6: Leverage nonstandard S3 storage classes.

Step 7: Minimize the need to create multiple copies of the same objects.

Step 8: Use AWS S3 Select.

Step 9: Sign an enterprise support contract when it makes sense.

4.2 Optimize EC2 Baseline Costs

4.2.1 Introduction

For EC2 instances, there are four different pricing models you need to understand to ensure you are leveraging the right one for you:

- Dedicated Hosts and Instances
- On-Demand Instances
- Spot Instances
- Reserved Instances

Depending on your business needs, you may end up choosing different pricing models for different workloads.

4.2.1.1 Dedicated Hosts and Instances

AWS runs your compute workload on hardware that is dedicated only to you and is not shared with any other customer of AWS. Therefore, this is the most expensive pricing model.

One reason to use dedicated instances is that some regulations require you to run your applications on dedicated hardware.

4.2.1.2 On-Demand Instances

This is the most common pricing model. It requires less effort to implement since it is given right out of the box.

You only pay for what you use, you are not required to make a commitment or make upfront payment. You can start or stop instances at any time.

4.2.1.3 Spot Instances

Spot Instances are basically spare compute capacity that AWS sells at deep discount with the caveat that AWS may interrupt your workload and take back the resource with a two-minute notice.

In order to take advantage of this pricing model, you need to ensure that your workloads are stateless or that you can pause and resume your workload.

4.2.1.4 Reserved Instances

You can reserve capacity starting from one-year up to three-year with or without an upfront payment. You get a discount depending on the term and upfront payment.

There are two types of Reserved Instances:

- Standard Reserved Instance
- Convertible Reserved Instance

With Reserved Instances, you are committing to pay for all the hours for the term regardless of whether you use it or not.

You have to make sure that you track your Reserved Instance (RI) Utilization in AWS Cost Explorer.

4.2.1.5 Standard Reserved Instance

After you purchase a standard Reserved Instance, you can only modify the instance size, not the instance type. However, if you decide you do not need to use it anymore, you can sell it back on the Amazon EC2 Reserved Instances Marketplace

Only purchase standard Reserved Instance types if you are sure about the instance family and type that your workload needs and don't expect this to change for the duration of the term.

4.2.1.6 Convertible Reserved Instance

You can modify the instance family, type, platform, scope and tenancy after being purchased but they can't be sold back.

If you are not 100% sure about the instance type or if it is something that may change in the future, you may consider Convertible Reserved Instances.

If you ever need to change any of the reservation attributes, you'll have to go through the process of exchanging Convertible Reserved Instances.

4.2.2 Choose the Right Type and Size

AWS offers many options in configurations when you purchase an EC2 instance.

First, there are five categories of EC2 instances:

1. General Purpose
2. Compute Optimized
3. Memory Optimized
4. Storage Optimized
5. Accelerated Computing

For each category, there are multiple types of instances. For each type, there is a list of models with a different mix of memory, CPUs, storage and networking capacity.

For example, a General Purpose instance has T series (such as T4 and T3) and M series (such as M5 and M4) of instances. T3 has different models: t3.large, t3.xlarge, t3.2xlarge, and so on.

Selecting the right type and the right size depends on the requirements of your application.

Make your decisions based on the demands of memory, CPUs, storage, and networking capacity. Make the trade-off between them if the distinctions are not clear. For example, your application is memory intensive and also demands a lot of CPUs.

Should you choose memory-optimized r5.xlarge with four vCPUs and 32g of memory, or should you choose computing optimized c5.2xlarge with eight vCPUs and 16g of memory?

Usually, t3.xlarge is twice the cost of t3.large, t3.2xlarge is twice the cost of t3.xlarge, and so on. One common question is whether to use two EC2 instances of t3.xlarge, or one EC2 instance of t3.2xlarge. You can test on each instance and pick the right type and size for your needs.

The focus of this chapter is not on the correct sizing strategy, which requires deep knowledge of the applications, but on finding room for optimization.

4.2.3 On-Demand Instances or Spot Instances

> Optimize Baseline Costs
>
> Step 1: Maximize the utilization of Spot Instances.

The first step to optimizing the cost of the EC2 unit price is to maximize the utilization of Spot Instances. Spot Instances typically cost you 70 percent to 90 percent less than On-Demand Instances.

On-Demand Instances are purchased at a fixed rate per hour. You pay as you go, and you own them until you terminate them. Unlike Spot Instances, they are uninterrupted although they are much more expensive.

Amazon offers its excess capacity in EC2 instances to customers. You can place bids to use the excess capacity at a tremendous discount, with typical savings of 70 percent to 90percent over On-Demand Instances. However, the tremendous savings come at a cost. Spot Instances can be reclaimed by Amazon at any moment with a two-minute notification.

One misconception is that your Spot Instances could be reclaimed by Amazon when someone bids a higher price for your instances. This is not true. The bid price is not a factor. Supply and demand determine whether a Spot Instance is reclaimed.

You pay the Spot price that is in effect for the current hour for the instances that you launch. The Spot prices adjust slowly over days and weeks. You can control your costs by setting the maximum price that you are willing to pay.

Since Spot Instances are so much cheaper than On-Demand Instances, why don't we use Spot Instances all the time? Unfortunately, not every application can use Spot Instances.

4.2.3.1 What Workload Is Appropriate to Run on Spot Instances?

If your application is stateless, it is a candidate for using Spot Instances. If your application saves client data generated in one session and uses that data in the next session, your application is not stateless. Spot Instances may not be good for your application.

When a Spot Instance is reclaimed by AWS, the sessions are gone. The client data are gone. The client (user or application) has to start over.

Please keep in mind that such interruptions do not happen every day and you have a two-minute advanced warning.

If you are running a task on a single EC2 instance that takes five days to finish, you may not be able to afford to use Spot Instances. If the five-day task has been running for two days and is interrupted, you have wasted two days of time and money.

4.2.3.2 Architect Applications to Run on Spot Instances

However, for this five-day task, you can save your progress somewhere in the S3, in the database, or in an On-Demand Instance. If the task is interrupted, you can launch another task to restart the task right from the point at which it was interrupted. In this case, your application manages its own state and Spot Instances may be used.

You can also take advantage of the two-minute window (EC2 Spot Instance Termination Notice) to save your state and progress, upload final log files, or remove your work from a load balancer, and hand it off to another session in an efficient manner.

So, if your workload is not suitable to run on Spot Instances, can you architect your application to run on Spot Instances? If the answer is yes, you can save up to 70 percent to 90 percent of the EC2 instance costs.

Optimize EC2 Baseline Costs

Architect your application to run on Spot Instances.

The Cost Optimization pillar in the AWS Well-Architected Framework provides guidance and best practices on how to design and run systems on the AWS Cloud at minimal cost.

LINK: Follow AWS Well-Architected Framework - Cost Optimization Pillar

4.2.3.3 How to Maximize the Utilization of Spot Instances

You can work on the following list to maximize the utilization of Spot Instances.

- To reduce the impact of interruptions, set up Spot Instances and Spot Fleets to respond to an interruption notice. Stop or hibernate rather than terminate instances when capacity is no longer available.

- To reduce the impact of interruptions, diversify and run your application across multiple capacity pools. Each instance family, each instance size, in each AZ (Availability Zone), in each Region is a separate Spot pool.

- Use third-party tools to optimize your EC2 instances to take advantage of Spot Instances. Take advantage of On-Demand Instances and Reserved Instances to work with Spot Instances.

- Design your applications so that your applications can be run on Spot Instances. For example, let your application manage the state so that it can continue from where it stops when Spot Instances are reclaimed by EC2.

- Automate the two-minute notifications you receive when Spot Instances are interrupted by Amazon EC2. For example, save the application state, upload the final log file, remove the instance from Elastic Load Balancer, push SNS notifications, drain your container instance, and so on.

- You can also review the Spot Instance Advisor for average frequency of interruption for different Spot pools.

- Containerize your workload. Containers are stateless, fault-tolerant, and a great fit for Amazon EC2 Spot Instances.

4.2.4 Reserved Instances

> Optimize Baseline Costs
>
> Step 2: Cover On-Demand Instances with RIs.

4.2.4.1 Introduction

Reserved Instances (RIs) are very complicated in an enterprise environment.

Because of the huge financial commitment, not only will you have to know what EC2 instances you currently have but you will also have to anticipate what you will need in the future. If you commit to more than you actually use, you may end up wasting instead of saving money.

It is very complicated because the attributes of your On-Demand Instances have to match the attributes of RIs.

There are also different types of RIs, each with different payment options (no upfront, one-year upfront, two-year upfront and three-year upfront).

You may run your own financial modeling to play with different scenarios to come up with ROIs and a breakeven point. The breakeven point is when your entire commitment has been recovered.

From that point you will start saving money because of the commitment.

If you have a support plan, you may rely on the AWS support team to do some of the work for you. They will assist you in calculating ROIs.

The RIs in this section are more for EC2 On-Demand Instances and RDS On-Demand Instances. Reserved Capacity for DynamoDB and other resources are not covered here.

4.2.4.2 Defining RIs

If you must use On-Demand Instances, you can still save up to 75 percent by purchasing Reserved Instances (RIs).

Reserved Instances (RI) are On-Demand Instances you commit to using for at least one year. In exchange for your commitment, Amazon gives you a significant discount, up to 75 percent over On-Demand Instances.

When you purchase RIs, you are not launching any instances. Rather, you are making a commitment to use the instances. Once you make the commitment, the RI discount will be applied to your instances.

You do not have to specify which instances are reserved and which are not. AWS billing will match your instances with the active RIs by attribute and apply the discounted hourly rates for you automatically.

4.2.4.3 The Instance Attributes Related to RIs

It is important to know which attributes are used to match your On-Demand Instances with your RIs.

Below are the four attributes with the examples from the time of writing:

Instance type:

> t2.4xlarge (If you do not reserve capacity, the size doesn't matter)

Platform:

> Linux/UNIX, SUSE Linux, Redhat Enterprise Linux, Microsoft Windows Server and Microsoft SQLServer.

Tenancy:

> This only matters when you choose dedicated instances.

Availability Zone:

> This only matters when you reserve the capacity in the specified Availability Zone.

4.2.4.4 Consolidated Billing and RIs

If you have multiple accounts, consolidate them in the billing. Then your RIs will be applied to all the consolidated billing accounts, as long as the above instance attributes match.

4.2.4.5 Standard RIs

There are three types of RIs: Standard RIs, Convertible RIs, and Scheduled RIs.

Standard RIs are the ones you should start with because they will save you the most. At the time of writing, Standard RIs save you up to 75 percent off On-Demand whereas Convertible RIs save you up to 54 percent off On-Demand. On average, Standard RIs save you 40 percent off On-Demand with a one-year commitment or 60 percent with a three-year commitment. Convertible RIs save you an average of 31 percent with a one-year commitment or 54 percent with a three-year commitment.

4.2.4.6 Convertible RIs

You want to leverage RIs as much as you can. However, you have to match the attributes of On-Demand Instances with those of RIs. You may hesitate to make a commitment. For example, you may not want to commit to a specific instance family (such as t2, m3, etc.) for your applications.

In this case, you can purchase Convertible RIs. With Convertible RIs, you can switch from t2 to m3 EC2 instances as long as the m3 instances have an equal or lower payment than t2.

One difference between Standard RIs and Convertible RIs is that, Standard RIs can't take advantage of the price reductions and Convertible RIs can. With Convertible RIs, you must stick to the same region. If you purchase Convertible RIs in the us-east-1 region, they will only be applied to On-Demand Instances in the us-east-1 region.

With Convertible RIs, you can also switch from a one-year payment option to a three-year payment option, or vice versa, to allow you flexibility on the length of commitment.

For example, you launched eight t2.4xlarge Linux instances in the us-west-2 region on January 10, 2018. You purchased four Standard RIs of t2.4xlarge Linux instances with a one-year-no-upfront on January

20, 2018. You will get a discount of approximately 35 percent for four of the eight instances, starting on January 20, 2018, for one year. Whether you are using these 4 instances for the full year or not, you are committing to paying for the full year.

RIs are applied across accounts as long as these accounts are in the consolidated AWS bill. It doesn't matter which Availability Zone the instances are in as long as the region of the instances matches the region of the RIs.

You have an option to reserve capacity in a specific Availability Zone. If you do, you must specify the Availability Zone.

If you do not reserve the capacity, your RIs will cover all the sizes. In the example above, the four RIs of t2.4xlarge Linux will cover sixteen t2.xlarge Linux On-Demand Instances as long as these instances are in the us-west-2 region.

4.2.4.7 Scheduled RIs

Scheduled Reserved Instances are the instances you run on a regular schedule (daily, weekly or monthly), at the specified start time and duration, for one year. As with other RIs, you pay for the reserved capacity whether you use the capacity or not. If you have Scheduled Instances, you should evaluate the ROIs of the Scheduled RIs.

4.2.4.8 Things to Consider When Purchasing RIs

Before you purchase RIs, please consider the following:

- ROI of RIs

In general, if you need On-Demand Instances longer than seven months of the year, consider purchasing Reserved Instances (RIs). The final decision should be based on your own calculations. The seven months are a roughly estimated breakeven time when RIs will not result in wasting money. If you purchase them (and commit to pay for one year to get the discount) but you do not need the instances any more after seven months, you end up paying more than the On-Demand price.

- Price reductions

    Amazon has announced price reductions over sixty times in its history although the pace has slowed.

    One difference between Standard RIs and Convertible RIs is that Standard RIs can't take advantage of the price reductions whereas Convertible RIs can.

- Administrative costs of RIs

    There are three major administrative costs:

    o Tracking the expiration dates.

        If you have RIs with different expiration dates, you will have to keep track of them and renew them in a timely manner. That is why it is important to document all RIs and share the documentation with the stakeholders.

        If you have access to AWS Cost Explorer, you can go to "Reservation Summary." This page includes "Total Reservations," "Net Savings (last 30 days)," and "Reservations expiring (next 30 days)." You should check this page for all the reservations that will expire in the next thirty days.

- Renewing the RIs. AWS does not have the automatic renew feature, nor can you purchase RIs in advance.

  The price of RIs is set at the time of purchase. You must purchase RIs on the expiration date or the date you are ready to renew them.

  It is important to plan ahead. The EC2 instances or RDS instances can be reviewed before renewal. They may be subject to the new approval process. Thus, make a plan and get ready for renewal well before the expiration date.

- Tracking the RI utilization and RI coverage.

  The RI Utilization Report tells you what percentage of your RIs is utilized.

  For example, you have four t2.4xlarge Linux RIs but you have ten t2.4xlarge Linux at this moment. Your RI Utilization at this point is 100 percent because all four RIs are utilized. Every dollar you paid for RIs is being utilized at this moment.

  In the same example, your RI Coverage for t2.4xlarge Linux is 40 percent because only four of ten t2.4xlarge instances are being covered by the RIs. You may have the opportunity to save more by purchasing more RIs.

  It is important to watch the RI utilization report and RI coverage report on Cost Explorer.

  An ideal RI Utilization is 100 percent, which means all of your RIs have been utilized.

Your RI Coverage indicates what percentage of your active EC2 instances or RDS instances are using the RIs.

For details, please check the following link:

LINK: Implementation #7: How to Monitor RI Utilization and RI Coverage.

- Should you purchase RIs for small instances?

    With large EC2 or RDS instances, it makes sense to have RIs to cover them if they are to be active for over seven months (depending on the purchase price).

    Considering the administrative costs of RIs, should you purchase the RIs for the smaller instances?

    If you cover smaller instances with RIs but these instances are used for less than seven months, purchasing RIs has cost you more.

    If you are using only a few types of instances, the decision is easier. For example, you may have one hundred t2.small Linux instances and forty t2.small Windows instances. You are sure an average of 50% of them will be online. Then you can purchase RIs for fifty t2.small Linux instances and twenty t2.small Windows instances.

- Enterprise Support Plan Subscription

    The ROIs for RIs could be different if you have an Enterprise Support Agreement, which provides tiered discounts based on AWS expenditure. Talk to your AWS account managers.

    If you have upfront payments for RIs when or before you sign up for one of the support plans, these upfront payments will be included in the calculation of your support bill. For more details, please see "Effects of RIs" below.

4.2.4.9 How to Maximize RI Utilization

It is a challenge in an enterprise environment to keep track of On-Demand Instances and RIs.

The following is a list of things to do to maximize RI utilization.

- Document all your RIs and keep the documentation up to date.

    Documenting all the RIs allows you to review the purchase decisions of each RI and renew it promptly when it expires.

- Share the RI documentation with the stakeholders and beyond.

    Sharing the RIs encourages others to utilize the RIs whenever they can. One application can run on either t3.xlarge or m5.xlarge, both with two vCPUs and 8g memory; there are RIs for t3.xlarge but not for m5.xlarge. Therefore, choosing t3.xlarge could potentially save a lot.

- Renew RIs promptly.

    It takes time to review RIs and obtain approvals for renewal. Make a plan early and renew RIs promptly.

- Monitor RI Utilization and RI Coverage.

    Generate a report every month of all the EC2 instances or RDS instances that are not covered by RIs. Evaluate them and purchase RIs if necessary.

    For details, please check the following:

LINK: Implementation #7: How to Monitor RI Utilization and RI Coverage.

4.2.4.10 Effect of RIs

Your AWS bills and the cost allocations will become more difficult to understand when you purchase RIs. When you sign up for a Support Plan, your first month's support bill may be more than you expected. That is because the earlier one-time upfront charges for RIs are prorated and included in the calculation for the first month of AWS support.

For example, if you purchase a one-year reserved instance on January 1 and sign up for Business Support plan on October 1 of the same year, 75 percent of the upfront fee you paid in January is included in the calculation of support costs for October.

This complicates cost estimation. Now you have to go all the way back to get the total upfront payments to calculate the cost of signing up for a support plan.

4.3 Use Serverless Architecture or Managed Services

You can choose Spot Instances over On-Demand Instances and purchase RIs to minimize the cost of On-Demand Instances.

You could go much further with cost optimization and not use any instances at all with the serverless architecture or managed services.

> Optimize Baseline Costs
>
> Step 3: Use Serverless Architecture or Managed Services.

4.3.1 AWS Managed Services

AWS offers a list of managed services.

- Managed services for databases:

    Amazon RDS

    Amazon DynamoDB

- Managed services for search, analytics and others:

    Amazon Elasticsearch Service

    AWS Athena and AWS Glue

    Amazon EMR

- Serverless or application-level services:

    AWS Lambda

    Amazon Simple Queue Service (Amazon SQS)

    Amazon Simple Notification Service (Amazon SNS)

Amazon Simple Email Service (Amazon SES)

With the managed services, AWS manages the infrastructure for you.

For example, with AWS Athena, you do not have to launch an EMR (Elastic Map Reduce) cluster to do the computing. AWS does that for you behind the scenes at a cost of $5 per TB of data scanned. If your query scans 10.24 GB of data, the cost of your query is only $0.05. There are no EC2 instances or EMR clusters to launch and manage. There are no upfront payments. This service is readily available on demand.

Managed services could save you time and money. Leverage them if you can.

4.3.2 Serverless Architecture

With serverless architecture, no server is needed to run your application. AWS scales your application for you. In many cases, automation is easier with serverless architecture than with server-based architecture.

For example, you could launch an EC2 instance and run cron jobs on that instance. The EC2 instance acts as a server. You pay for the EC2 instance.

With Serverless architecture, you can create an AWS Lambda function and schedule it to run. The Lambda function can also be triggered by CloudWatch events.

Instead of using your database to store data and track activities, you could use S3 for storage and SNS or SQS for a message-queuing service, notification, and workflow.

For less than $20, you can allocate 128MB of memory to your Lambda function and execute it 30,000,000 times in one month, if it runs for 200ms each time.

For details on AWS Serverless, please visit:

https://aws.amazon.com/serverless/

4.4 Choose a Free OS Platform

> Optimize Baseline Costs
>
> Step 4: Choose a free OS platform for EC2 instances when possible.

In the table below, at the time of writing, the Linux platform for your EC2 instances was the cheapest of all the platforms. Windows costs 33% more, and SLES costs 76% more.

t3.large	Linux	RHAL	SLES	Windows
On-Demand per hour	$0.0832	$0.1432	$0.1462	$0.1108
Relative Cost	100%	172%	176%	133%

Choose the Linux platform whenever you can.

4.5 Choose a Free Database Software

> Optimize Baseline Costs
>
> Step 5: Choose a free database software for RDS instances when possible.

The following table shows you how much it costs to use an open source database such as MySQL or PostgreSQL and how much more it costs to use the proprietary database software. For example, if you are using RDS for SQL Server Standard Edition, you are spending over three times as much as for RDS for MySQL.

Table 5 1: Price Comparison - Free vs. Proprietary

db.r3.xlarge	RDS for MySQL	RDS for PostgreSQL	RDS for SQL Server (Standard)	RDS for Oracle (Standard 1)	Aurora with MySQL
On-Demand per hour, Single Zone (Except for Aurora)	$0.475	$0.50	$1.52	$0.91	$0.58
Relative Cost	100%	105%	320%	192%	122%

According to AWS, compared to MySQL, you could save 90 percent of your costs by using Aurora with MySQL. Aurora with MySQL or Aurora with PostgreSQL runs on a cluster. It is more expensive than RDS in the table because it has built-in and managed high availability.

In many cases, developers choose the database they are familiar with. If they are using Microsoft Visual Studio for development, they prefer SQL Server because it is tightly integrated with Visual Studio.

A decentralized organization could end up with several types of databases are being deployed. This creates two issues:

1. You are paying a lot for the license costs when proprietary databases are deployed, but open source databases may work just as well.

2. When you purchase RIs to cover these RDS instances, not only is the RI utilization lower, but the administration (the tracking, reviewing and renewing) is also more difficult.

Work with product managers, software architects, and engineers. When they evaluate databases, encourage them to use open source database software, the ones for which you already have RIs, or the ones you are already using.

It may also make sense to break up a big database into a few smaller ones for scalability and cost savings.

You may also be able to consolidate several databases into one for cost savings, especially when a license is required for proprietary database software. Consolidation reduces expensive software license costs.

4.6 Leverage Nonstandard S3 Storage Classes

> Optimize Baseline Costs
>
> Step 6: Leverage nonstandard S3 storage classes.

4.6.1 Four Main Classes of S3 Storage

There are four main classes of S3 storage: Standard, Standard IA, One Zone IA and Glacier. Standard IA is for files of "Infrequent Access." One Zone IA is similar to Standard IA, except that the files will be available in a single zone. If that zone is not available, the files are not available.

Files in Glacier are not online, and they are not available. You must create a request to have AWS restore the files to bring them online.

On April 4, 2019, Amazon announced the availability of Amazon S3 Glacier Deep Archive. According to the announcement from Amazon, this is a new storage class "for long-term data retention and digital preservation for data that may be accessed once or twice a year". The price is $0.00099 per GB-month, or about $1 per TB-month.

4.6.2 Cost Savings over Standard Storage Class

As seen from the S3 pricing table below, you could save 45.65 percent by moving Standard storage to Standard IA, 56.52 percent to One Zone IA, or 82.61 percent if you change to Glacier. Any one of the nonstandard storage classes represents significant savings.

Table 4-1: Four S3 Storage Classes - Cost Comparison

Storage Class	Price (US East Ohio)	Relative Cost	Savings over Standard
Standard	$0.023 per GB per month (for the first 50 TB)	100%	-
Standard IA	$0.0125 per GB per month	54.35%	**45.65%**
One Zone IA	$0.01 per GB per month	43.48%	**56.52%**
Glacier	$0.004 per GB per month	17.39%	**82.61%**
Glacier Deep Archive	$0.00099 per GB-month	4.30%	**95.70%**

When files are moved to Standard IA and One Zone IA, you must pay the cost of data retrievals (this is not the same as data transfer) at $0.01 per GB in the US East Ohio region. In addition, you must pay higher cost for PUT, COPY or POST requests, at $0.01 per 1,000 requests. The PUT, COPY, and POST requests for Standard storage are $0.005 per 1,000 requests.

4.6.3 Identify Candidate Objects for Standard IA and One Zone IA

To leverage the lower pricing of Standard IA and One Zone IA storage, you need to identify which buckets, prefixes or objects can be moved to Standard IA or One Zone IA.

Here is the approach we took to identify which buckets and which prefixes should be changed to Standard IA. This approach is for someone who knows how to write basic database queries. It may only make sense if you have a large S3 storage bill.

You will need some business intelligence on your S3 storage: the number of objects that are over six or twelve months old, the type of objects they are, and whether it is a good idea to move them from Standard to Standard IA. You can use S3 Inventory and AWS Athena to analyze the data and get your answers.

Please see the following sections for instructions:

Implementation #9: How to Set Up and Use AWS S3 Inventory for AWS Cost Optimization

Implementation #8: How to Set Up and Use AWS Athena for Cost Optimization

Analyze AWS S3 Inventory Data

Report #4: Six-Month-Old Objects Summary Report

Report #5: Twelve-Month-Old Objects Summary Report

4.6.4 Standard Vs. Standard IA - the Optimization Model

To leverage the lower pricing of Standard IA and One Zone IA storage, you also need to estimate how much data retrievals and how many requests you may have. With that information, you can calculate the potential savings by moving objects into Standard IA or One Zone IA storage.

Here is an example in a simplified model:

There is a bucket called "Clinical-Docs" in the US East Ohio region. This bucket stores the clinical documents from partners and clients, which include hospitals and clinics. One of the prefixes is Medical-Images, which stores the medical images you receive at the beginning of every quarter.

Region:	US East Ohio
Bucket:	Clinical-Docs
Prefix:	Medical-Images

These images are retrieved and analyzed at the end of each quarter, but are not used for three months in between. There are 10 TB (or 10,240 GB) of medical images with an average size of 1 MB each.

The question is whether you should move the files to Standard IA at the beginning of the quarter in which you receive these files. After all, these files will not be analyzed until the end of quarter.

Let's calculate the total costs for two scenarios:

(1) doing nothing - keeping the files on Standard storage class;

(2) moving the files to Standard IA.

In comparing the total costs for three months for each case, with the pricing information from AWS, we make two assumptions:

1. On average, each image will be requested five times for analysis using GET requests, mostly the GetObjects requests.
2. On average, each image will be retrieved 1.5 times for analysis.

Table 4-2: Standard vs. Standard IA Optimization Model - Variables and Assumptions

Model Variables		
Standard Pricing - Storage	$ 0.0230	per GB per month
Standard IA Pricing - Storage	$ 0.0125	per GB per month
Standard - Requests	$ 0.0050	per 1,000 requests
Standard IA Pricing - Requests	$ 0.0100	per 1,000 requests
Standard IA - Data Retrievals	$ 0.0100	per GB per month
Average # of Requests	5	requests per file
Average # of Data Retrievals	1.50	retrievals per file

Now we have the necessary information to calculate the costs for three months. The "total number of requests" for Month 1 are the requests to change each file object's storage class from Standard to Standard IA. Assume that it takes one attempt for each file, which is the same as the

"File Count." The "total number of requests" for Month 3 is the GET requests for image analysis, which is five times the "File Count."

Table 4-3: Table 5 2: Standard vs. Standard IA Optimization Model - Key inputs

	Month #1	Month #2	Month #3
Average File Size (KB)	1,024	1,024	1,024
File Count	1,048,576	1,048,576	1,048,576
Total Size (in GB)	102,400	102,400	102,400
Total # of requests	1,048,576	-	5,242,880
Data Retrievals (in GB)	-	-	153,600

With the variables and assumptions above, we have the total costs for three months.

Table 4-4: Standard vs. Standard IA Optimization Model - Calculation

Standard - Cost Estimate	Month #1	Month #2	Month #3	Total Cost
Storage	$2,355.20	$2,355.20	$2,355.20	$7,065.60
Requests			$26.21	$26.21
Data Retrievals				
Total	$2,355.20	$2,355.20	$2,381.41	$7,091.81

Standard IA - Cost Estimate	Month #1	Month #2	Month #3	Total Cost

Storage	$1,280.00	$1,280.00	$1,280.00	$3,840.00
Requests	$10.49		$52.43	$62.91
Data Retrievals			$1,536.00	$1,536.00
Total	**$1,290.49**	**$1,280.00**	**$2,868.43**	**$5,438.91**

3 Months Total Savings - Standard IA:	**$ 1,652.90**
12 Months Total Savings - Standard IA:	**$ 6,611.60**

Based on the above analysis, you will save $1,652.90 each quarter by moving the ten TB medical images to Standard IA, or $6,611.60 of savings every twelve months.

If these medical images are only used every six months or every twelve months, you will save more. If they will never be used once they are analyzed, you can move them to Glacier or Glacier Deep Archive for archiving.

Of course, this is a simplified model. To be accurate, you can calculate the net present value (NPV) of each scenario and base your decision on the NPVs.

You may receive medical images continuously. In this case, you have to estimate how many files are eligible to be moved to Standard IA. You may also estimate the growth rate of the prefix for each month.

If you are really into the optimization, you can also run a simulation model in Excel to get the breakeven points for each variable.

For example, holding all other variables constant, at how many requests per file will there be no difference between Standard IA and Standard? What if the image files are analyzed every four months, six months or twelve months?

Using the same approach, you can make decisions regarding whether to archive some files to Glacier.

With Glacier, there is an initial cost of transition requests into Glacier. Then when you need to access to the objects, you first have to make requests to restore the objects.

Table 4-5: AWS S3 Glacier - Cost

Lifecycle Transition Requests into Glacier	$0.05 per 1,000 requests (US East Ohio)
Glacier Retrieval request pricing	Standard - $0.05 per 1,000 requests (US East Ohio) Expedited - $10.00 per 1,000 requests (US East Ohio) Bulk - $0.025 per 1,000 requests (US East Ohio)
Glacier Retrieval pricing	Standard - $0.01 per GB (US East Ohio) Expedited - $0.03 per GB (US East Ohio) Bulk - $0.0205 per GB (US East Ohio)

If you want to further reduce the archiving costs, you may create a model to analyze whether to transfer the data off AWS to your own infrastructure.

4.6.5 Save Data Transfer Costs with AWS Snowball

If you have a large amount of data to be transferred to or from AWS Cloud, AWS Snowball could save you a lot on data transfer.

You submit a request for Snowball data transfer. A Snowball device is shipped to you. When you receive the Snowball device, plug it into your network, download and run the "Snowball Client," and select the files to be transferred to the AWS Cloud. The "Snowball Client" encrypts the files and transfers them to the device. You return the device to AWS with the pre-printed mailing label.

If you transfer files from AWS Cloud to your network, the files will be in the device and you will be able to decrypt the files and transfer the files to your local network.

4.7 Avoid Creating Multiple Copies of the Same Objects

Optimize Baseline Costs
Step 7: Minimize the need to create multiple copies of the same objects.

One object may end up in different buckets owned by different groups. This is not unusual in an enterprise environment when there are multiple groups handling the same data.

When the research department needs to analyze the object, they make a copy of the object so that they can manipulate and process the object however they can. A data scientist from the software development makes another copy. An engineer in the QA department makes another copy. You see the problem.

This is a big problem in addressing the cost of S3 storage, not even considering the regulatory compliance challenges in protecting sensitive customer data.

There is no cost-effective way to determine how many identical objects exist across all buckets, even with the MD5 Checksum of each object.

Since there is no easy way to track the copies of an object, the only way seems to be preventing an object from being copied in the first place.

Motives to create copies of objects vary. Some people would like to get around access control. Some would like to have a snapshot of a bucket or a prefix in a bucket. Some would like to have a subset of the data in a bucket.

You could create a policy that any COPY requests must go through the approval process. With such an approval process, people will consider whether they really want to make a copy.

Such an approval process also provides documentation on the flow of S3 objects. When you try to delete an object, you may use the documentation to find other identical copies and delete them as well.

Another way is to create a trigger to listen to the COPY event of an object and log its source and destination of the COPY event. Now you have a single place to search for copies of an object and audit the COPY requests periodically.

4.8 Use AWS Select

> Optimize Baseline Costs
>
> Step 8: Use AWS S3 Select.

AWS Data Transfer is expensive, especially when you are delivering files from S3 to the Internet, or between regions.

The cost to transfer files from US East Ohio to US West Oregon is $0.02 per GB, and to the Internet the cost is from $0.05 to $0.09 per GB (free for the first GB).

Your application may only need a portion of data in some files that meet certain criteria.

Typically, your application may download 100 files, open each one of them, and find thirty that have the data to match your criteria. You are paying for the downloading of all 100 files.

With S3 Select, you can pull out only the data you need from an object, which can dramatically improve performance and reduce the cost of applications that need to access data in S3.

You only need to download those 30 files that meet your criteria. In some cases, you don't need to download the files at all. You only pull out the data you need from an object.

Table 4-6: AWS S3 Select - Cost

Data Returned by S3 Select (US East Ohio)	$0.0007 per GB
Data Scanned by S3 Select (US East Ohio)	$0.002 per GB

If your S3 Select scans 10 GB of data and returns 1 GB of data, the cost of S3 Select is $0.002*10 + $0.0007*1 = $0.0207. The cost of data transfer over the Internet is 1 GB * $0.05 per GB = $0.05.

The total cost is $0.0207 + $0.05 = $0.0707.

If you download the 10 GB over the Internet, your estimated cost is 10 GB * $0.05 per GB = $0.50, which is over 600% more than S3 Select, not even considering the time it takes to download the data.

Therefore, educate your teams and encourage them to use S3 Select.

4.9 Consider Business or Enterprise Support Contract

> Optimize Baseline Costs
>
> Step 9: Sign an Enterprise Support Contract when it makes sense.

There are four AWS Support Plans: Basic, Developer, Business, and Enterprise. Other than the Basic Plan, each plan is charged as the percentage of your AWS bill, with a minimum commitment. For example, the Enterprise Support Plan has a minimum of $15,000 per month. The exact amount could be calculated with a tiered pricing model.

With an Enterprise Support Plan, the more you save on your AWS bill, the more you will be rewarded by the reduced cost of Enterprise Support.

As the table below shows, when you cut your AWS bill from $1,000,000 to $600,000, your enterprise support plan fee is also cut by $20,000 (from $64,500 to $44,500).

Table 4-7: Cost Optimization and Enterprise Support Fees

If your AWS Bill is:		$1 M		$600K	
Enterprise Support Plan - Fees:					
Greater of $15,000					
- or -		Amount in the Tier	Fees	Amount in the Tier	Fees
10% of monthly AWS usage for the first $0–$150K	10%	150,000	15,000	150,000	15,000
7% of monthly AWS usage from $150K–$500K	7%	350,000	24,500	350,000	24,500
5% of monthly AWS usage from $500K–$1M	5%	500,000	25,000	100,000	5,000
3% of monthly AWS usage over $1M	3%	-	-	-	-
		Total Fees		64,500	44,500

4.10 Chapter Summary

In this chapter, you learned to optimize the baseline cost with a focus on optimizing compute and storage costs.

For EC2 instances, you can use one of three ways to save: use Spot Instances, purchase RIs for On-Demand Instances, or don't use EC2 instances at all by using serverless architecture.

For storage, move as many of your objects out of the Standard storage class as you can. Leverage a cheaper storage class such as Glacier or Glacier Deep Archive for data retention.

This chapter presents nine steps to optimizing baseline costs:

Summary

Step 1: Maximize utilization of Spot Instances.

Step 2: Cover On-Demand Instances with RIs.

Step 3: Use managed services or serverless architecture.

Step 4: Choose a free OS Platform for EC2 instances.

Step 5: Choose free database software for RDS instances when possible.

Step 6: Leverage nonstandard S3 storage classes.

Step 7: Minimize the need to create multiple copies of the same objects.

Step 8: Use AWS S3 Select.

Step 9: Sign an enterprise support contract when it makes sense.

Chapter 5. Optimize Cloud Costs with 10 Step-by-Step Implementations

Quick links in this chapter:

Chapter 5.   Optimize Cloud Costs with 10 Step-by-Step Implementations 137

5.1   Introduction 139

5.2   Implementation #1: How to Estimate the Monthly AWS Cost, Save It and Share It 140

5.3   Implementation #2: How to Set Up AWS Budget Alerts 150

5.4   Implementation #3: How to Implement a Schedule to Start and Stop an EC2 or RDS Instance 177

5.5   Implementation #4: How to Implement S3 Lifecycle Policies for AWS Cost Optimization 182

5.6   Implementation #5: How to Implement Data Lifecycle Management 204

5.7   Implementation #6: How to Tag AWS Resources for Cost Optimization 218

5.8   Implementation #7: How to Monitor RI Utilization and RI Coverage 237

5.9   Implementation #8: How to Set Up and Use AWS Athena for Cost Optimization 246

5.10   Implementation #9: How to Set Up and Use AWS S3 Inventory for AWS Cost Optimization 273

5.11   Implementation #10: How to Set Up and Use AWS S3 Server Access Logging for AWS Cost Optimization 298

5.12   Chapter Summary 318

5.1 Introduction

The previous chapters presented *what* to do to optimize AWS Cloud costs.

In this chapter, you will learn *how* to use the tools to optimize AWS Cloud costs.

This is a chapter about hands-on technical implementation. You will learn to use the tools step by step.

For engineers:

> You can get started immediately. You can go beyond this book and dig deeper on your own.

For managers:

> You can understand what AWS tools are available for AWS cost optimization.

This is not a replacement for the AWS User Guide for each AWS service or product.

Unlike the instructions in the AWS User Guides, these implementation steps are very short and very practical within the context of AWS cost optimization.

Please note that our AWS account for the writing of this book is quite small. The screenshots show very little data. However, you should be able to follow the steps in your own AWS environment.

5.2 Implementation #1: How to Estimate the Monthly AWS Cost, Save It and Share It

5.2.1 Introduction

Let's start with something simple and very important: how to estimate your monthly cost.

Before you launch any AWS services, you should get an estimate of what your monthly bill will be. This is not just good practice. Most people use this tool for a one-time estimate of a specific AWS service, such as EC2. This tool could in fact give you estimates for your entire project.

In addition, you can save the estimates and send your teammates the link to the estimates. You can embed the estimates in your project plan or other documentation. You can publish the estimates to your internal work space, such as Confluence, SharePoint, and so on.

5.2.2 Instructions

The following example illustrates how useful this tool can be.

Project: Monthly Medical Imaging Processing
AWS Services Required:
Region: U.S. East (N. Virginia)

- Compute: 8 EC2 On-Demand Instances, c4.4xlarge, on Linux.
- EBS: 8 EBS volumes with 200g of SSD GP2 each.
- Storage: 2 TB of S3 standard storage.
- Database for applications: RDS Aurora with MySQL r3.4xlarge, 50g storage, on-demand.
- Database for imaging processing: DynamoDB with 25g storage, on-demand.

We will ignore the data transfer cost and other costs that may or may not be significant.

Go to the website:

You could estimate your AWS cost by using the "AWS Simple Monthly Calculator":

https://calculator.s3.amazonaws.com/index.html

This calculator will tell you how much you will spend per month for the AWS services you choose.

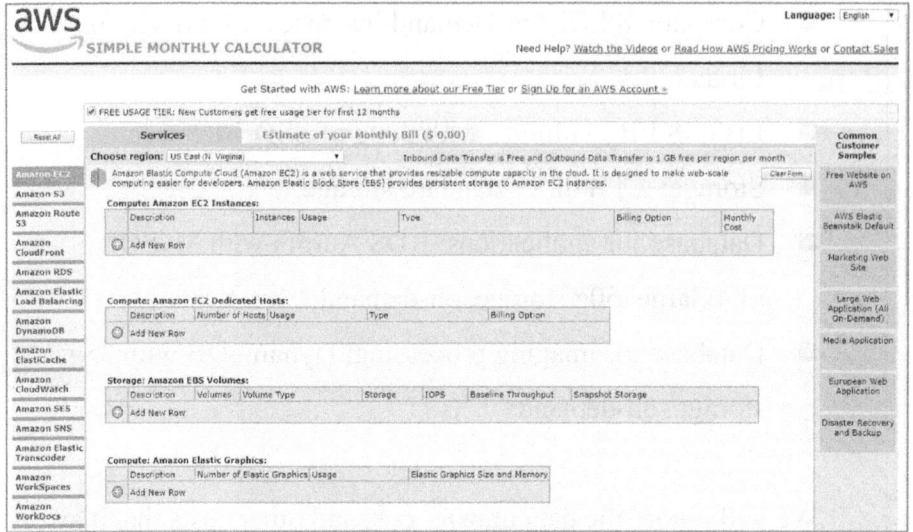

Figure 5.1: AWS Simple Monthly Calculator - Main

There is a link at the top of this page: "Read How AWS Pricing Works." You are encouraged to read this page to understand how AWS pricing works for major AWS services such as EC2, S3, RDS, DynamoDB, and so on.

As shown above, you can select AWS services on the left. Then specify what you need in the "Services" tab in the main panel. As you add more to the services, the amount in the second tab, "Estimate of your Monthly Bill (<new amount>)," is updated.

Please note that when you select a new AWS service on the left, you are not throwing away the previous estimates. Rather, you are adding the new selection to your current estimates. You can keep adding AWS services to your portfolio. The amount for your portfolio is updated on the second tab.

If you click on the second tab, "Estimate of your Monthly Bill (<new amount>)," you will see the components of your portfolio and their respective costs.

Estimate EC2 and EBS costs:

We begin with an EC2 instance.

Click on "Amazon EC2" on the left. Then add the following to Services:

Compute: Amazon EC2 Instances: 8 Instances, Linux on c4.4xlarge, On-Demand. You can see that the monthly cost is $4661.44.

EBS: On the same page, now add 8 EBS volumes of GP2 with 200 GB each. You can see that the amount in the tab "Estimate of Your Monthly Bill" is updated from $4661.44 to $5300.29.

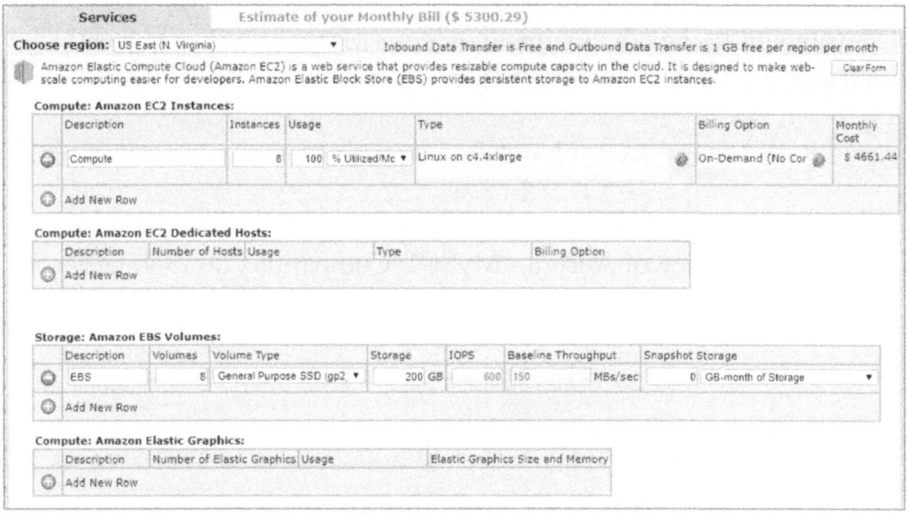

Figure 5.2: AWS Simple Monthly Calculator - EC2 and EBS

Add S3 Storage Cost Estimate:

You don't have to click the "Save" button to save your work. There is no such a button because your work is automatically saved. You can see it by going to the second tab, "Estimate of your Monthly Bill ($ xxxx.xx)."

Click on "Amazon S3" on the left. Then add the following to "Services":

S3 Standard Storage and Requests: 2048 GB.

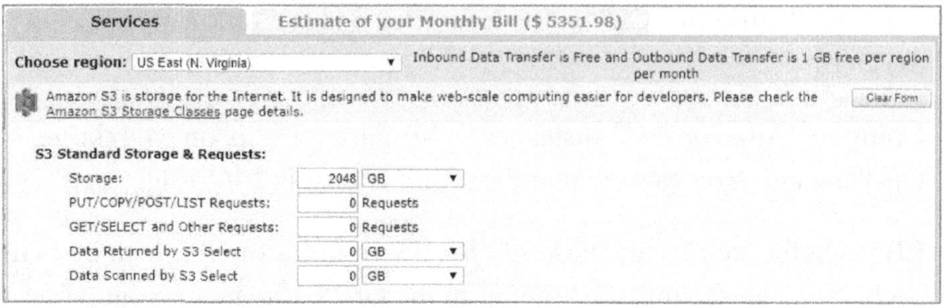

Figure 5.3: AWS Simple Monthly Calculator - S3

The amount in the tab "Estimate of Your Monthly Bill" has been updated from $5300.29 to $5351.98.

Add RDS Database Cost Estimate:

Click on "Amazon RDS" on the left. Then under the "Services" tab, add 1 DB Instance of Aurora - MySQL Compatible, db r3.4xlarge, 50 GB.

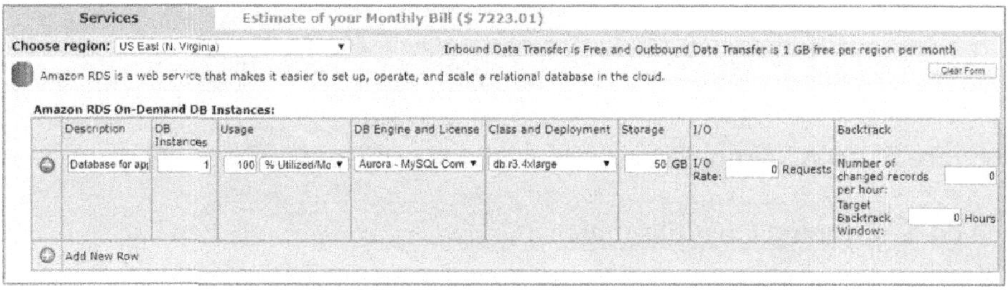

Figure 5.4: AWS Simple Monthly Calculator - RDS

The amount in the tab "Estimate of Your Monthly Bill" has been updated from $5300.29 to $7223.01.

Add DynamoDB Cost Estimate:

Click on "Amazon DynamoDB" on the left. Under the "Services" tab, add the following:

Dataset size of 25 GB, item size of 20 KB. Total number of items read per month: 5 in millions.

![AWS Simple Monthly Calculator DynamoDB screenshot showing Estimate of your Monthly Bill $7227.27, with Indexed Data Storage Dataset Size 25 GB, Item Size 20 KB, Eventually Consistent, Total number of items read per month 5 in millions]

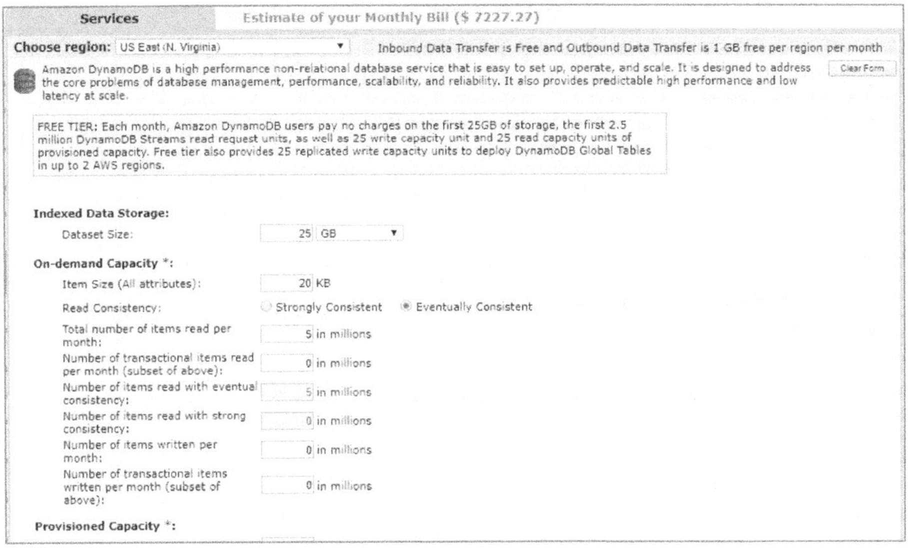

Figure 5.5: AWS Simple Monthly Calculator - DynamoDB

The amount in the tab "Estimate of Your Monthly Bill" has been updated from $7223.01 to $7227.27. This is a small increase because we have not provisioned any capacity for reading and writing. The provisioned capacity is the most significant cost.

If you are curious, we can provision 150 reads / second and 150 writes / second. As shown below, the total cost increases from $7227.27 to $8820.33. The cost of the provisioned capacity is $1593.06 per month.

[AWS Simple Monthly Calculator screenshot for Amazon DynamoDB — Estimate of your Monthly Bill ($ 8820.33)]

- Choose region: US East (N. Virginia)
- Inbound Data Transfer is Free and Outbound Data Transfer is 1 GB free per region per month

Indexed Data Storage:
- Dataset Size: 25 GB

On-demand Capacity *:
- Item Size (All attributes): 20 KB
- Read Consistency: Eventually Consistent
- Total number of items read per month: 5 in millions
- Number of transactional items read per month (subset of above): 0 in millions
- Number of items read with eventual consistency: 5 in millions
- Number of items read with strong consistency: 0 in millions
- Number of items written per month: 0 in millions
- Number of transactional items written per month (subset of above): 0 in millions

Provisioned Capacity *:
- Item Size (All attributes): 20 KB
- Read Consistency: Eventually Consistent
- Total number of items read per second: 150 Reads/Second
- Number of transactional items read per second (subset of above): 0 Reads/Second
- Number of items read with eventual consistency: 150 Reads/Second
- Number of items read with strong consistency: 0 Reads/Second
- Number of items written per second: 150 Writes/Second

Estimate of the portfolio of services:

Now we have added all the services we need for the project.

Click on the second tab, "Estimate of Your Monthly Bill ($7227.27)." All of the component costs are present, as shown below.

Services	Estimate of your Monthly Bill ($ 7227.27)		
Estimate of Your Monthly Bill			
☑ Show First Month's Bill (include all one-time fees, if any)			
Below you will see an estimate of your monthly bill. Expand each line item to see cost breakout of each service. To save this bill and input values, click on 'Save and Share' button. To remove the service from the estimate, jump back to the service and clear the specific service's form.			
Export to CSV			Save and Share
Amazon EC2 Service (US East (N. Virginia))			$ 4821.44
Compute:		$ 4661.44	
EBS Volumes:		$ 160.00	
EBS IOPS:		$ 0.00	
Amazon S3 Service (US East (N. Virginia))			$ 47.11
S3 Standard Storage:		$ 47.11	
Amazon RDS Service (US East (N. Virginia))			$ 1703.24
DB instances:		$ 1698.24	
Storage:		$ 5.00	
I/O:		$ 0.00	
Amazon DynamoDB Service (US East (N. Virginia))			$ 3.87
On-demand Capacity:		$ 3.25	
Provisioned Capacity:		$ 0.00	
Indexed Data Storage:		$ 0.62	
DynamoDB Streams:		$ 0.00	
On-demand backup:		$ 0.00	
Continuous backup (PITR):		$ 0.00	
Restoring a table:		$ 0.00	
Global Tables:		$ 0.00	
AWS Support (Business)			$ 657.03
Free Tier Discount:			$ -5.42
Total Monthly Payment:			$ 7227.27

Figure 5.6: AWS Simple Monthly Calculator - Portfolio

Please note that these are estimates. You may add new items such as provisioned capacity for DynamoDB (as mentioned before) and data transfers. You may also remove items such as "AWS Support (Business)" if you don't subscribe to AWS Support (Business).

Save and share configuration:

Now you can export the estimate of your portfolio of services to a CSV file by clicking on the "Export to CSV" button in the top left corner under the "Services" tab. Then you can share the CSV file with your teammates.

However, if your teammates would like to change the instance type or instance class, it is difficult to change from the CSV file because the pricing data is on the web.

The correct way to save and share is to save the link and share the link with your teammates.

Click on the "Save and Share" button in the upper right corner. You will see the screen below.

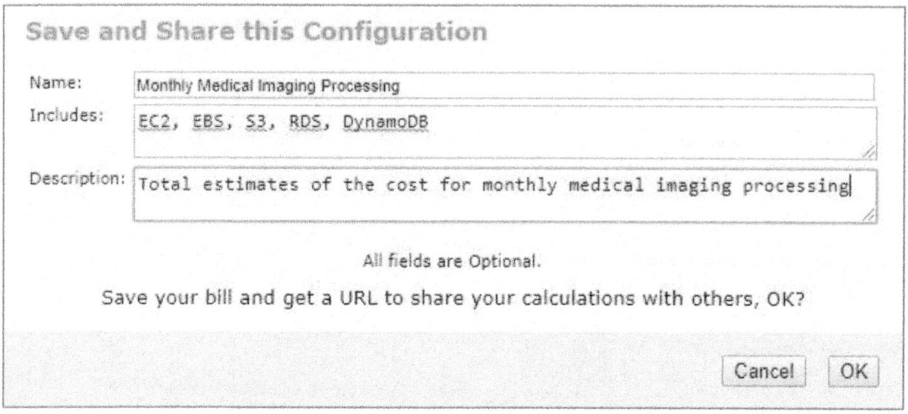

Figure 5.7: AWS Simple Monthly Calculator - Save and Share Configuration

Enter the name, then click "OK." Now you are presented with a web URL.

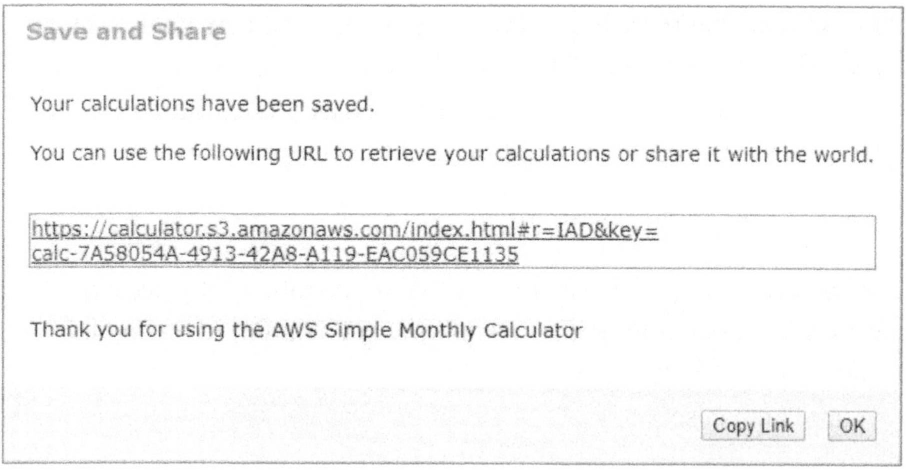

Figure 5.8: AWS Simple Monthly Calculator - Save and Share Link

Now you can save the link, send the link to others, or embed the link in your documentation.

If you receive a link from your teammate, you can open it, modify it and save it as a new link, or send the revised link back to your teammate.

Please note that the web URL is the only way you can come back to your cost estimate. This web URL is not saved anywhere, whether you are logged in or not. When you leave this site, all of the estimates are gone.

5.2.3 Summary

It is a best practice to estimate the cost of AWS services you need for a project. There are several benefits to doing cost estimates with the AWS Simple Monthly Calculator:

- Estimates unmask the true monthly cost of seemingly insignificant unit costs such as "$0.08 per hour."
- Estimates provide documentation for your project plan.
- Estimates enhance the communication among your team members.
- Estimates provide a baseline for your cost optimization.

5.3 Implementation #2: How to Set Up AWS Budget Alerts

5.3.1 Introduction

AWS Budget lets you create a budget for usage.

You can see the usage to date and compare it against the predicted usage at the end of the month.

You can also set up alerts when the budget limit is reached.

There are four types of budgets you can create:

- cost budgets
- usage budgets
- RI utilization budgets
- RI coverage budgets

Having budget alerts allows you to catch the unexpected sooner. The following are two incidents that made us wish we had budget alerts in place.

One incident was that hundreds of EC2 instances were launched by mistake and ran for over five days. These instances were launched by a loop in the code, and the maximum number of instances was not set.

Another incident was that billions of GET requests were made to S3 objects. Again, the requests were made via a code that was not carefully written. At $0.0004 per 1,000 requests, an extra $1,400 a day accrued for fifteen days. If we had had budget alerts in place, we might have caught the mistakes earlier.

5.3.2 Give Teams Permissions to Create Budgets

To empower teams to control their costs, they need more access and control.

To allow IAM users to create budgets, the user must have IAM permission to view your Billing and Cost Management console.

To allow IAM users to create budgets in the Billing and Cost Management console, the IAM user must have permissions to view billing information, create CloudWatch alarms, and create Amazon SNS notifications.

Here is an example of a policy to allow an IAM user to modify the Budget console page:

```
{
  "Version": "2012-10-17",
  "Statement": [
    {
      "Sid": "Stmt1435216493000",
      "Effect": "Allow",
      "Action": [
        "aws-portal:ViewBilling",
        "aws-portal:ModifyBilling",
        "budgets:ViewBudget",
        "budgets:ModifyBudget"
      ],
      "Resource": [
        "*"
      ]
    },
    {
      "Sid": "Stmt1435216514000",
      "Effect": "Allow",
      "Action": [
        "cloudwatch:*"
      ],
```

```
      "Resource": [
        "*"
      ]
    },
    {
      "Sid": "Stmt1435216552000",
      "Effect": "Allow",
      "Action": [
        "sns:*"
      ],
      "Resource": [
        "arn:aws:sns:us-east-1"
      ]
    }
  ]
}
```

5.3.3 Create a Budget and an Alert to Monitor EC2 Costs by Project

As mentioned earlier, we need to receive alerts when a research project is using too many EC2 resources. Let's create a Cost Budget to track that project.

In this example, we assume that all the EC2 instances related to this research project are tagged with "project" with the value of "Research."

Go to the AWS Billing dashboard. Click on "Budgets" on the left. You will see all the existing budgets you have created so far.

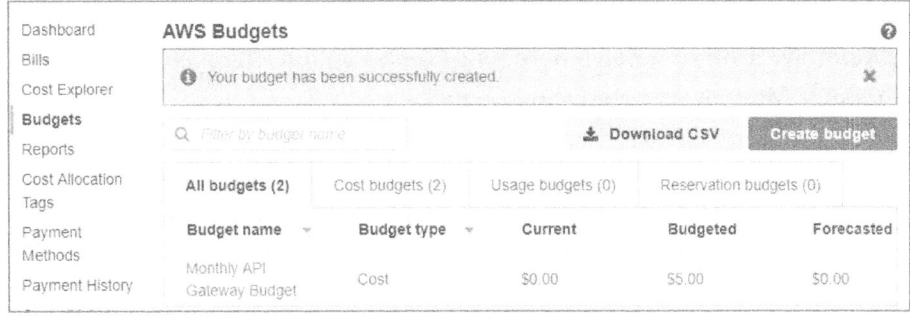

Figure 5.9: AWS Budget - main

Click on "Create budget" in the upper right corner. You'll see the screen below. Select "Cost budget" as the budget type. Then click "Set your budget" at the bottom.

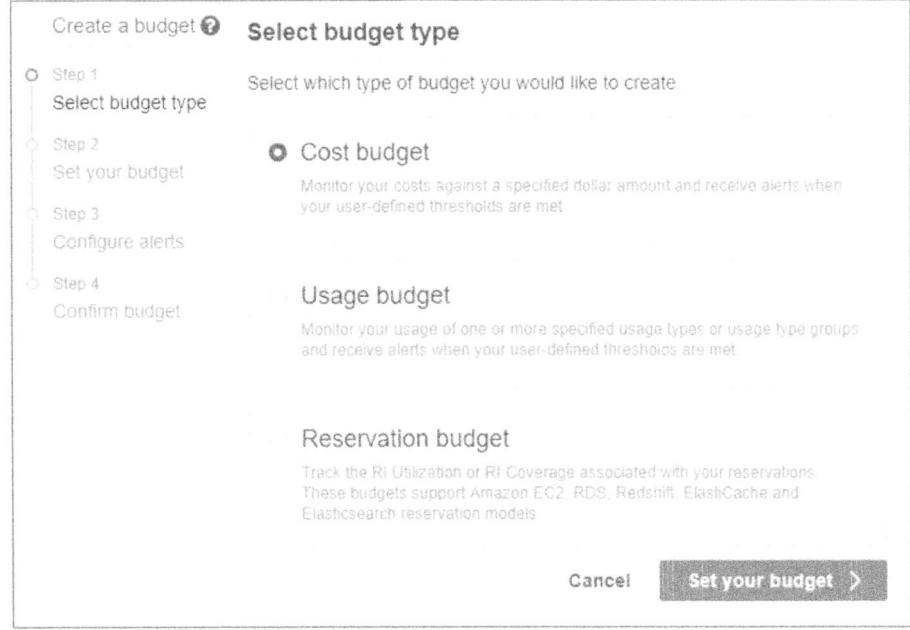

Figure 5.10: AWS Budget - Select budget type

Next, set your budget.

Enter the name "Monthly EC2 Budget - Research." Specify the period "Monthly." Unfortunately, there is no "Daily" option. There are only three options: Monthly, Quarterly and Annually.

Enter the budgeted amount. You will see the cost of the previous month on the right for reference. Please note that this amount will change once you specify the filter by using tags. You will come to that later.

Make this a recurring budget for every month, starting this month.

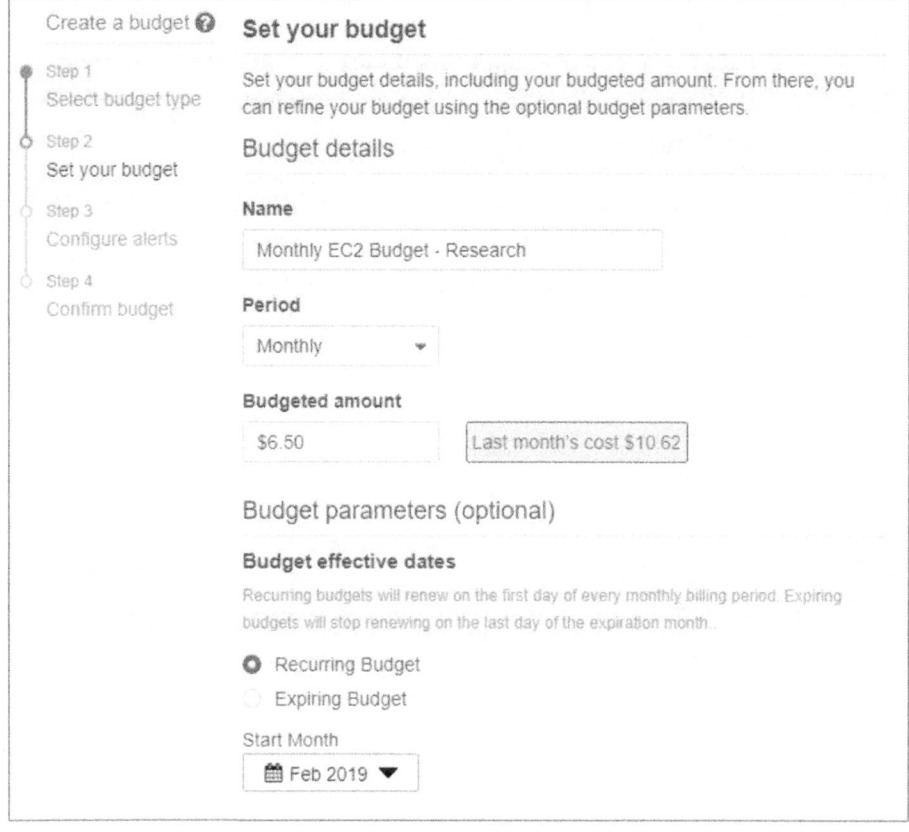

Figure 5.11: AWS Budget - Cost Budget - Set your budget - name and amount

Now you can specify filters. In this case, we need to filter by the tag "project" and by the service EC2.

Under Filtering, Tag, select "project" from the dropdown. You will see a list of values for the "project" tag. Select "research" from the dropdown. Click "Apply filters."

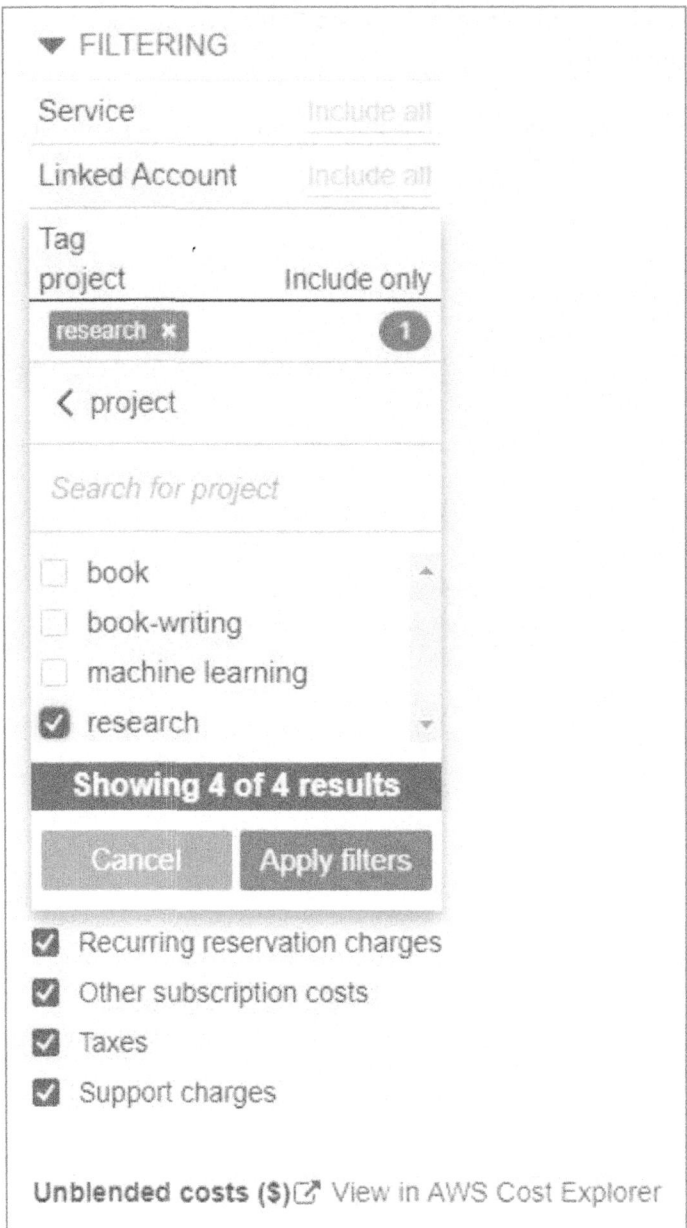

Figure 5.12: AWS Budget - Cost Budget - Set your budget - filter by tag

Now let's add another filter for EC2 only. Click "Service" under FILTERING. Select "EC2-Instances (Elastic Compute Cloud - Compute)." Then click "Apply filters."

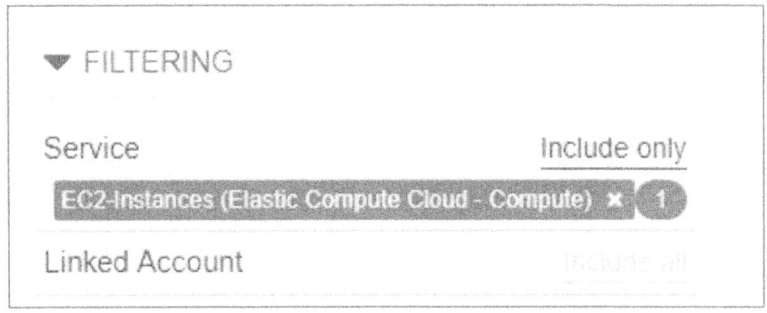

Figure 5.13: AWS Budget - Cost Budget - Set your budget - filter by service

Each time you apply a new filter, the amount in "Last month's cost" under "Budgeted amount" is updated. Without filters, the button label is "Last month's cost $10.62." After filters are applied, the button label is changed to "Last month's cost $5.12."

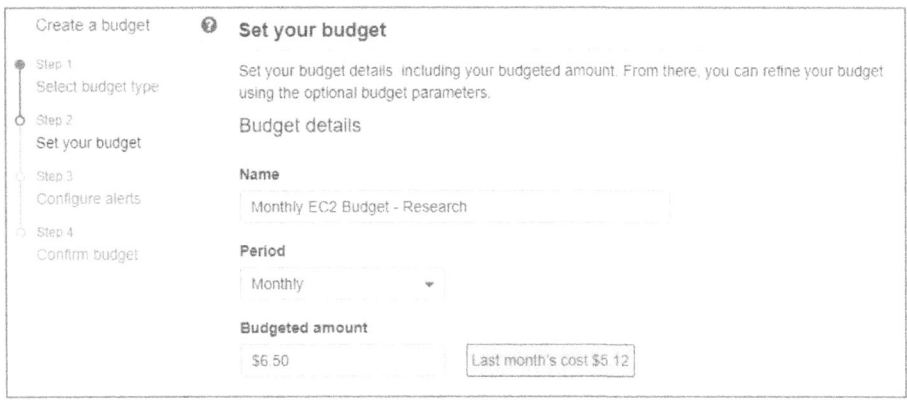

Figure 5.14: AWS Budget - Cost Budget - Set your budget - amount change after filtering

Below the filters, you will see costs for the last twelve months and the month-to-date cost of the current month. This is pulled from Cost Explorer if you have Cost Explorer configured. If not, you will see an empty chart here.

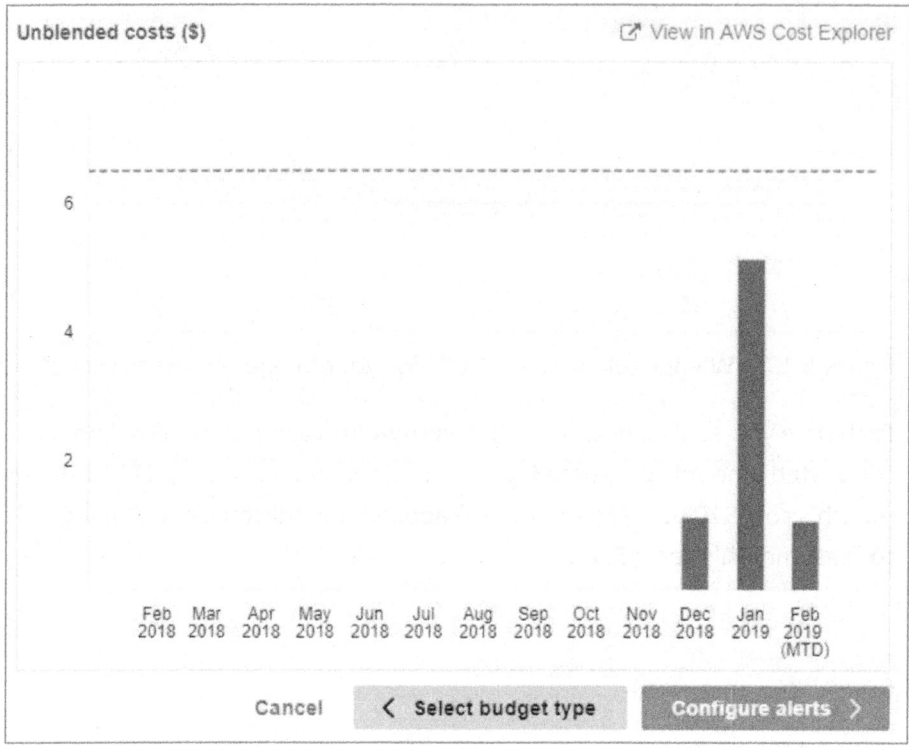

Figure 5.15: AWS Budget - Cost Budget - Set your budget - cost explorer

Now you have the budget amount set. Next, configure the alert. Click "Configure alerts" it the bottom right corner.

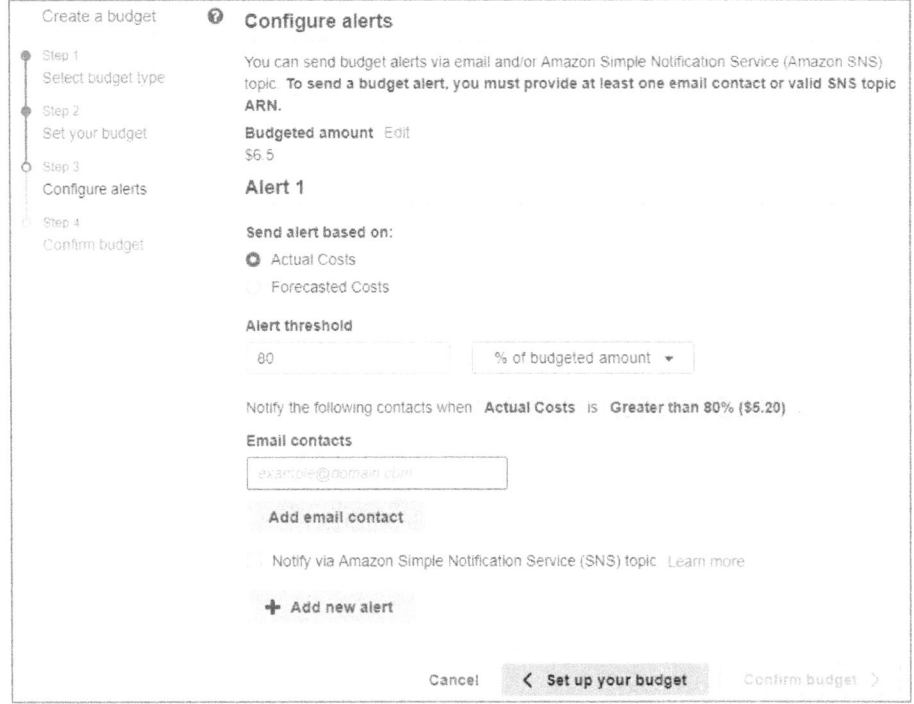

Figure 5.16: AWS Budget - Cost Budget - Configure alerts

Select "Actual Cost" under "Send alert based on." You may want to select "Forecasted Costs" if that is a better way to capture the abnormal spending earlier.

Specify 80% as your threshold. Once the cost reaches 80% of the budgeted amount, an alert will be sent to you.

Enter the email address, then click "Confirm budget" to continue.

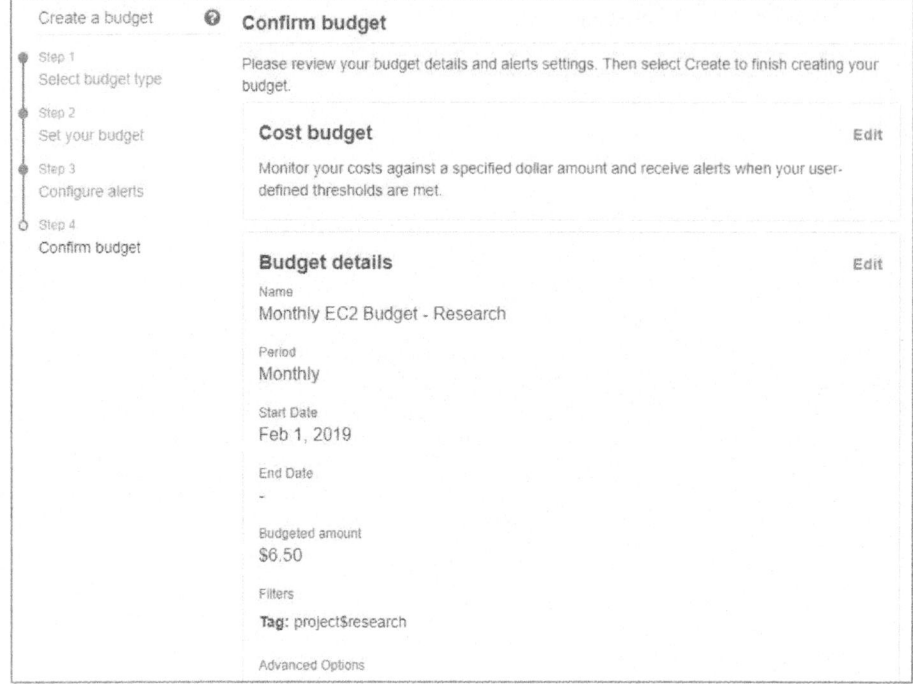

Figure 5.17: AWS Budget - Cost Budget - Confirm budget - 1

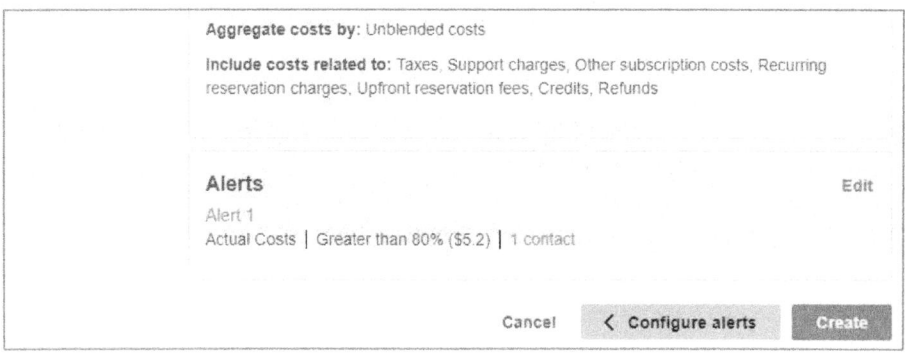

Figure 5.18: AWS Budget - Cost Budget - Confirm budget - 2

Now review your setting, then click "Create."

Your Cost Budget "Monthly EC2 Budget - Research" has been created. You can see the budgeted amount ($6.50). You will see the current and forecasted amounts soon after the creation.

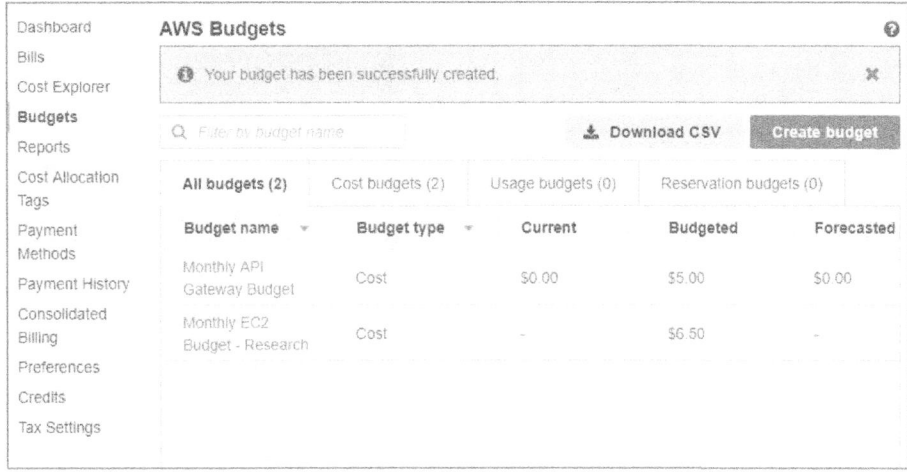

Figure 5.19: AWS Budge - main - with new budget

You can come back later and click on the budget you just created to see the details. Now you see "Current vs. Budgeted" and "Forecasted vs. Budgeted" as well as your budget history from the past twelve months in a chart.

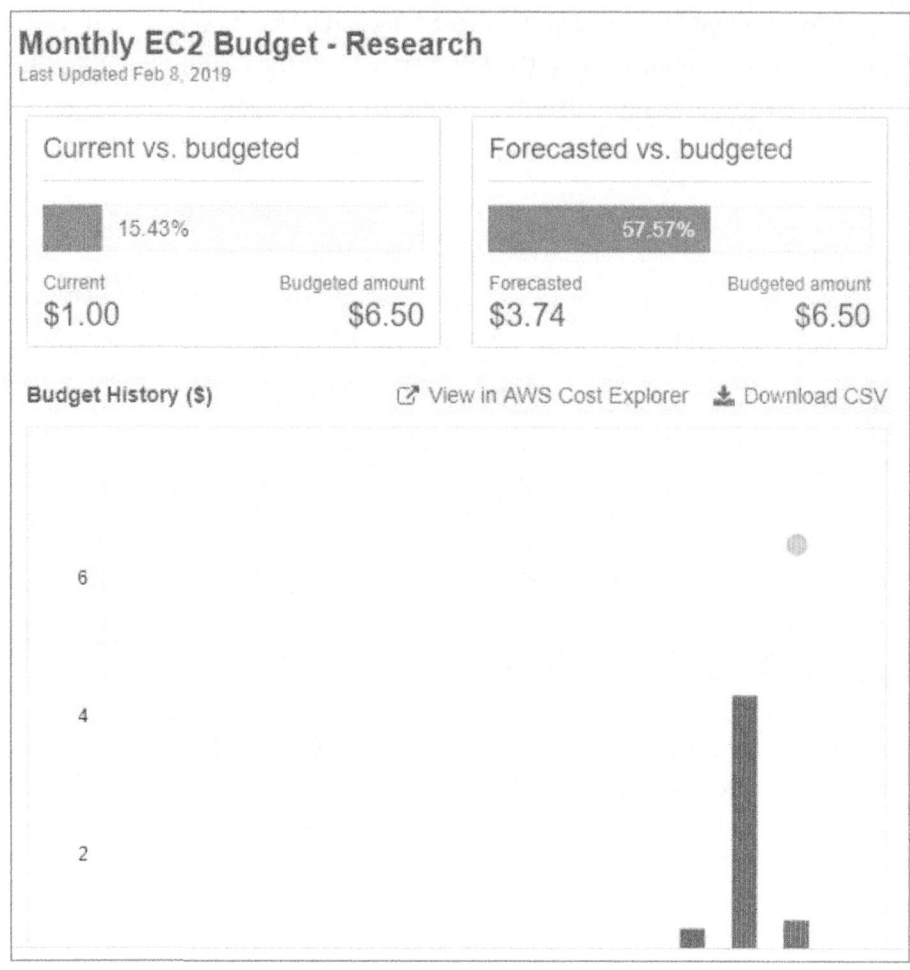

Figure 5.20: AWS Budget - Detail View

In the chart you can see what your actual cost was and what your budget was in each of the last 12 months. This gives you some idea whether your monthly costs have previously run over budget.

Please note that, since this alert threshold is set for the monthly budget, rather a daily budget, you may not receive alerts as early as you want.

For example, say your budget for the current month is $1,000. Your budget alert threshold is 80%, which means, you will not be notified until the accumulated cost reaches $800.

Let's assume the expected spending for the first 5 days of this month is $200. However, the actual spending for the first 5 days of this month is $500.

Unfortunately, since the actual spending of $500 has not met the threshold of $800 yet, your budget alert will not be triggered.

However, although the alert may not be soon enough, it may still be better than not having the budget alert at all.

In addition, you can always rely on the "Current vs. budgeted" and "Forecasted vs. budgeted" sections to detect any abnormal spending early in the month.

5.3.4 Create a Usage Budget to Monitor S3 GET Object Requests

In the second case mentioned earlier, there were billions of GET requests for S3 objects every day for fifteen days. This is nearly 500 times the normal number of GET requests.

To be alerted earlier of such an abnormal usage, consider a budget alert to monitor S3 GET object requests.

First, go to the main page of AWS Budget. Click "Create budget."

Now select "Usage budget" as the budget type.

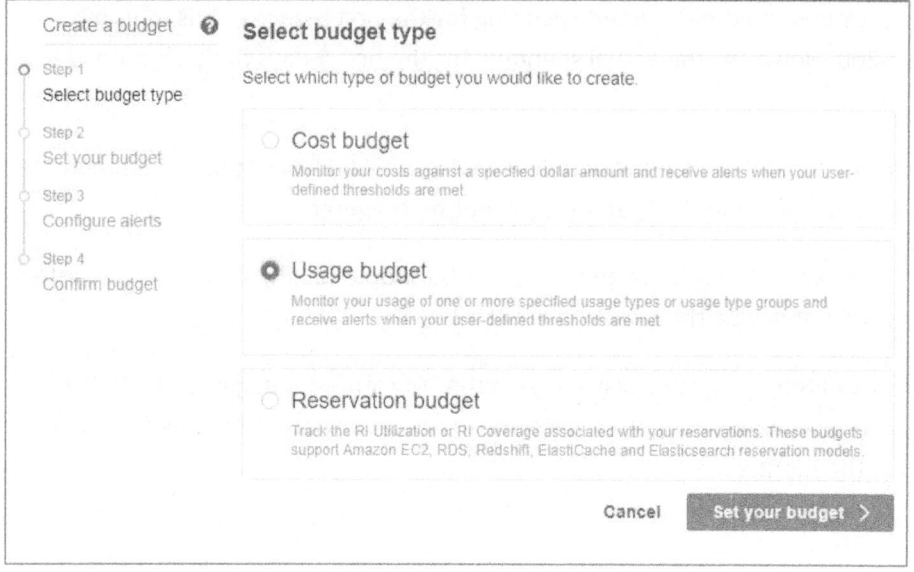

Figure 5.21: Usage Budget - select budget type

Give this budget a name: "Monthly S3 Object Requests - Machine Learning."

Select "Monthly" as the period. Unfortunately, there is no "Daily" option. There are only three options: Monthly, Quarterly and Annually.

Then select "Usage Type."

Select "S3 (Simple Storage Service)" on the left; then select "Requests-Tier2 (Requests)" on the right. This will capture all the "Get and other requests" from all regions.

About S3 Tier Requests:

> AWS Billing for S3 Requests is broken down into three tiers that indicate the type of request:
>
> Tier 1 = PUT, COPY, POST, or LIST requests
> Tier 2 = GET and other requests

Tier 3 = Glacier Archive and Restore Requests

Now enter 1,000,000 requests as the budgeted amount. As a reference, you see "Last month's usage" on the right. This number will change after you apply the filters later.

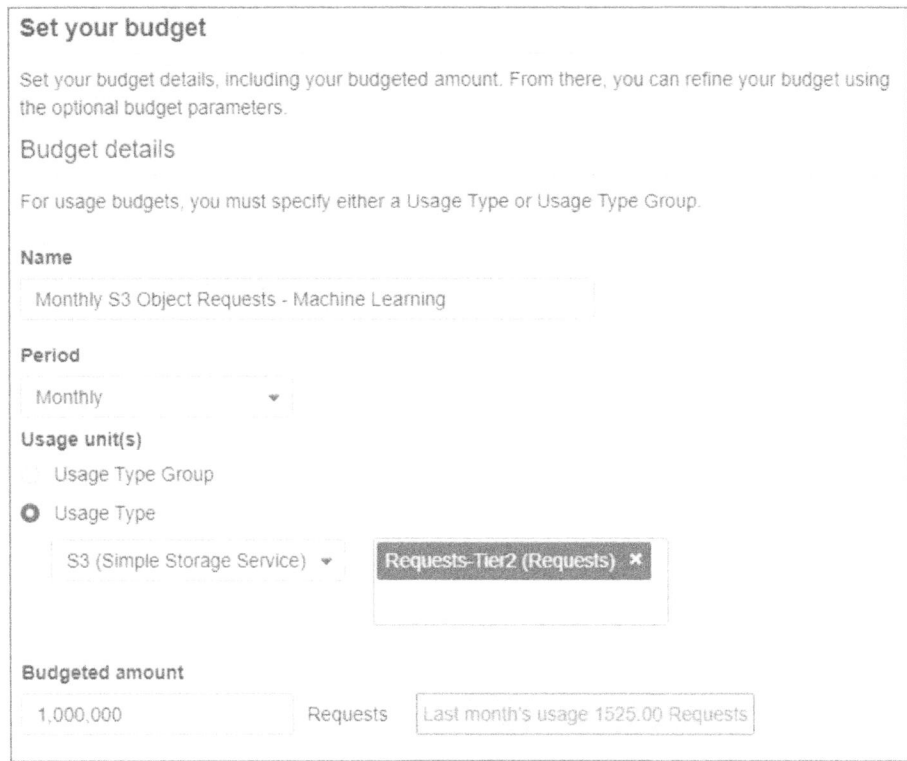

Figure 5.22: Usage Budget - Set your budget - name and amount

Enter additional budget parameters. Select "Recurring Budget," starting in the current month.

Now click "Tag," select "project," and then select "Machine Learning." Apply the filters.

Your budget will only be applied to those S3 Tier 2 requests related to the Machine Learning project.

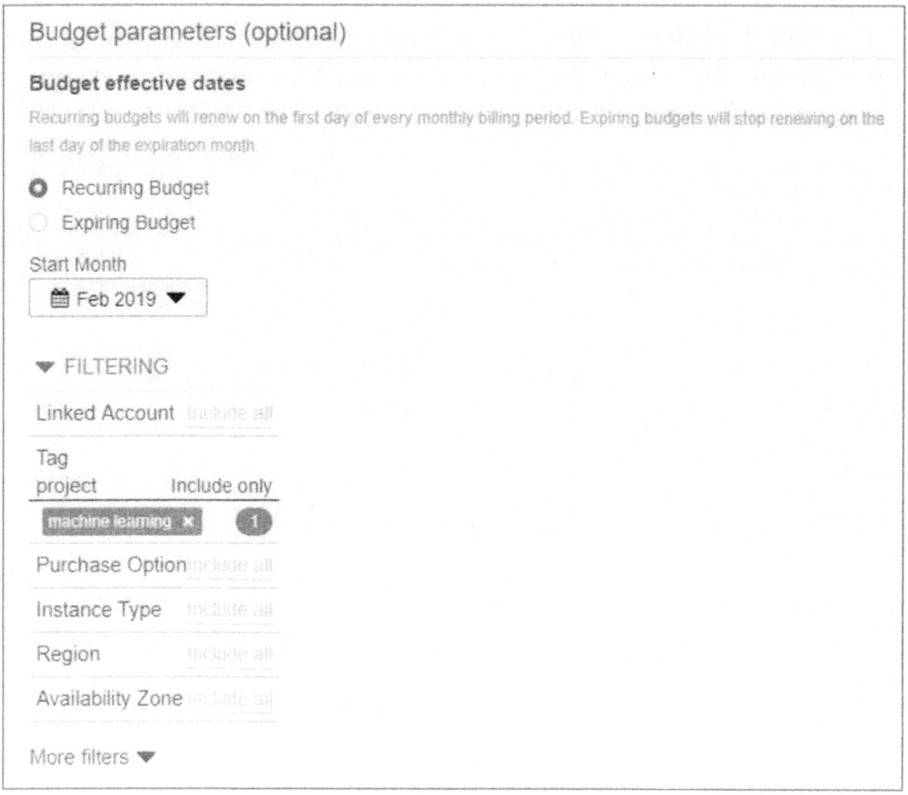

Figure 5.23: Usage Budget - Set your budget - filter by tag

The cost related to this budget setting is displayed below in a chart for your reference.

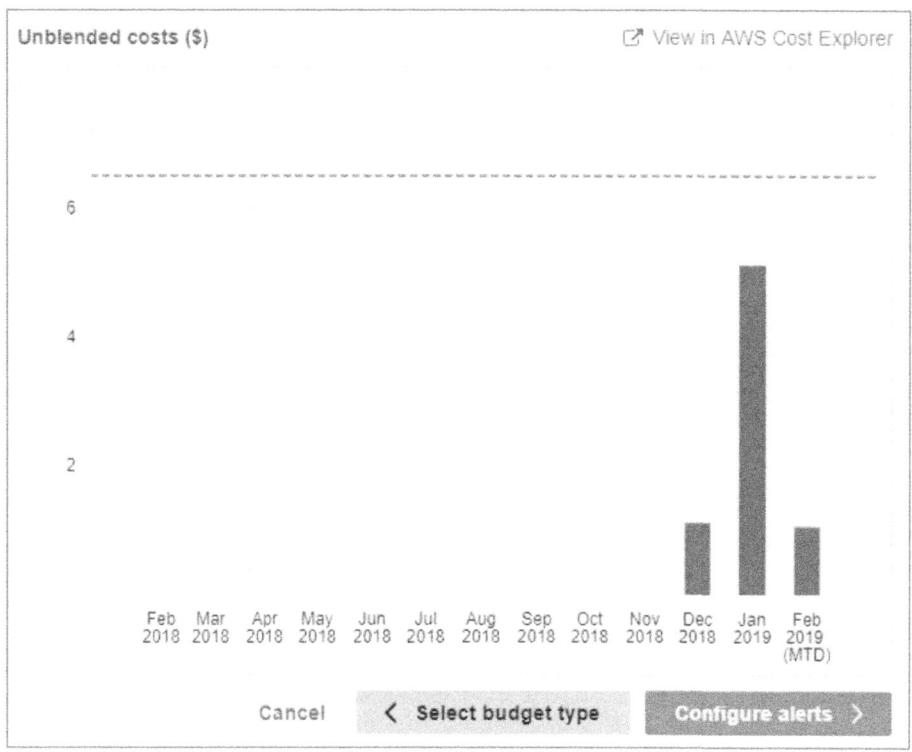

Figure 5.24: Usage Budget - Cost Explorer chart

Click "Configure alerts."

Select "Forecast usage."

Enter 80% as the threshold. When the forecasted usage reaches 80% of the budgeted amount, the alert will be triggered, and an email notification will be sent.

Enter your email.

Click "Confirm budget" to continue.

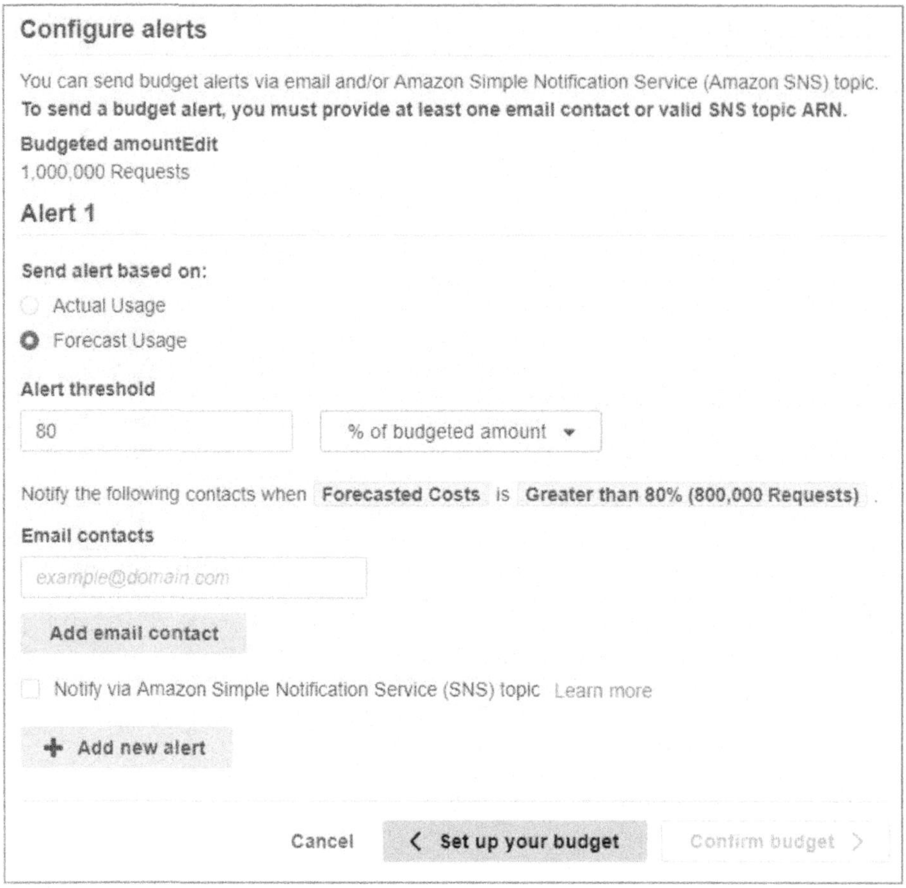

Configure alerts

You can send budget alerts via email and/or Amazon Simple Notification Service (Amazon SNS) topic. To send a budget alert, you must provide at least one email contact or valid SNS topic ARN.

Budgeted amount Edit
1,000,000 Requests

Alert 1

Send alert based on:
- ○ Actual Usage
- ● Forecast Usage

Alert threshold

| 80 | % of budgeted amount ▼ |

Notify the following contacts when **Forecasted Costs** is **Greater than 80% (800,000 Requests)**.

Email contacts

example@domain.com

[Add email contact]

☐ Notify via Amazon Simple Notification Service (SNS) topic   Learn more

+ Add new alert

Cancel   < Set up your budget   Confirm budget >

Figure 5.25: Usage Budget - Configure alerts

Review your setting. Click "Create" to create the budget.

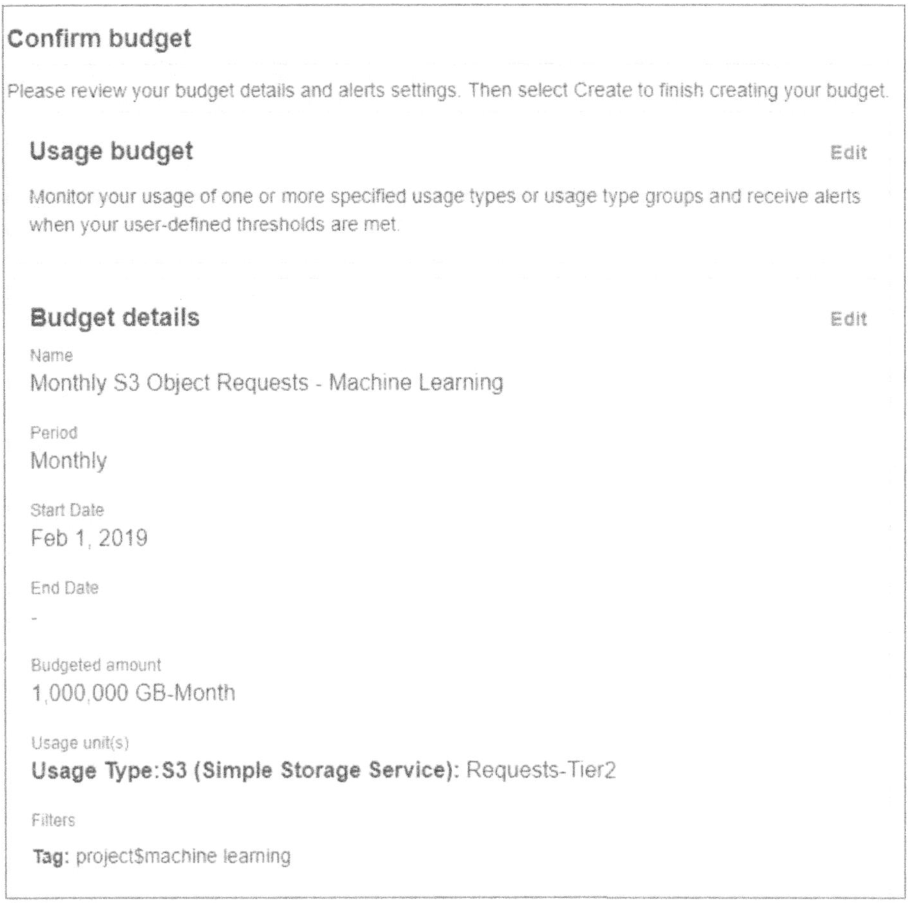
Confirm budget
Please review your budget details and alerts settings. Then select Create to finish creating your budget.
Usage budget
Edit
Monitor your usage of one or more specified usage types or usage type groups and receive alerts when your user-defined thresholds are met.
Budget details
Edit
Name
Monthly S3 Object Requests - Machine Learning
Period
Monthly
Start Date
Feb 1, 2019
End Date
-
Budgeted amount
1,000,000 GB-Month
Usage unit(s)
Usage Type:S3 (Simple Storage Service): Requests-Tier2
Filters
Tag: project$machine learning

Figure 5.26: Usage Budget - Confirm budget - part 1

Alerts
Edit
Alert 1
Forecasted Usage | Greater than 80% (800,000 Requests) | 1 contact
Cancel
Configure alerts
Create

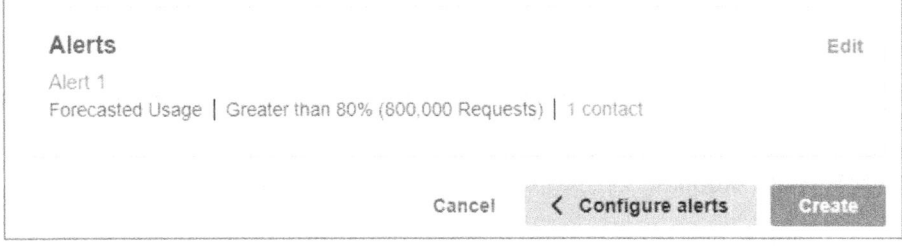

Figure 5.27: Usage Budget - Confirm budget - part 2

Below is the new budget on the "AWS Budgets" main page.

Budget name	Budget type	Current	Budgeted	Forecasted
Monthly EC2 Budget - Research	Cost	$1.00	$6.50	$3.74
Monthly API Gateway Budget	Cost	$0.00	$5.00	$0.00
Monthly S3 Object Requests - Machine Learning	Usage	-	1,000,000 Requests	-

Figure 5.28: AWS Budget - Main

As with the previous cost budget alert, you may not get notified soon enough when the abnormal usage occurs early in the month.

You can click on the usage budget and check the "Current vs. budgeted" and "Forecasted vs. budgeted" to spot unusual usage, especially in the early part of the month.

5.3.5   Create a Reservation Budget and an Alert for RI Utilization of a Project

LINK: Defining RI

LINK: RI Coverage

LINK: RI Utilization

LINK: Implementation #7: How to Monitor RI Utilization and RI Coverage

Assume a yearlong machine learning project. You use a lot of On-Demand EC2 instances for this project. You purchase RIs to cover 90% of the On-

Demand instances. You want to be notified daily when the RI Coverage is *below* 80%. In this case, you can create a reservation budget.

Go to AWS Budget main page. Click "Create budget."

Now select "Reservation budget."

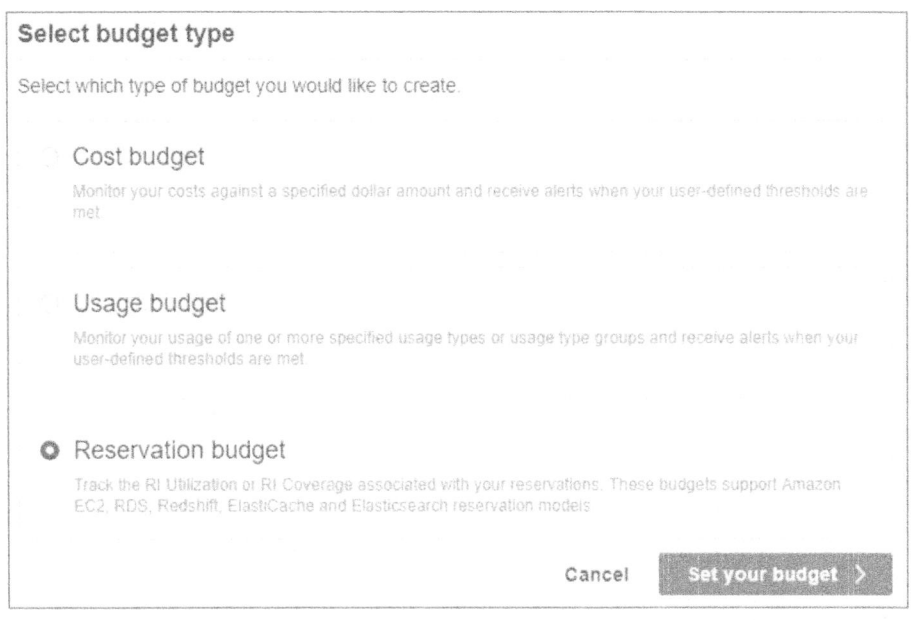

Figure 5.29: AWS Budget - Reservation Budget - select budget type

Enter the name of your budget: "Daily RI Coverage - Machine Learning."

Select "Daily."

Choose "RI Coverage."

Under Service, select "EC2-instances (Elastic Compute Cloud - Compute)."

Enter 80% as the coverage threshold. Please note that you will be notified when the RI Coverage is *below* 80%.

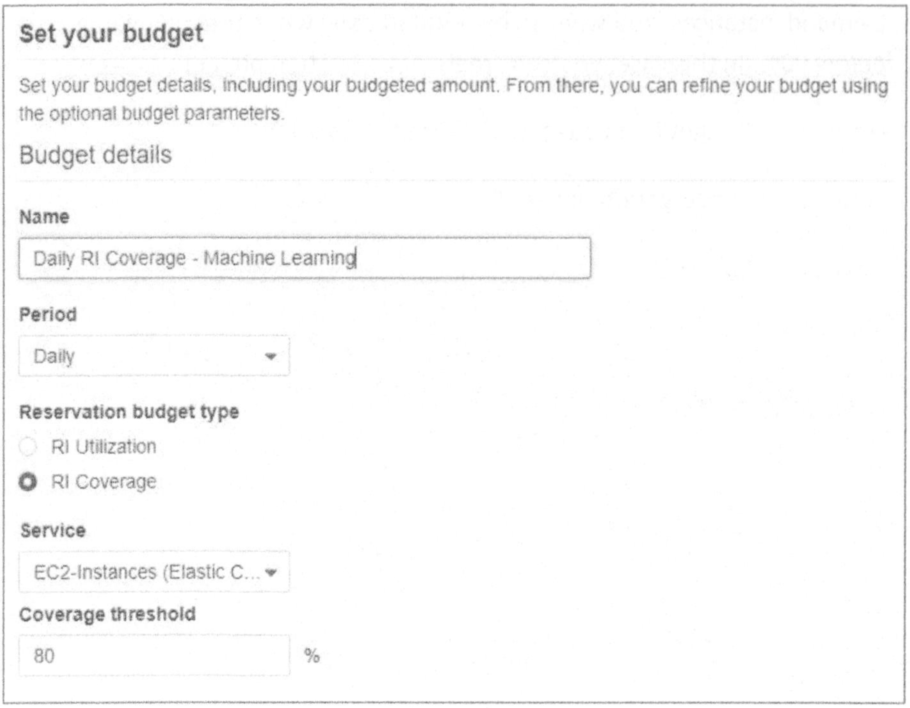

Set your budget

Set your budget details, including your budgeted amount. From there, you can refine your budget using the optional budget parameters.

Budget details

Name

[Daily RI Coverage - Machine Learning]

Period

[Daily ▼]

Reservation budget type
- ○ RI Utilization
- ● RI Coverage

Service

[EC2-Instances (Elastic C... ▼]

Coverage threshold

[80] %

Figure 5.30: AWS Budget - Reservation Budget - budget name and threshold

Click "Tag," select "project," select "Machine Learning," and click "Apply filters." Your budget will only be applied to those EC2 instances with the "project" tag whose value is "Machine Learning."

Click "Configure alerts."

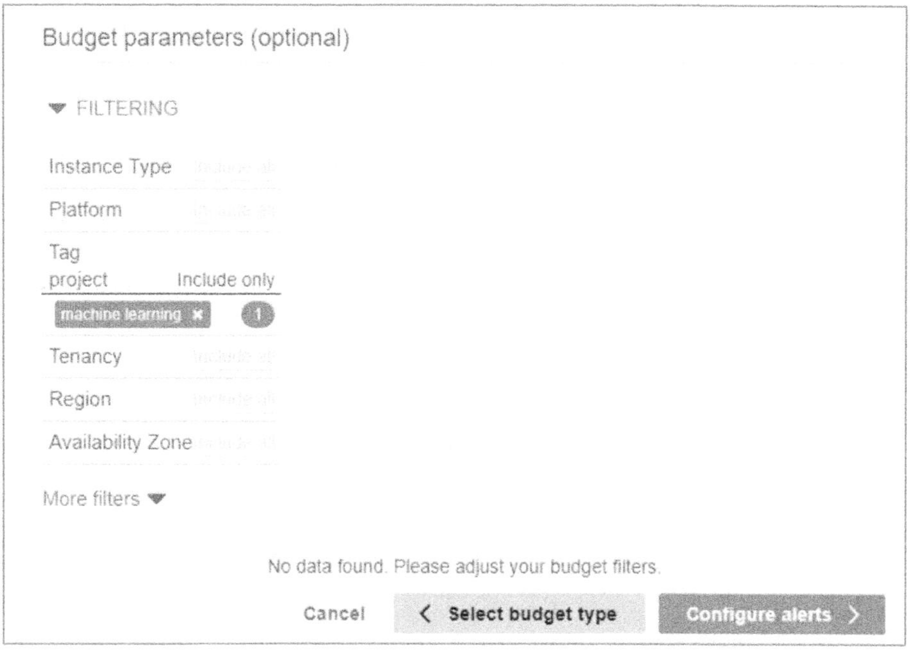

Figure 5.31: AWS Budget - Reservation Budget - filter by tag

Enter email. Click "Confirm budget."

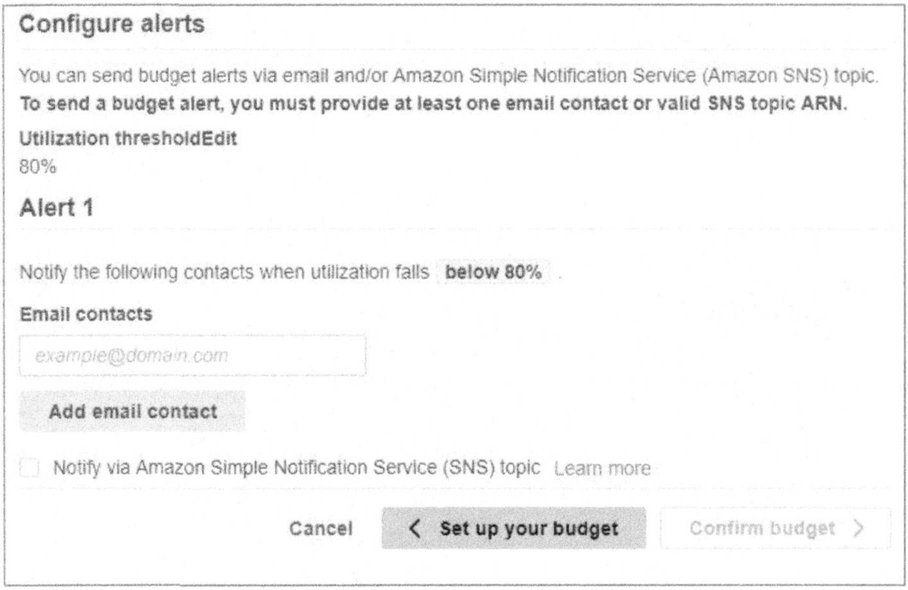

> **Configure alerts**
>
> You can send budget alerts via email and/or Amazon Simple Notification Service (Amazon SNS) topic. To send a budget alert, you must provide at least one email contact or valid SNS topic ARN.
>
> Utilization thresholdEdit
> 80%
>
> **Alert 1**
>
> Notify the following contacts when utilization falls **below 80%**.
>
> Email contacts
>
> [example@domain.com]
>
> [Add email contact]
>
> ☐ Notify via Amazon Simple Notification Service (SNS) topic Learn more
>
> Cancel   < Set up your budget   Confirm budget >

Figure 5.32: AWS Budget - Reservation Budget - configure alerts

Review your budget setting. Please note the "Tag: project$machine learning" under "Filters." You also see "RI Coverage | Below 80%" at the bottom of the page.

Click "Create."

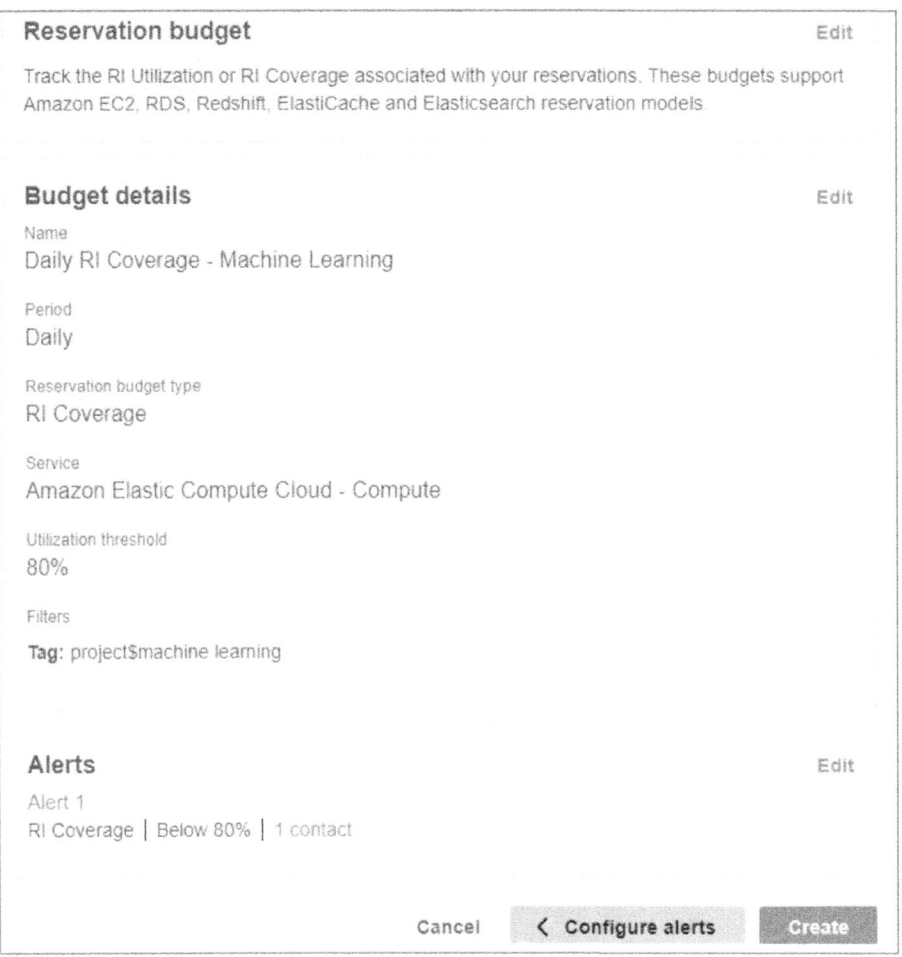

Figure 5.33: AWS Budget - Reservation Budget - confirm

The new budget is now visible on the AWS Budget main page.

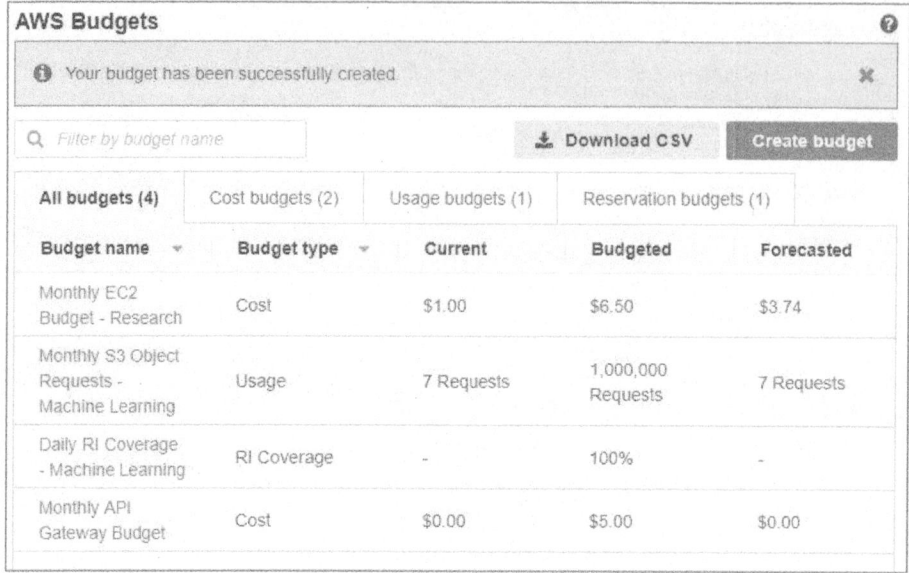

Figure 5.34: AWS Budget - Reservation Budget - main

Now you will receive email alerts when the RI coverage is below 80%.

5.3.6 Summary

When abnormal spending occurs, you wish you could have caught it sooner. AWS Budget with alerts gives you one way to accomplish that. It may not be ideal because most of the budgets are monthly, which means you may not catch the abnormal activities by the next day.

AWS Budget also tracks your month-to-date spending and the forecasted spending for the month. You know where you are in terms of your spending based on your budget.

5.4 Implementation #3: How to Implement a Schedule to Start and Stop an EC2 or RDS Instance

5.4.1 Introduction

One of the quick and easy ways to reduce AWS costs is to keep EC2 or RDS instances from running constantly when they don't need to be.

For example, some EC2 or RDS instances in the development environment do not have to be running after regular business hours, which are 8:00 a.m. to 6:00 p.m. Monday through Friday.

On weekdays, you can stop these instances at 6:00 p.m. and start them at 8:00 a.m. There are several ways to implement the auto-start and auto-stop.

5.4.2 Auto Start and Auto Stop Using Tags

One way is to use lambda function and tags. The tags could be "auto-start" and "auto-stop". For example, if the value of "auto-start" is "0 8 * * 1-5," the instance will be auto-started at 8:00 a.m. UTC, Monday through Friday (please adjust for your time zone).

If the value of "auto-stop" is "0 18 * * 1-5," the instance will be auto-stopped at 18:00 UTC, Monday through Friday (please adjust for your time zone). The instance will not be running over the weekend and will resume the next Monday at 8:00 a.m. UTC.

You can create a lambda function that is scheduled to run every 5 minutes. It can evaluate all the EC2 and RDS instances and check the tags "auto-start" and "auto-stop." Based on the tags and values, the lambda function can start an instance or stop an instance.

This approach is quite flexible, and you hand control over to the owners of the instance, who can add or modify the tags. All they have to do is to add the "auto-start" and "auto-stop" tags to an EC2 or RDS instance.

Be aware that your instance may be accidentally stopped. Whoever can add or modify the tags can also stop your instance.

5.4.3 Auto Start and Auto Stop Using AWS Instance Scheduler

AWS Instance Scheduler is a similar solution. It also relies on tags. Again, proper tagging is the foundation for a lot of cost optimization techniques.

The slight difference is that you define a schedule first, then attach the schedule to your instance. The pre-defined schedules are saved to DynamoDB, which incurs additional costs.

For example, you could designate a tag "Schedule." The value of this "Schedule" tag could be "new-york-office-hour," "san-francisco-office-hour," and so on.

The lambda function checks the "Schedule" tag of all EC2 and RDS instances every 5 minutes. Based on the value of the "Schedule" tag, the instance will be started or stopped according to the schedule.

The schedules are stored in a DynamoDB table, in which you have some control over the behaviors.

For example, if you set "enforced=true" in the table, the scheduler will stop the instance when someone manually starts the instance outside of the running period. Similarly, the scheduler will start the instance when someone manually stops the instance during the running period.

For the documentation, step-by-step implementation, automated deployment and scheduler-cli commands, please visit:

https://aws.amazon.com/answers/infrastructure-management/instance-scheduler/

Amazon Web Services – AWS Instance Scheduler	October 2018

View template **instance-scheduler-remote.template:** Use this template to configure permissions for instances in secondary accounts. The default configuration creates the AWS Identity and Access Management (IAM) roles necessary to start and stop instances in a secondary account.

Automated Deployment

Before you launch the automated deployment, please review the architecture, configuration, and other considerations discussed in this guide. Follow the step-by-step instructions in this section to configure and deploy the Instance Scheduler into your account.

Time to deploy: Approximately five (5) minutes.

What We'll Cover

The procedure for deploying this architecture on AWS consists of the following steps. For detailed instructions, follow the links for each step.

Figure 5.35: Schedule to start and stop an EC2 instance - AWS Instance Scheduler

5.4.4 Things to Consider When Implementing Auto-Start and Auto-Stop Schedules

- Communication:

Before you implement the auto-start and auto-stop scheduler, make sure you have established adequate communication with the stakeholders on how this works and when it will be implemented. Stakeholders must be informed.

- Time Zone:

  Pay attention to the time zone.

- Tracing events:

  Log each event and leave a record whenever the instance is started or stopped by the scheduler. You then have a history of when the instance was started and stopped. This is very helpful for troubleshooting of your applications.

- Notification:

  Send the email notification via SNS to the stakeholders after the instance is started or stopped.

- When Multi-AZ is enabled:

  For Aurora databases and other RDS instances with Multi-AZ enabled, the instances will not be stopped because stopping in one node or one zone will automatically start another node or another zone.

- RDS Instance will restart after 7 days of being stopped:

  AWS automatically brings a stopped RDS instance online after 7 days of being stopped.

  Don't be surprised to see that an RDS instance you stopped a month ago is in fact running.

You can prevent this with an auto-stop scheduler. For example, create a scheduler that stops an RDS instance every day. That way, an RDS instance will automatically be stopped again the day it is restarted by AWS. You may have to watch the timing so that there is minimal gap between the stopping time of the scheduler and the AWS restarting time.

5.4.5 Summary

As covered in the "Time Multiplier," changing the running period from 24/7 to 8:00 a.m. - 6:00 p.m. on weekdays saves 70.24%.

You can implement the scheduler with the "auto-start" and "auto-stop" tags, or use the AWS Instance Scheduler. A lambda function will control the auto-stop and auto-start.

Please ensure that the stakeholders are notified and take extra care of the production systems. You don't want to disrupt your normal business activities.

5.5 Implementation #4: How to Implement S3 Lifecycle Policies for AWS Cost Optimization

5.5.1 Introduction

The objects in S3 should have a lifecycle - from the time the object is created to the time the object is no longer needed. In between, there could be multiple versions of the object if you have versioning enabled for the bucket.

The lifecycle policy is what you tell AWS to do to the objects during the life of the object.

- You can delete objects and their versions after certain days.
- You can move objects to a cheaper storage class after certain days.
- You can archive objects after certain days by changing the storage type to Glacier.
- You can replicate objects to another region for backup and recovery and delete the objects from the source.

5.5.2 Lifecycle Policies and Cost Optimization

One of the easiest ways to keep the storage costs down is to implement the lifecycle policy.

Here are a few examples of lifecycle policies you can implement.

- Move objects from Standard to Standard IA after 30 days from object creation.
- Archive objects to Glacier after 60 days from object creation.
- Delete objects and their versions after 90 days from object creation.
- Archive objects to another region using CRR (cross region replication) immediately.

5.5.3 A note on Multipart Upload:

The best practice is, check this checkbox when you see it: "Clean up incomplete multipart uploads."

You initiate a multipart upload and begin uploading parts. Amazon S3 stores these parts, but it creates the object from the parts only after you upload all of them and send a successful request to complete the multipart upload. If you don't send the complete multipart upload request successfully, Amazon S3 will not assemble the parts and will not create any object. Therefore, the parts remain in Amazon S3 and you pay for the parts that are stored in Amazon S3.

Use lifecycle policies to instruct Amazon S3 to abort the multipart upload (and deletes the parts associated with the multipart upload).

5.5.4 Lifecycle Policies Implementation

Here is the step-by-step guide to implement the lifecycle policies above.

5.5.4.1 Move Objects from Standard to Standard IA after 30 Days.

Go to S3 bucket's Management tab.

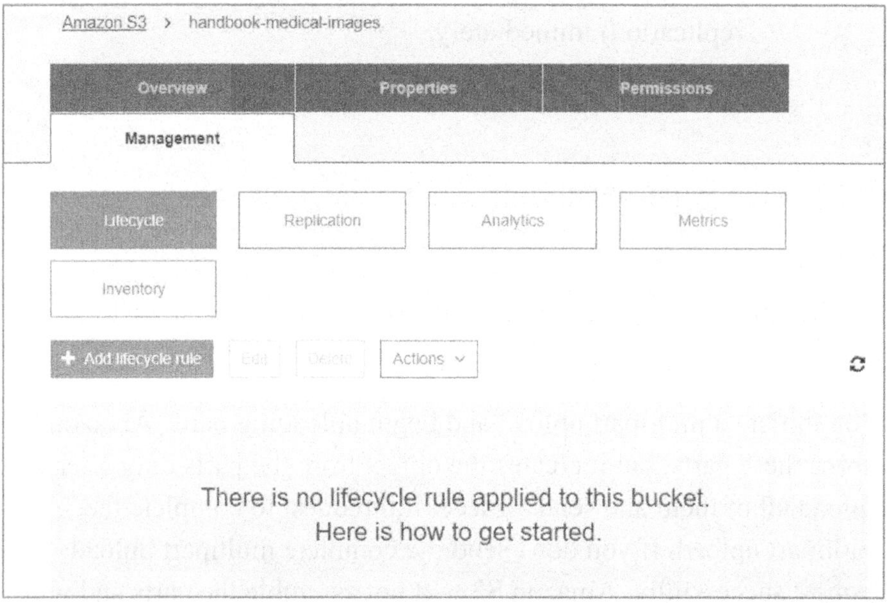

Figure 5.36: - S3 Lifecycle Policy - Add lifecycle rule

Click on "Add lifecycle rule"; then enter the rule name, "Move objects from Standard to Standard IA." Click on "Next."

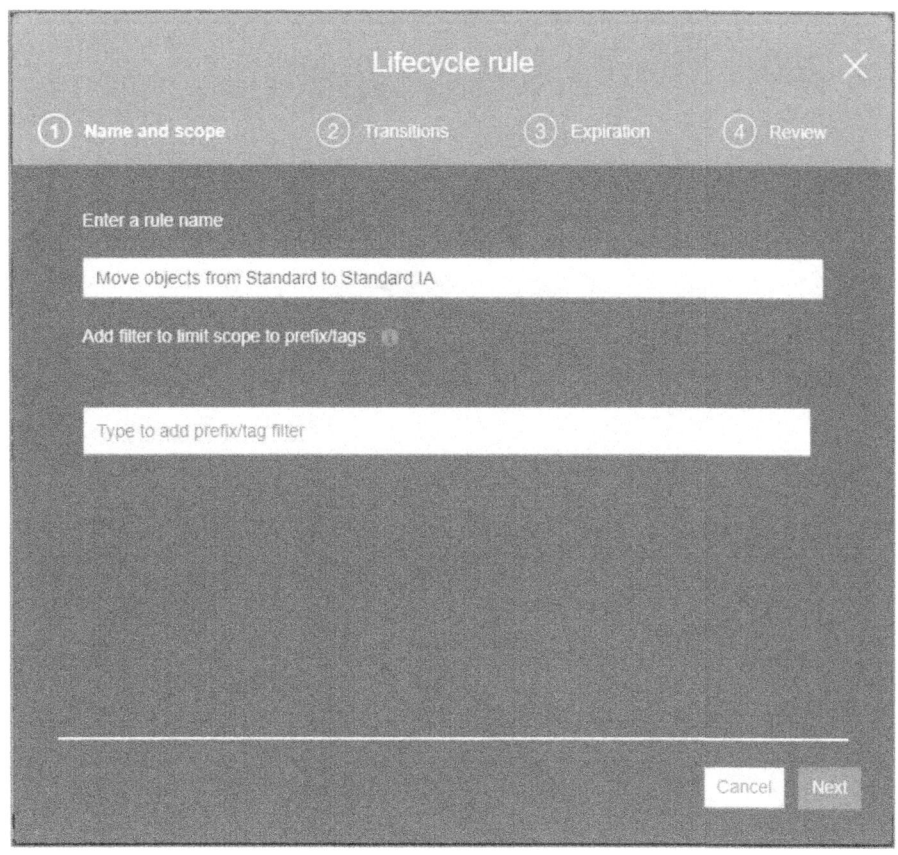

Figure 5.37: S3 Lifecycle Policy - Add lifecycle rule - step 1: Name and scope

Add transitions to the policy: Transition to Standard IA after 30 days, for both current version and previous versions.

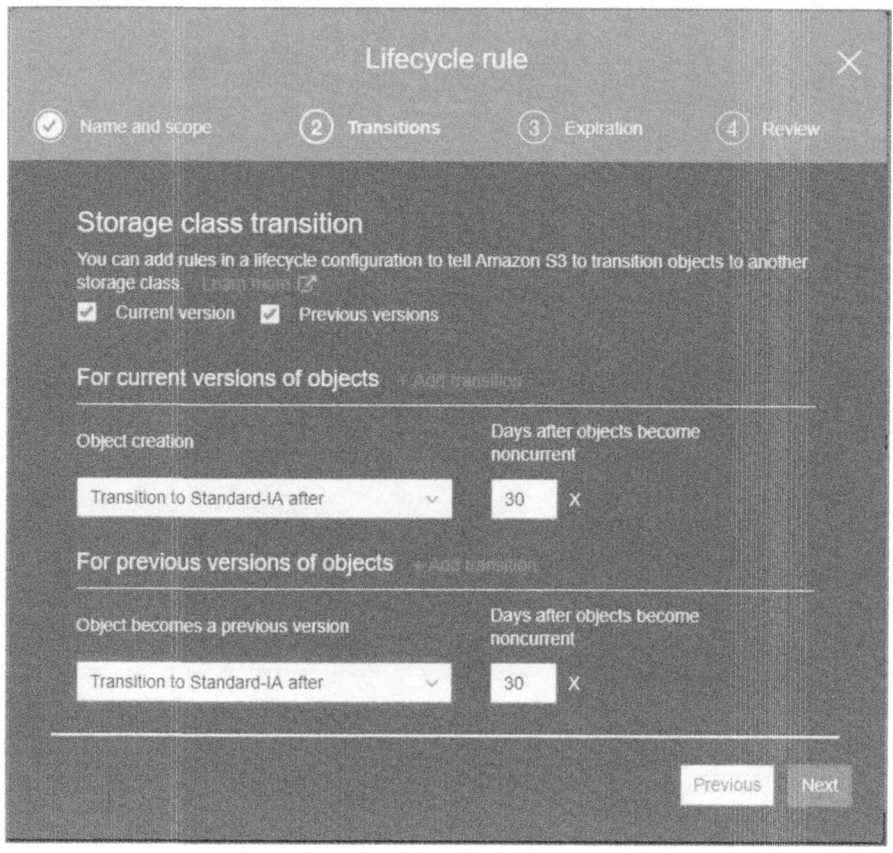

Figure 5.38: S3 Lifecycle Policy - Add lifecycle rule - step 2: Transition

Set expiration. Objects will be deleted once the object is expired.

Do not set expiration for Current Versions and Previous Versions. We don't want to delete the objects; we just want to change the storage type from Standard to Standard-IA.

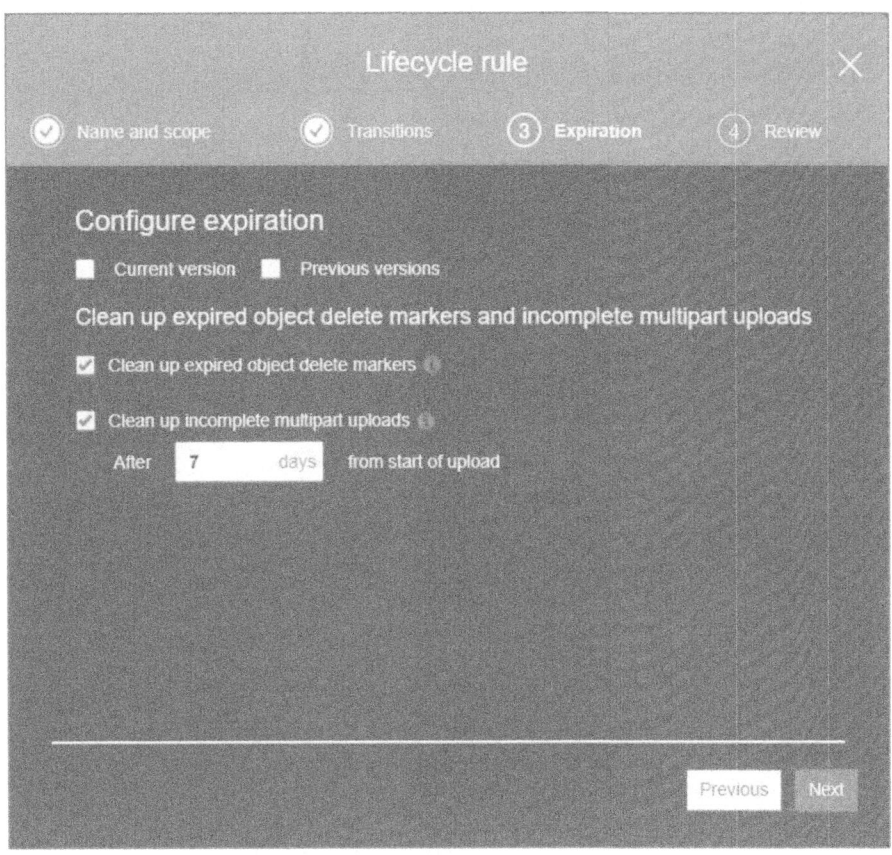

Figure 5.39: S3 Lifecycle Policy - Add lifecycle rule - step 3: Expiration

Review your policy; then click "Save."

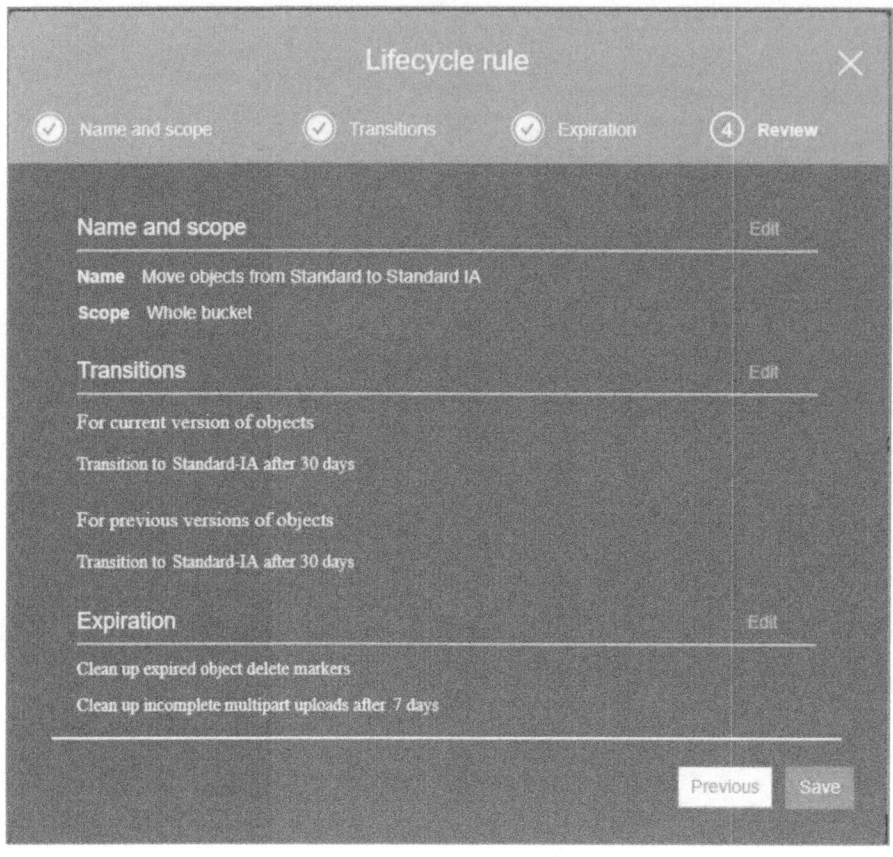

Figure 5.40: S3 Lifecycle Policy - Add lifecycle rule - step 4: Review and Save

You now have a lifecycle policy attached to your bucket.

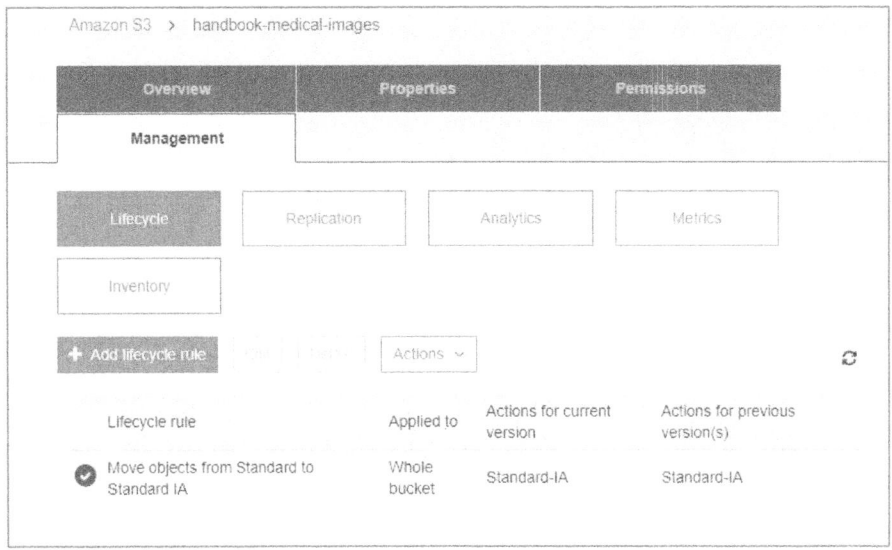

Figure 5.41: S3 Lifecycle Policy - Add lifecycle rule - result

The storage class for the object below is "Standard." After 30 days, the storage class will be changed to "Standard IA." Your storage cost will be reduced significantly as long as these objects are only accessed "infrequently."

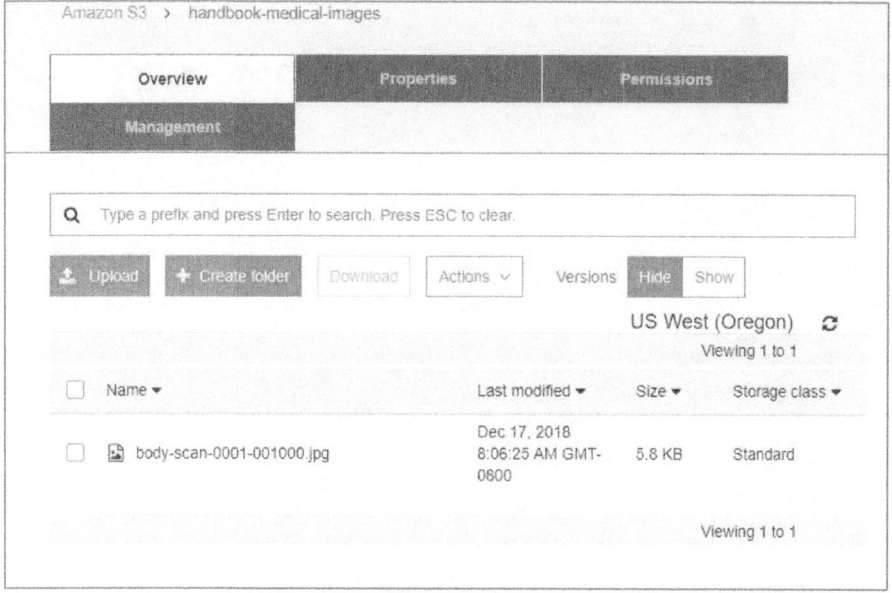

Figure 5.42: S3 Lifecycle Policy - with lifecycle rule - Storage class

5.5.4.2 Archive Objects to Glacier After Sixty Days.

Just as you can change the storage class from Standard to Standard-IA, you can archive objects to Glacier after 60 days.

This time, on the "Transitions" page, select "Transition to Amazon Glacier after," and enter 60 days.

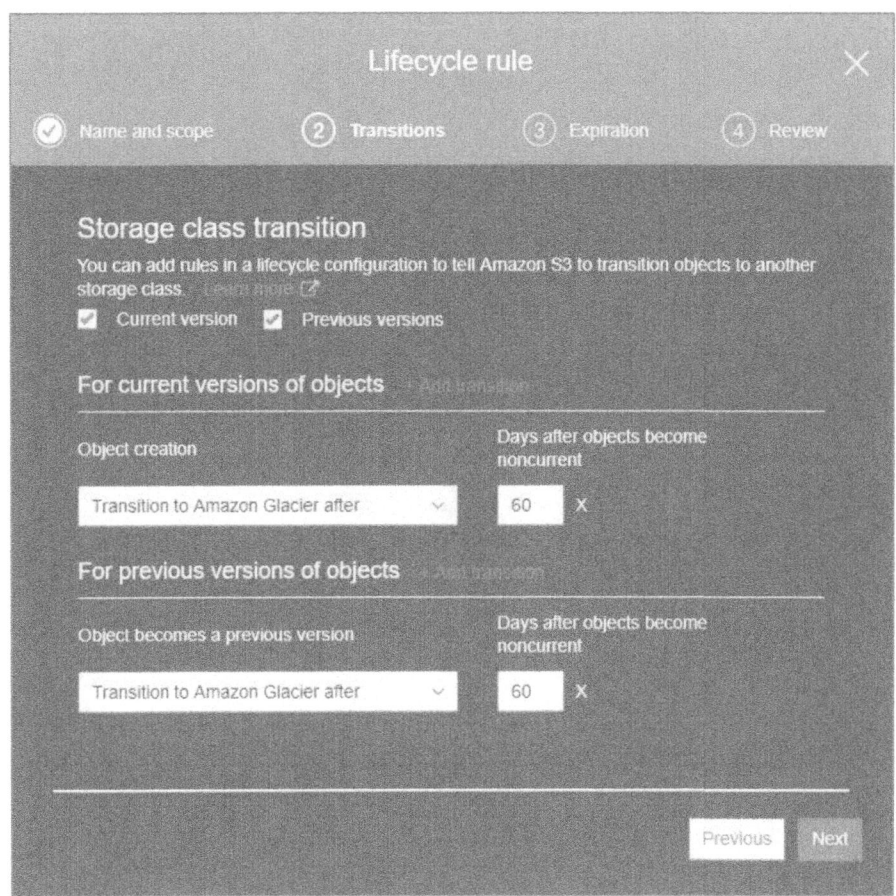

Figure 5.43: S3 Lifecycle Policy - Add lifecycle rule - Transition to Glacier

With this policy, the objects in this bucket will be stored in Glacier 60 days after creation.

5.5.4.3 Delete Objects and Their Versions After Ninety Days.

Now create a new lifecycle rule. This time set the expiration days to 90 days from object creation.

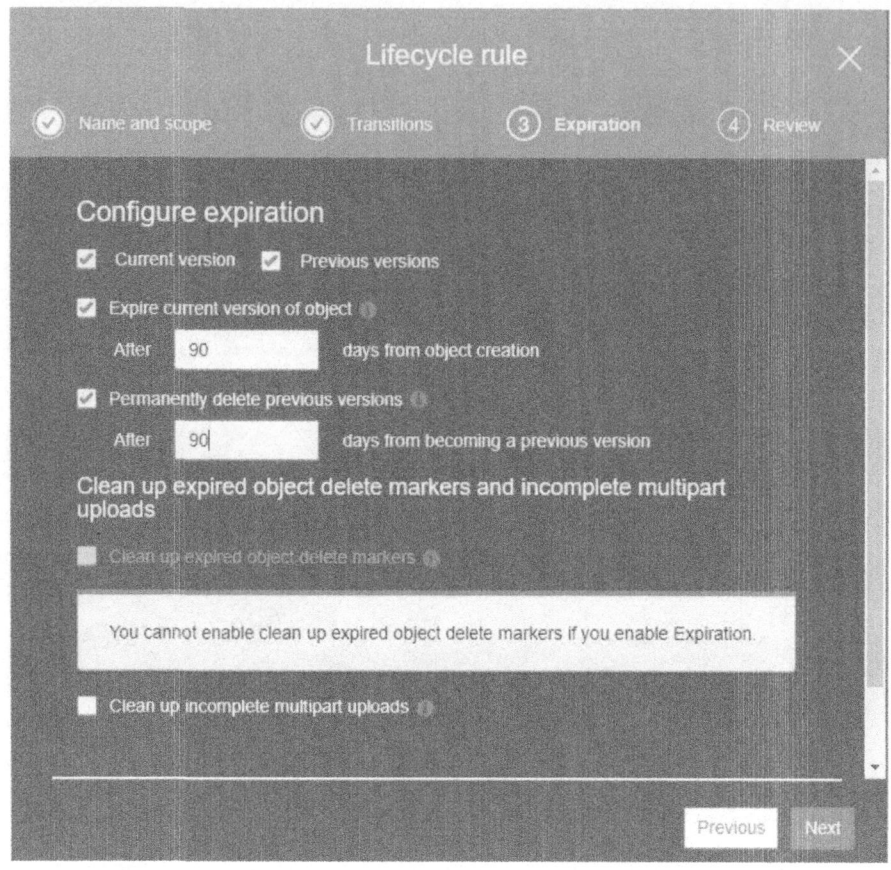

Figure 5.44: S3 Lifecycle Policy - Add lifecycle rule - Delete objects after 90 days

With this policy, objects in this bucket will be deleted permanently after 90 days of object creation.

Now you have three lifecycle policies attached to the bucket:

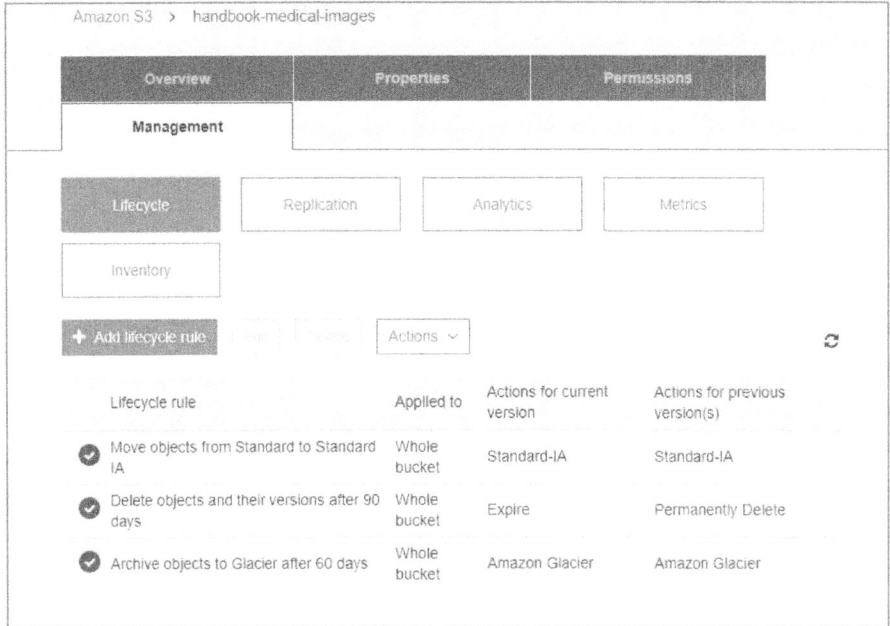

Figure 5.45: S3 Lifecycle Policy - Add lifecycle rule - all rules

5.5.4.4 Archive Objects to Another Region Using CRR

Now let's copy objects to another region using CRR (Cross-Region Replication). This is a common implementation for disaster recovery.

In certain industries such as healthcare, the data may be required to be stored for 15 years or longer. CRR is used to archive the data to another site.

Create the following bucket to store the backup copy of "handbook-medical-images":

> Bucket name: handbook-medical-images-backup
>
> Region: US-EAST (N. Virginia)

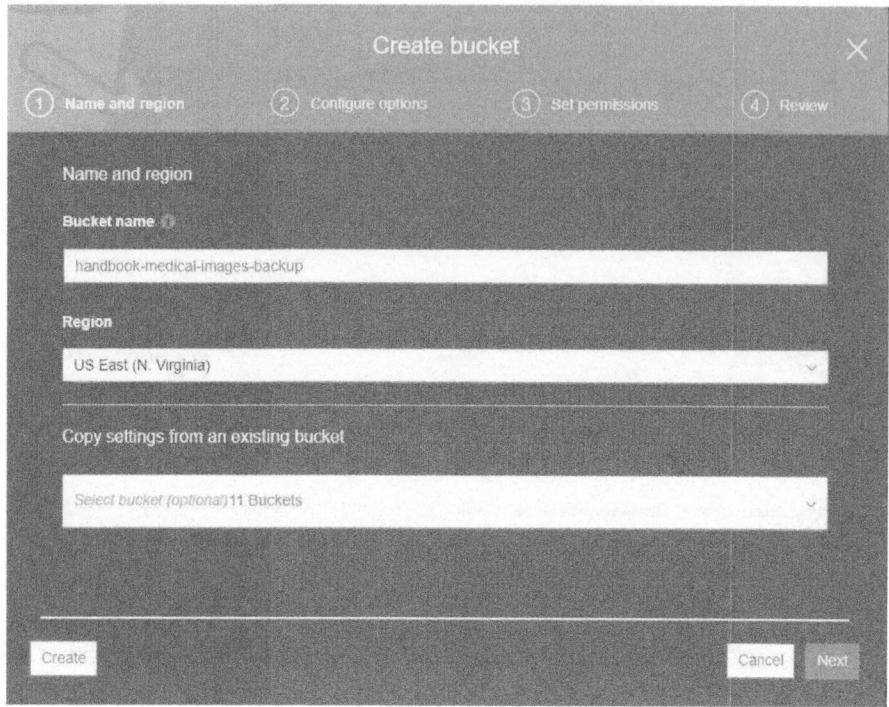

Figure 5.46: S3 Cross Region Replication - Create a bucket

Go to the bucket property of "handbook-medical-images," then "Replication," then "Add rule":

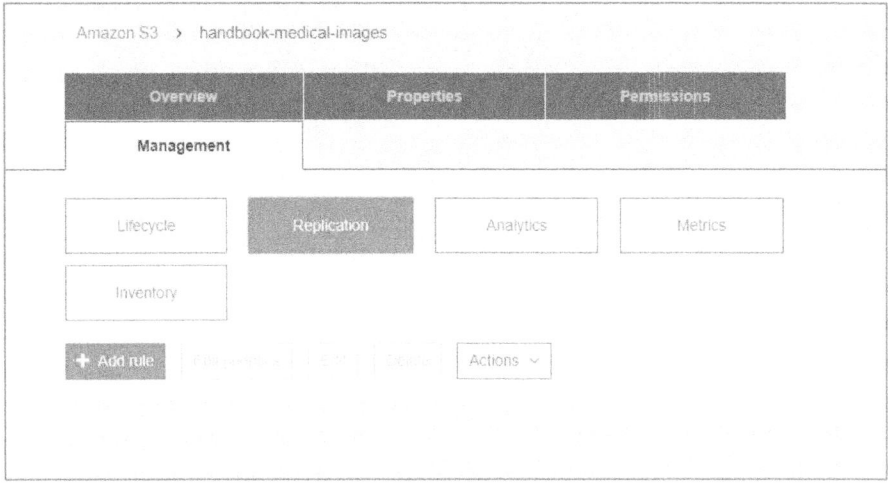

Figure 5.47: S3 Cross Region Replication - Add rule

Follow the steps to create the Cross-Region Replication rule:

- Select what to replicate.

    You can replicate the entire bucket or a prefix or objects with the tags you specify.

    You can't select the file type. If you only want to replicate the image files in the bucket "handbook-medical-images," you can store all the images in the prefix "images", and replicate the "images" prefix. You can also tag all the images and replicate by tags.

    For example, the following selection allows AWS to replicate the prefix "images" plus all objects with the tag of "project=research" or "project=marketing."

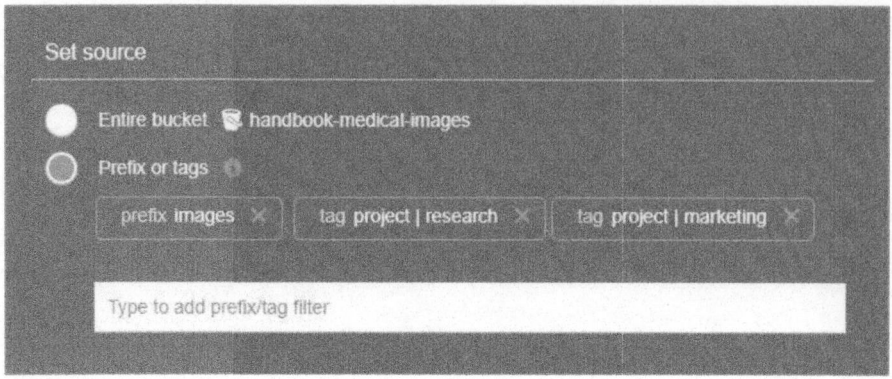

Figure 5.48: S3 Cross Region Replication - Set source

You can have multiple Cross-Region Replication rules: one to replicate a prefix, one to replicate by tags, and so on.

For now, let's replicate the entire bucket:

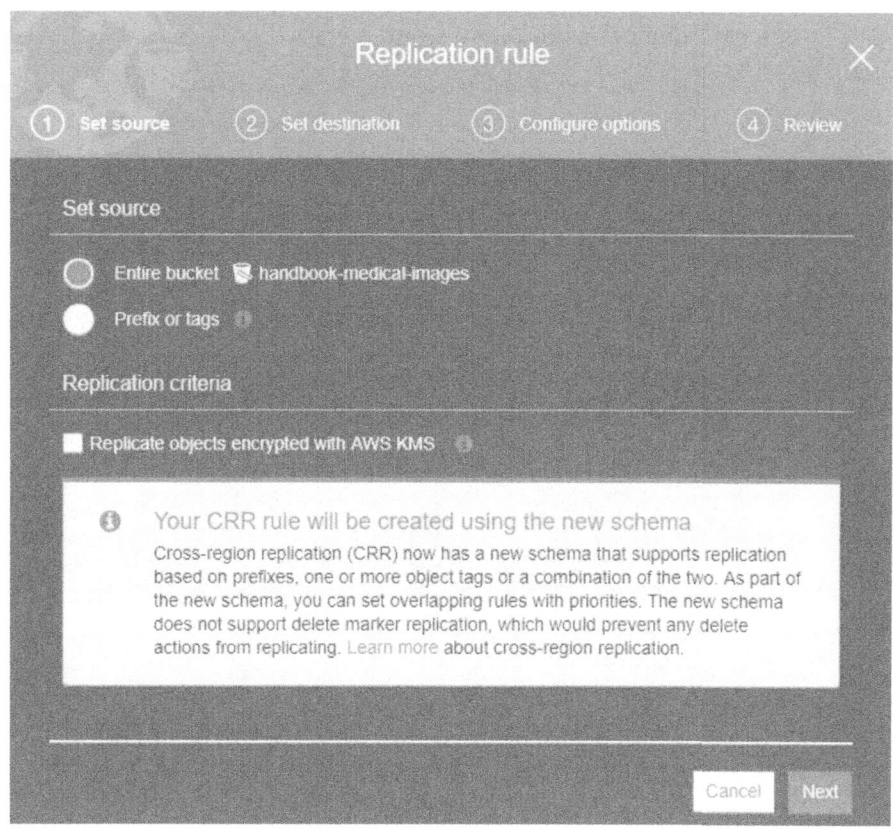

Figure 5.49: S3 Cross Region Replication - Set source 2

- Now set the destination.

    The destination is the backup bucket in the US_EAST (N. Virginia).

    Do you want to move the objects to Glacier immediately to save storage costs? If this is just a backup for disaster recovery or compliance with regulations, you may do so.

    If this is a colocation strategy to reduce the latency of your application in another region, do not change the storage class.

    Move objects to Glacier if the objects don't need to be online and will not be retrieved in the foreseeable future.

Select "Glacier" as the new storage class.

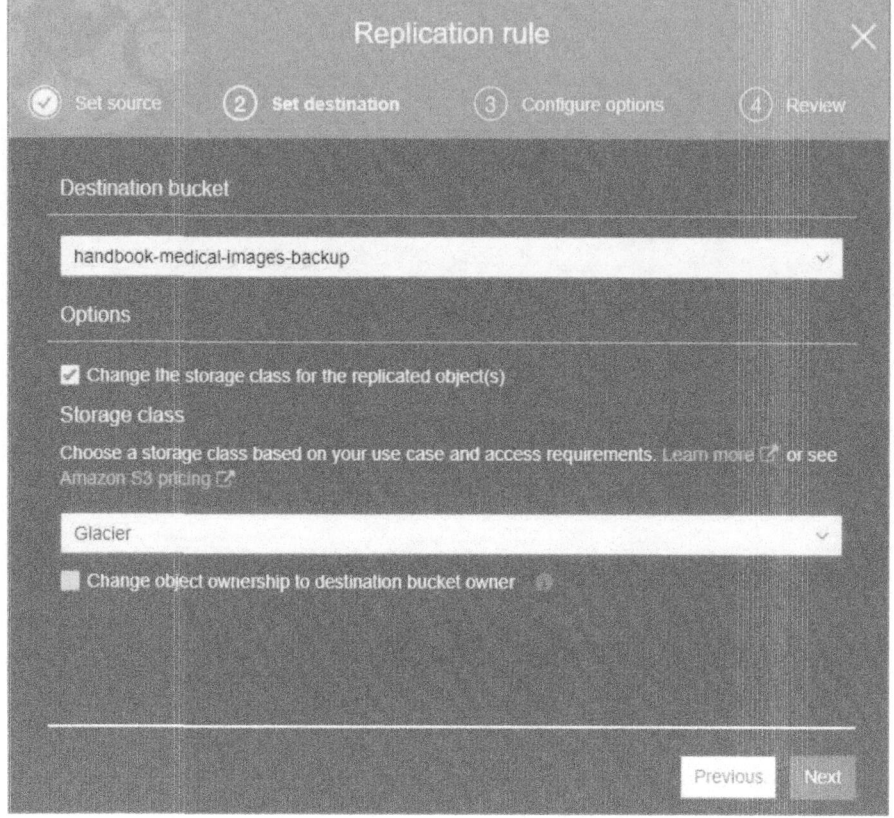

Figure 5.50: S3 Cross Region Replication - Set destination

The next step is to specify the IAM role for the replication. Let's create a new role called "role-crr-medical-image."

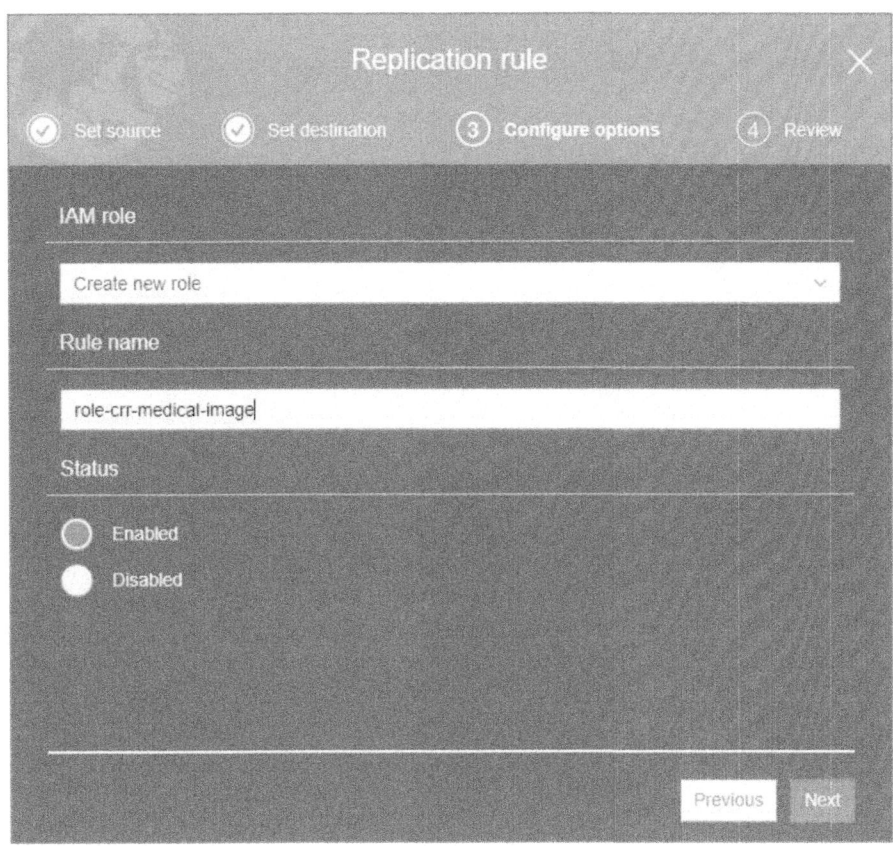

Figure 5.51: S3 Cross Region Replication - Configure options

Review your rule and save it.

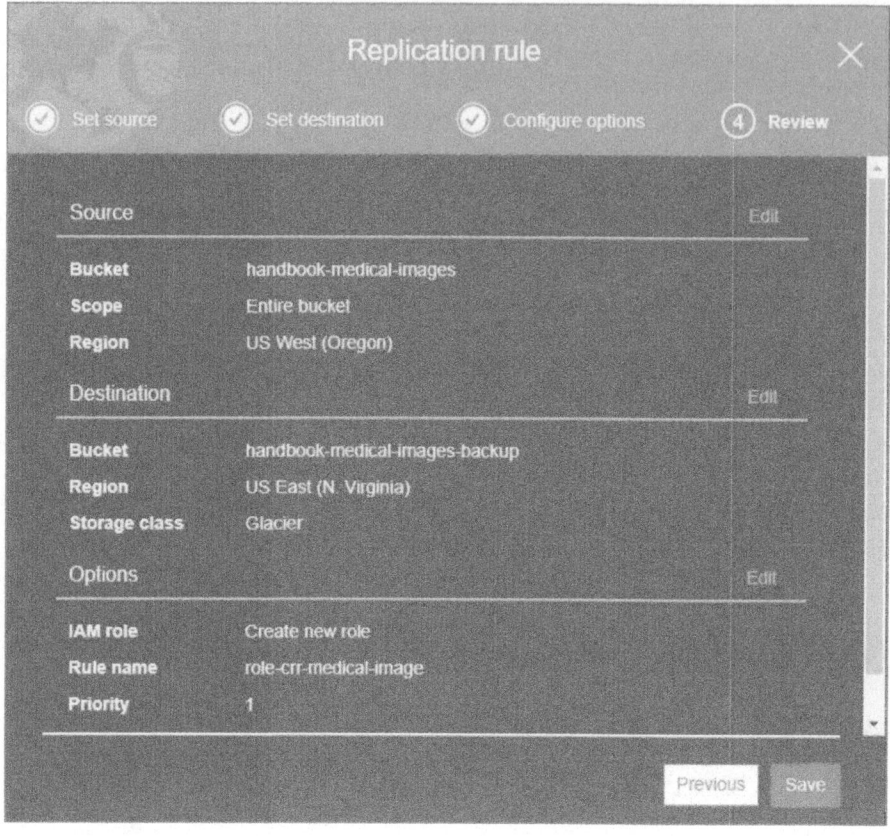

Figure 5.52: S3 Cross Region Replication - Review and Save

Now you have the CRR rule as shown below. You have a backup copy of the entire bucket "handbook-medical-images." The backup copy has the storage type of "Glacier" which is much cheaper than "Standard-IA."

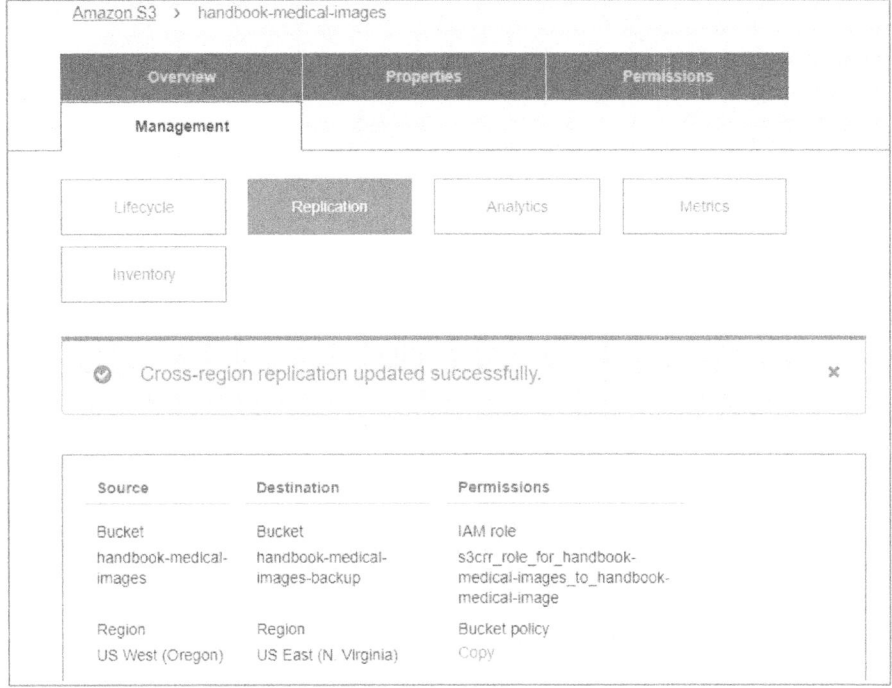

Figure 5.53: S3 Cross Region Replication - Rule added

Your objects will now be replicated to another region. You have peace of mind because the objects are backed up in another region. You can perform numerous operations on the source bucket without worrying about losing the objects.

Please note that both source bucket and destination bucket must have versioning enabled.

Deleting an object in the source bucket will set a delete marker for the object. With the latest version of the AWS replication rule, which is V2 at the time of writing, the delete marker will not be replicated. Please check AWS CRR documentation for more details.

You can pause the CRR by disabling the rule.

5.5.5 Things to Consider When Adding Lifecycle Rules

Documentation:

> Document all of your lifecycle policies in all buckets. Share the documentation with the teams and the stakeholders. Keep the history of changes so that all changes can be audited.

Communications:

> The lifecycle policies move objects and delete objects permanently. The stakeholders should be notified before and after each implementation.

Data retention policy and disaster recovery requirements:

> Keep your lifecycle policies consistent with your corporate data-retention policy and disaster recovery requirements.

Risks:

> Don't disrupt your normal business operation when you implement the lifecycle policies.
>
> When you have an Infrastructure-as-Code environment, your infrastructure is managed by the code. Any changes should be reviewed to prevent accidental changes when the code is executed.
>
> This is the case particularly when you have a CI/CD pipeline to promote the infrastructure code to a production environment.

5.5.6 Summary

It is easy to add lifecycle rules to S3 buckets. This is one of the first things to consider when you start the cost optimization.

Objects should be archived if they are not used frequently or deleted when they are no longer needed.

Cross Region Replication could be one of your data retention and disaster recovery options.

Communication, documentation and risk management are the key things to consider when you implement lifecycle policies.

5.6 Implementation #5: How to Implement Data Lifecycle Management

5.6.1 Introduction

Elastic Block Storage (EBS) is very expensive and quite difficult to manage.

If you check your AWS bill for EC2, EBS is usually a significant part of your compute costs.

▸ DynamoDB		$0.00
▾ Elastic Compute Cloud		$0.94
▾ US West (Oregon)		**$0.94**
Amazon Elastic Compute Cloud running Linux/UNIX		$0.78
$0.0058 per On Demand Linux t2.nano Instance Hour	134 Hrs	$0.78
EBS		$0.16
$0.10 per GB-month of General Purpose SSD (gp2) provisioned storage - US West (Oregon)	1.595 GB-Mo	$0.16
▸ Glue		$0.00

Figure 5.54: AWS Bill - EBS costs

The cost of EBS is based on the provision of the storage. If you provision 200 GB of General Purpose SSD (gp2), the cost is $20.00 a month at $0.10 per GB-month. If you provision IOPS, you have additional costs for the provisioned IOPS.

You also make snapshots of EBS volume for backup. In addition to the EBS storage costs, you are also paying for the storage of the EBS snapshots. The storage cost for Amazon EBS snapshots to S3 is $0.05 per GB-month of data storage.

The size of EBS snapshots will be significantly smaller than the provisioned volume size since EBS doesn't save empty blocks.

EBS is quite difficult to manage.

You may have many EC2 instances owned by different teams. Each team creates the snapshot of EBS as backup on its own schedule. The old snapshots may not be deleted in a timely fashion. The snapshots may be kept forever.

Amazon Data Management Lifecycle (DML) automates EBS snapshots for you.

Use DML to standardize how EBS snapshots are managed.

5.6.2 Create a Snapshot Lifecycle Policy

Before you get started, let's add a new tag to two volumes as illustrated below. Again, proper tagging is the foundation for a lot of cost optimization techniques. DML is based on tags.

Select a volume; then click on the tab "Tags." Then click on the button "Add/Edit Tags."

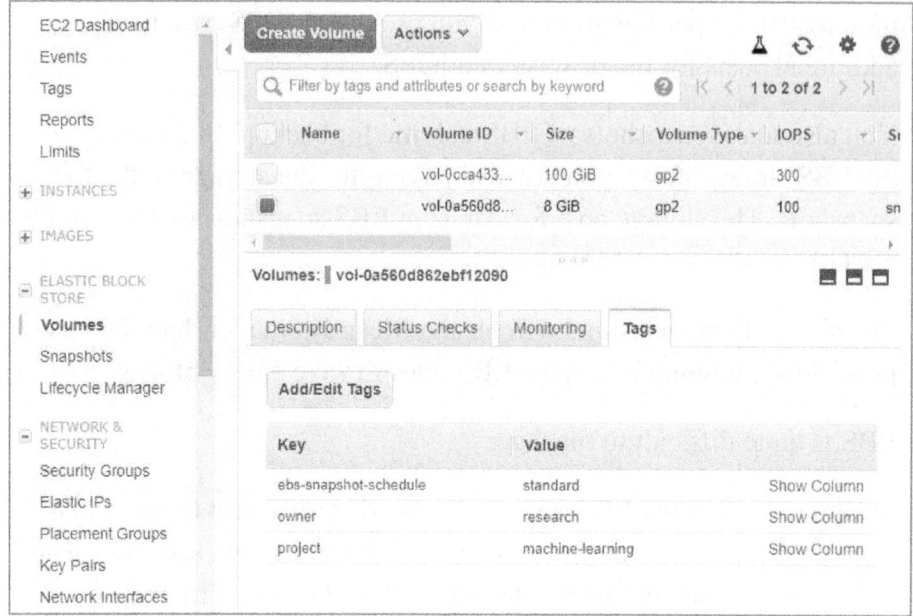

Figure 5.55: Add target tags to volumes for snapshot lifecycle policy

On the popup screen, add the tag "ebs-snapshot-schedule" and the value "standard." This is the standard EBS snapshot schedule.

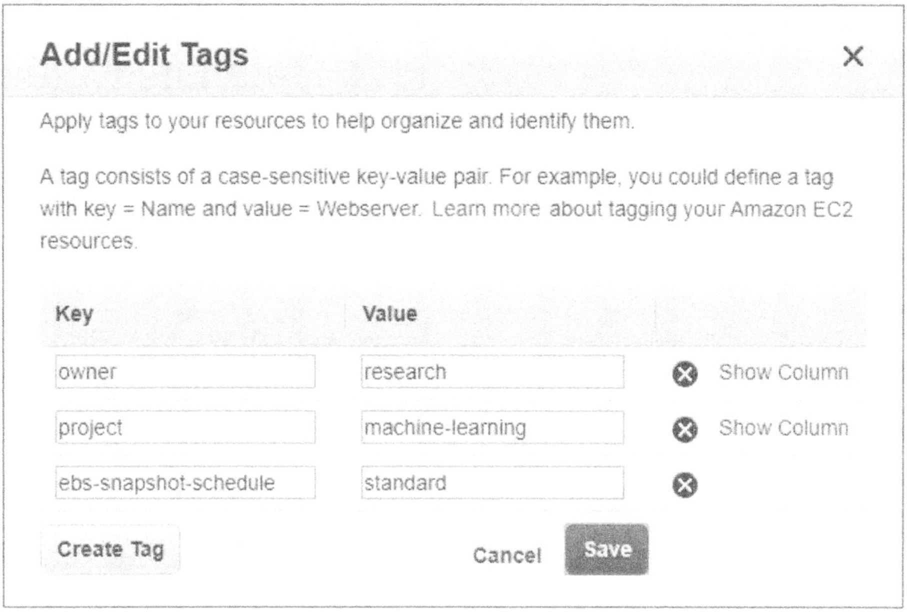

Add/Edit Tags

Apply tags to your resources to help organize and identify them.

A tag consists of a case-sensitive key-value pair. For example, you could define a tag with key = Name and value = Webserver. Learn more about tagging your Amazon EC2 resources.

Key	Value	
owner	research	Show Column
project	machine-learning	Show Column
ebs-snapshot-schedule	standard	

Create Tag   Cancel   Save

Figure 5.56: Add target tags to volumes

DML is based on tags. Now let's create a snapshot lifecycle policy that will take snapshots of all the volumes with the tag "ebs-snapshot-schedule" and the value "standard."

Go to EC2 "Lifecycle Manager" under "ELASTIC BLOCK STORE" on the left.

Click on the button "Create Snapshot Lifecycle Policy" on the main panel.

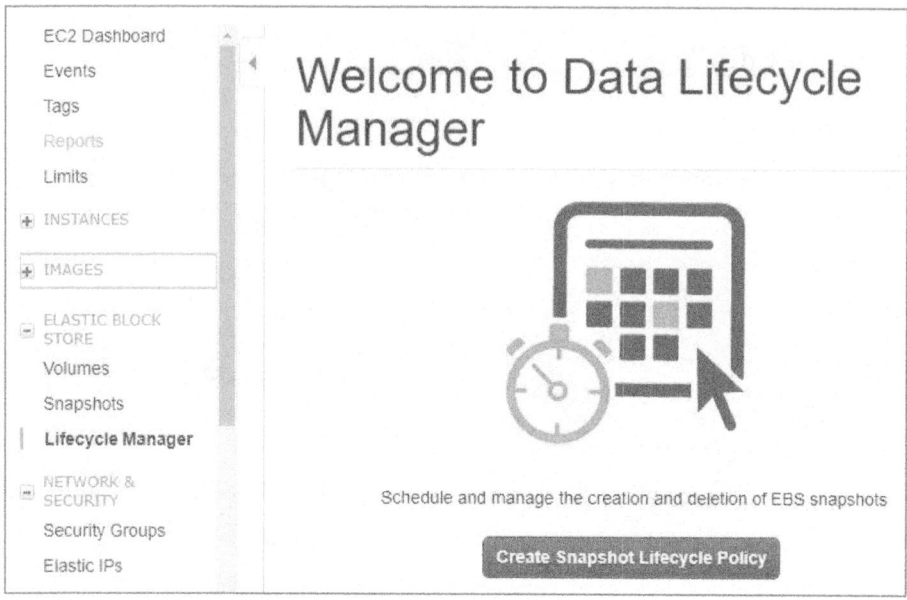

Figure 5.57: Lifecycle Manager

On this page, you will specify:

- the description of this policy
- targeted volumes with tags
- schedule
- tags of the snapshots
- IAM role used to create the snapshots
- "enable" or "disable" this policy after creation

First, enter the description "policy-standard-ebs-snapshot-schedule." Select the tag "ebs-snapshot-schedule" from the dropdown; then enter the value of the tag "standard."

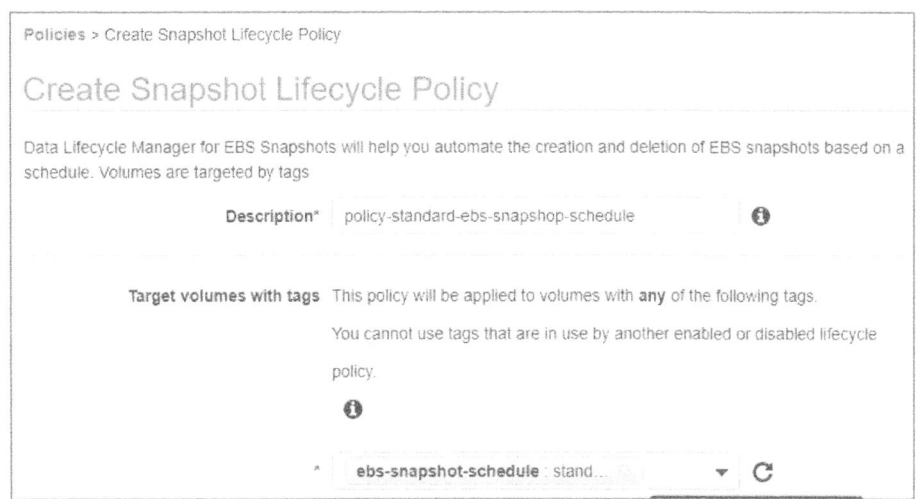

Figure 5.58: Create a snapshot lifecycle policy - description and target tags

Specify the schedule:

- Frequency: every 24 hours.
- Snapshot creation start time: 08:00 UTC.
- Retention rule: retaining 7 snapshots.

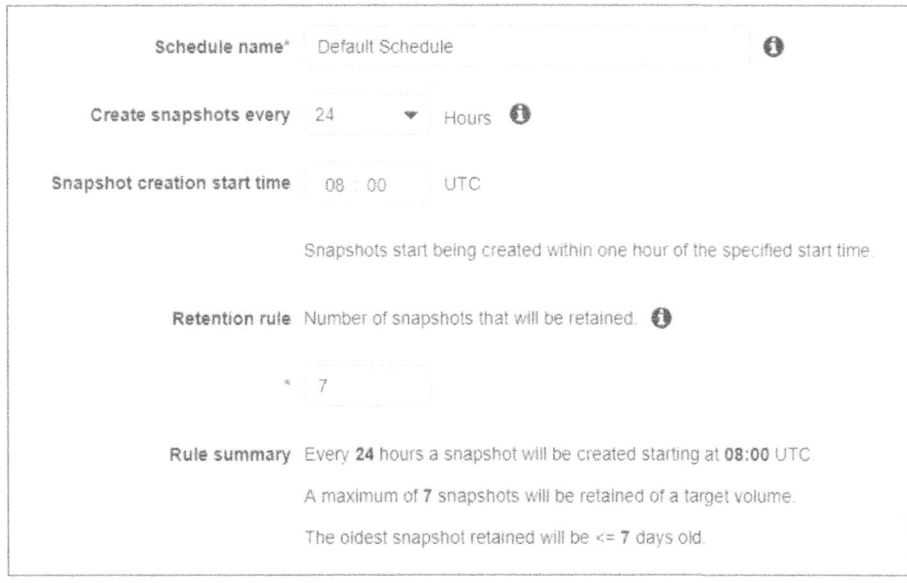

Figure 5.59: Create a snapshot lifecycle policy - schedule

Copy tags of the volume to the snapshots so that the snapshots have the same tags as the original volumes.

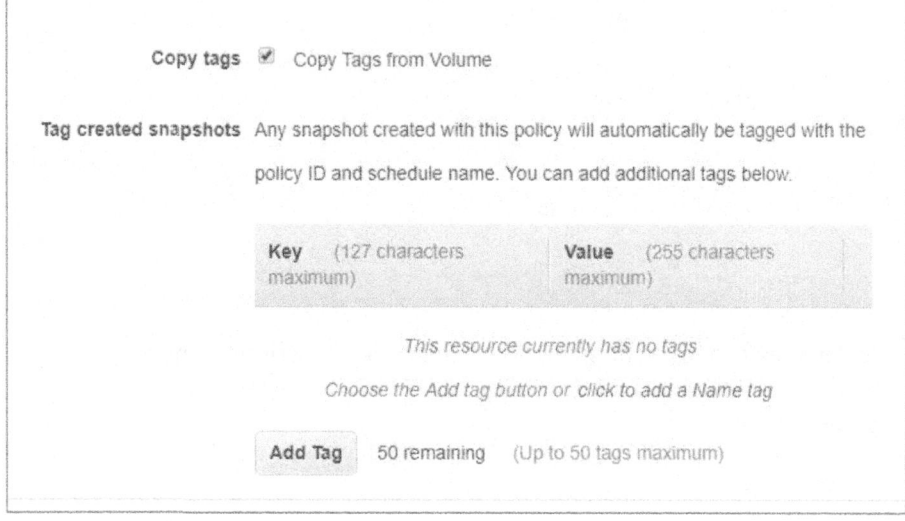

Figure 5.60: Create a snapshot lifecycle policy - copying tags to snapshots

Let AWS create a default IAM role to perform the snapshot creation and deletion. Enable this policy after creation.

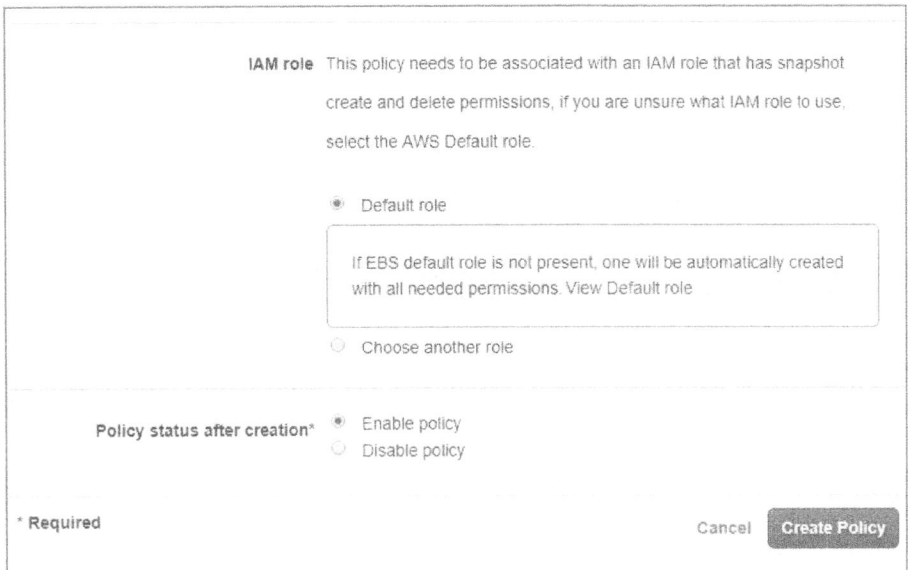

Figure 5.61: Create a snapshot lifecycle policy - IAM role

Click "Create Policy" to see the "success" message as below.

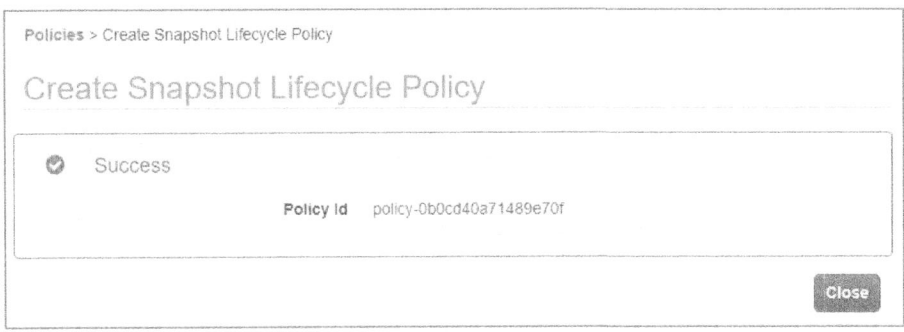

Figure 5.62: Create a snapshot lifecycle policy - success

Click the "Close" button. Go back to "Lifecycle Manager" page. You can now see the new snapshot lifecycle policy:

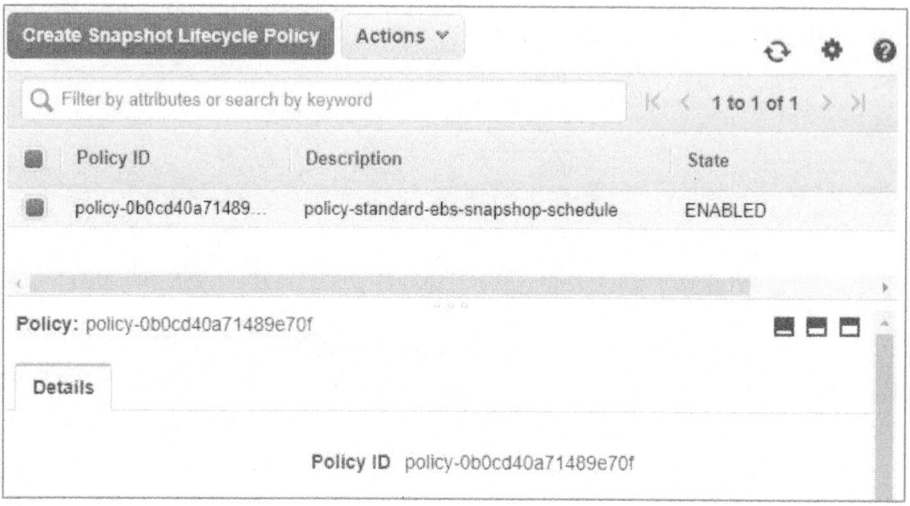

Policy ID	Description	State
policy-0b0cd40a71489...	policy-standard-ebs-snapshop-schedule	ENABLED

Policy: policy-0b0cd40a71489e70f

Details

Policy ID   policy-0b0cd40a71489e70f

Figure 5.63: List of snapshot lifecycle policies

If you check the policy detail, you will see that an execution role has been created:

"arn:aws:iam::<account id>:role/service-role/AWSDataLifecycleManagerDefaultRole"

If you go to IAM, then Roles, you will find the newly created role. This role has a policy attached to it. The policy name is "AWSDataLifecycleManagerServiceRole."

This is the definition of this policy:

```
{
  "Version": "2012-10-17",
  "Statement": [
    {
      "Effect": "Allow",
      "Action": [
        "ec2:CreateSnapshot",
        "ec2:DeleteSnapshot",
        "ec2:DescribeVolumes",
```

```
            "ec2:DescribeSnapshots"
         ],
         "Resource": "*"
      },
      {
         "Effect": "Allow",
         "Action": [
            "ec2:CreateTags"
         ],
         "Resource": "arn:aws:ec2:*::snapshot/*"
      }
   ]
}
```

If you choose to create your own IAM role policy for the snapshot lifecycle policy, the above definition is your reference.

Now you have the snapshot lifecycle policy.

Next, confirm that this snapshot lifecycle policy is working by checking the "Snapshots" page.

There are no snapshots yet.

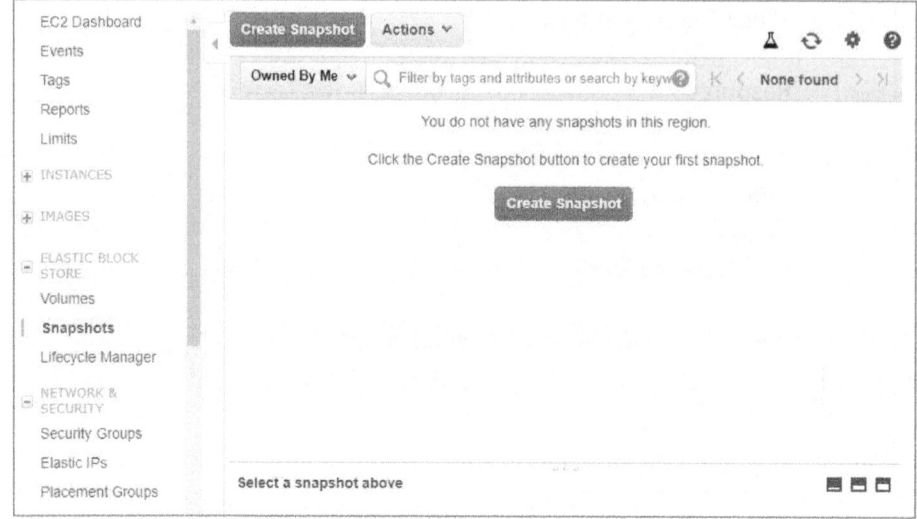

Figure 5.64: Snapshots before snapshot lifecycle policy

Confirm that the new DML is working as expected.

After 08:00 UTC, you will see the snapshots of those two volumes with the tag "ebs-snapshot-schedule" and the value "standard." The description of the snapshot has the policy ID and schedule name in it: "Created for policy: policy-0b0cd40a71489e70f schedule: Default Schedule."

Name	Snapshot ID	Size	Description
	snap-02c5560cf309...	100 GiB	Created for policy: policy-0b0cd40a71489e70f schedule: Default Schedule
	snap-0aa5a75baafa...	8 GiB	Created for policy: policy-0b0cd40a71489e70f schedule: Default Schedule

Figure 5.65: Snapshots created by snapshot lifecycle policy

If you look at the tags of these two snapshots, you will find that the three tags (owner, project, ebs-snapshot-schedule) in the original volumes have been copied over to the snapshots.

Figure 5.66: New tags in the snapshots created by snapshot lifecycle policy

In addition, two new tags have been added by AWS:

```
aws:dlm:lifecycle-policy-id: policy-0b0cd40a71489e70f
aws:dlm:lifecycle-schedule-name: Default Schedule
```

AWS DLM relies on these two tags to identify the series of the snapshots. If the schedule name is changed, the old series will not be covered by the lifecycle policy. As a result, the old series of snapshots will not be deleted by the new schedule.

5.6.3 Things to Consider When Implementing DLM

How are snapshots created?

The first time a snapshot is made, the full EBS volume is copied.

Successive snapshots are incremental - only new data and changed data are copied.

When you delete an incremental copy of the snapshot, only the data unique to that snapshot will be deleted.

When is a snapshot created?

Snapshots begin to be created by a policy within one hour following the specified start time.

If your schedule is 08:00 UTC every 24 hours, the snapshot may be created as late as 08:59 UTC.

What happens when the target tags are modified?

You can modify an existing snapshot lifecycle policy.

When the target tags are modified in this policy, the EBS volume with the old tags will no longer be covered by this policy. As a result, the old snapshots will not be deleted by this policy.

What happens when the schedule name is modified?

You can modify an existing snapshot lifecycle policy.

When the schedule name is modified in this policy, the snapshots made by the previous schedule name will no longer be covered by this policy. As a result, the old snapshots will not be deleted by this policy.

What happens when a snapshot is copied?

If a snapshot created by a policy is copied, the new copy will not be covered by the retention period of the policy.

If you want to keep a copy of a snapshot beyond the retention period, make a copy of it.

5.6.4 Summary

One of the biggest tasks when optimizing EC2 compute costs is to manage EBS volumes and their snapshots.

DLM helps you automate the EBS snapshot creation and retention. You do so by creating a snapshot lifecycle policy. With such a policy, AWS takes care of the snapshot creation and retention based on the schedule you specified. The policy will be only applied to those EBS volumes with the specified tags and values.

As with the lifecycle policy for S3 storage, with DML, you have peace of mind knowing you will keep your latest EBS snapshots and delete the old snapshots. Without such a policy, you may have accumulated many EBS snapshots, and you are paying for those snapshots that may no longer be needed.

5.7 Implementation #6: How to Tag AWS Resources for Cost Optimization

5.7.1 Introduction

A tag is a label for an AWS resource. Each tag consists of a key and a value. A key can have multiple values.

Tagging is extremely important in cost optimization in an enterprise environment.

- Proper tagging is the foundation of a lot of cost optimization techniques.
- Tagging is part of cost allocation strategy. You can identify, measure, and control AWS costs based on tags.
- Proper tagging creates transparency and accountability in using AWS resources.
- Tagging also helps in automation. You can create an auto-start and auto-stop policy on EC2 and RDS instances based on the tags.

Tagging is also quite challenging.

- If there are too many tags, maintenance is difficult. The marginal benefit decreases when the number of tags increases.
- Consistence is another challenge. Tags need to be consistent. The way to implement the tags must also be consistent.

How you implement tagging is also very important.

A tagging policy may be of considerable help in your organization to keep the tags clean and consistent.

5.7.2 The Benefits of Tagging in Cost Optimization

Tagging is very important in an enterprise environment. It gives you flexibility to identify and group AWS resources any way you prefer. You can perform an operation based on the tags. For example, you can create S3 cross-region replication policy based on the tags.

Tagging is also the foundation of enterprise Cloud cost management.

You will probably rely on tags in almost every major cost-saving effort in the enterprise Cloud environment.

In your efforts to drive down AWS costs, tags are definitely a primary source of information.

You can make owners accountable for their spending by using tags such as "owner" and "project."

In addition, you can empower owners with the tag-based billing information to inform them where they are in terms of AWS spending.

5.7.3 Cost Allocation with Tags

You can create tags and apply tags to your AWS resources. AWS can group the usage and costs by these tags once the tags are activated in the Billing and Cost Management console.

Now you can generate a cost allocation report group by tags. You can apply these tags to organize your costs across multiple services.

How to activate user-defined cost allocation tags:

On your "My Billing Dashboard" page, you can activate cost allocation tags.

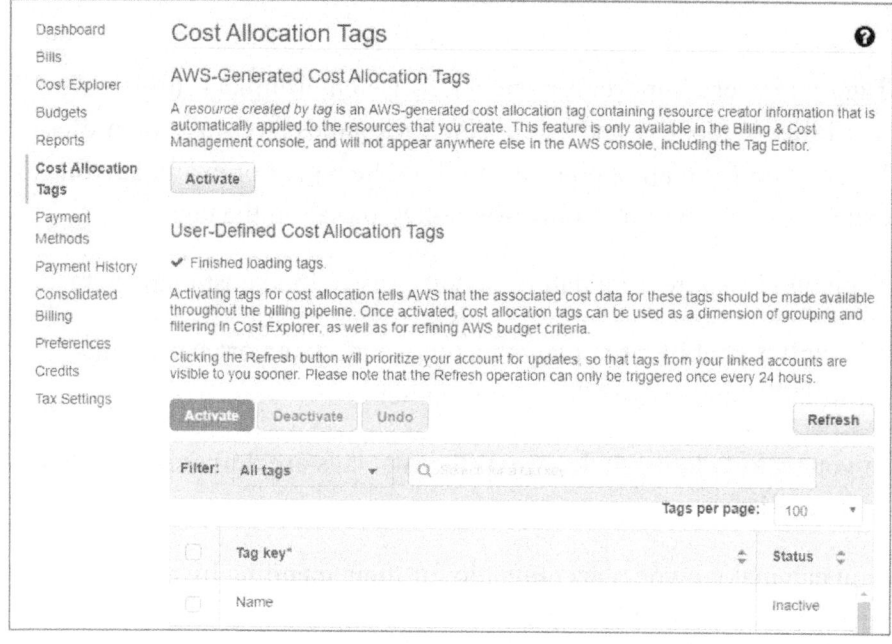

Figure 5.67: AWS Cost Allocation Tags - Activate

Select the tags you want to activate; then click "Activate."

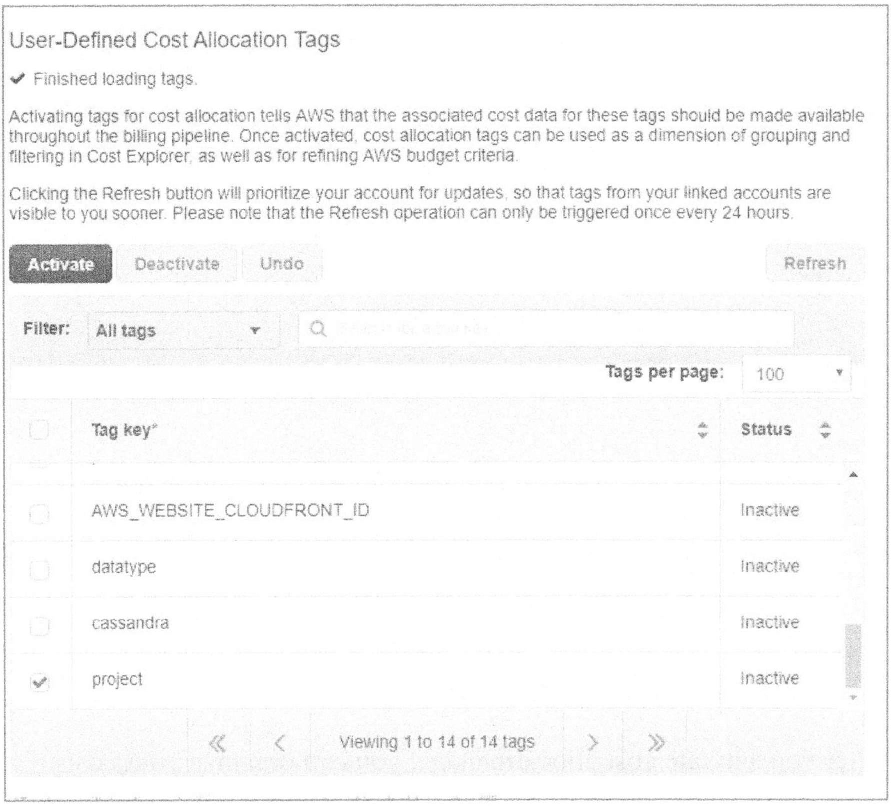

User-Defined Cost Allocation Tags

✔ Finished loading tags.

Activating tags for cost allocation tells AWS that the associated cost data for these tags should be made available throughout the billing pipeline. Once activated, cost allocation tags can be used as a dimension of grouping and filtering in Cost Explorer, as well as for refining AWS budget criteria.

Clicking the Refresh button will prioritize your account for updates, so that tags from your linked accounts are visible to you sooner. Please note that the Refresh operation can only be triggered once every 24 hours.

	Tag key	Status
☐	AWS_WEBSITE_CLOUDFRONT_ID	Inactive
☐	datatype	Inactive
☐	cassandra	Inactive
✔	project	Inactive

Figure 5.68: Cost Allocation Tags - Activate "project" and "owner" tags

Confirm to activate these two tags.

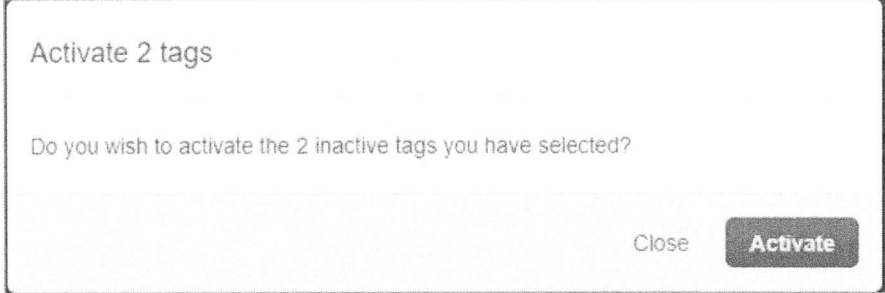

Figure 5.69: Cost Allocation Tags - Activate - Confirm

Now you have two cost allocation tags: "owner" and "project."

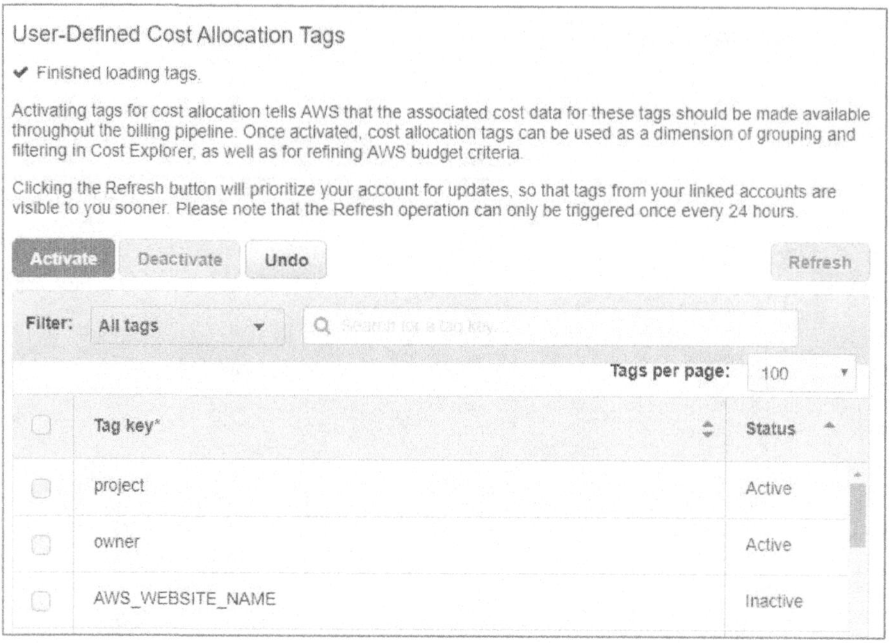

> **User-Defined Cost Allocation Tags**
>
> ✔ Finished loading tags.
>
> Activating tags for cost allocation tells AWS that the associated cost data for these tags should be made available throughout the billing pipeline. Once activated, cost allocation tags can be used as a dimension of grouping and filtering in Cost Explorer, as well as for refining AWS budget criteria.
>
> Clicking the Refresh button will prioritize your account for updates, so that tags from your linked accounts are visible to you sooner. Please note that the Refresh operation can only be triggered once every 24 hours.
>
> [**Activate**] [Deactivate] [Undo]   [Refresh]
>
> Filter: [All tags ▼] [🔍 Search for a tag key]
>
> Tags per page: [100 ▼]
>
> | ☐ | Tag key* | Status |
> |---|----------|--------|
> | ☐ | project | Active |
> | ☐ | owner | Active |
> | ☐ | AWS_WEBSITE_NAME | Inactive |

Figure 5.70: Cost Allocation Tags - results

After you activate cost allocation tags, you can organize your costs based on the cost allocation tags and create cost allocation reports to track costs by these tags.

With "project" and "owner" tags activated, you can now track costs by "project," or by "owner," or both.

The following section tells you how to track costs by tags.

LINK: Analyze Costs with AWS Cost Explorer

5.7.4 How to Tag AWS Resources

You can tag an S3 bucket, prefix, or object by going to the "Properties" of the object, "Advanced Settings," and then "Tags."

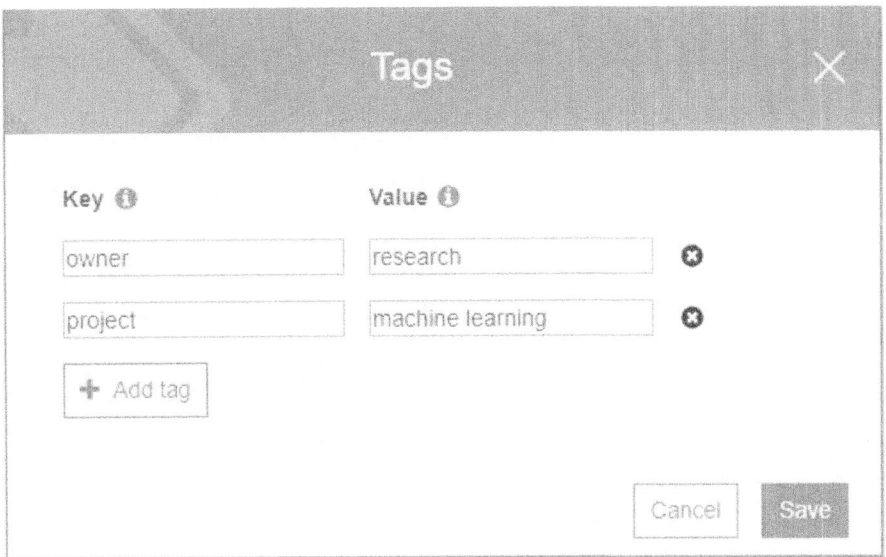

Figure 5.71: Tagging S3 Objects

You can tag an EC2 instance during the launch process:

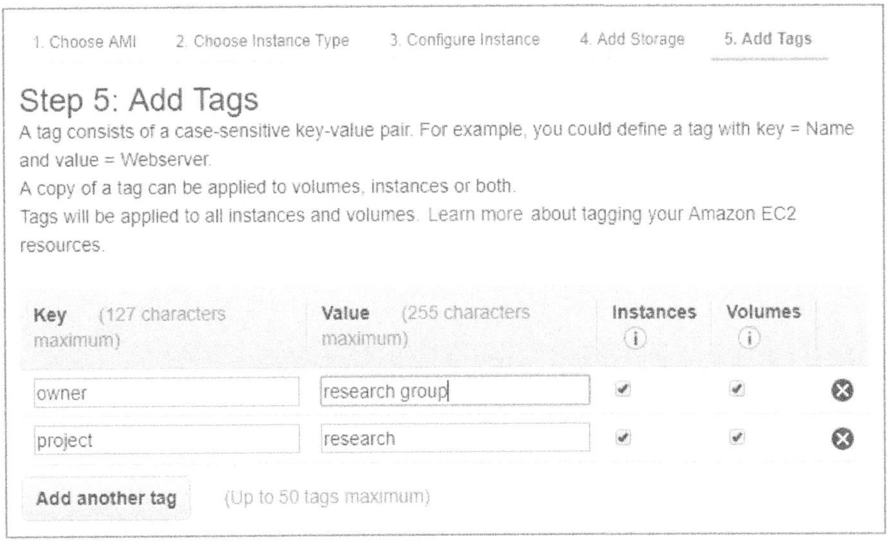

Figure 5.72: Tag EC2 instance during the launch process

You can add or edit tags for an existing EC2 instance, under the tab "Tags":

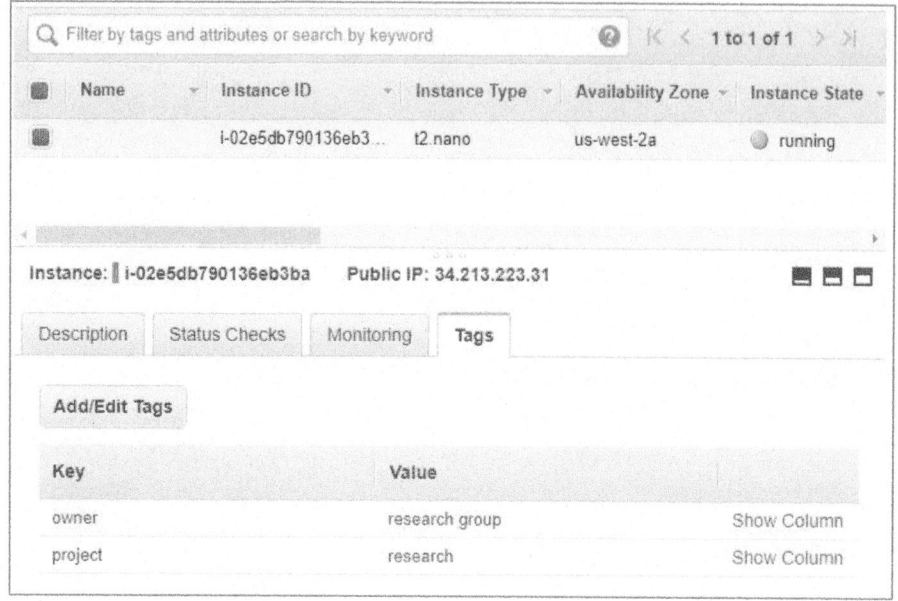

Figure 5.73: Tagging EC2 instance - Add/Edit tags

If you have an AWS Config rule that terminates an EC2 instance or deletes S3 objects without proper tagging, it is a good idea to tag the AWS resources during the creation.

If you are just beginning to implement a tagging policy, you may use AWS Tag Editor to tag AWS resources in bulk:

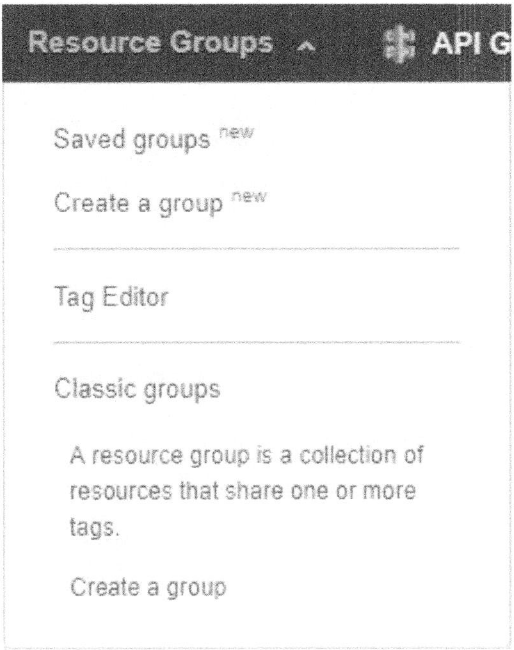

Figure 5.74: Tagging with Tag Editor - Launch Tag Editor

The following screen shows you how to find the AWS resources that have no "owner" tag or whose "owner" tag is empty (no value).

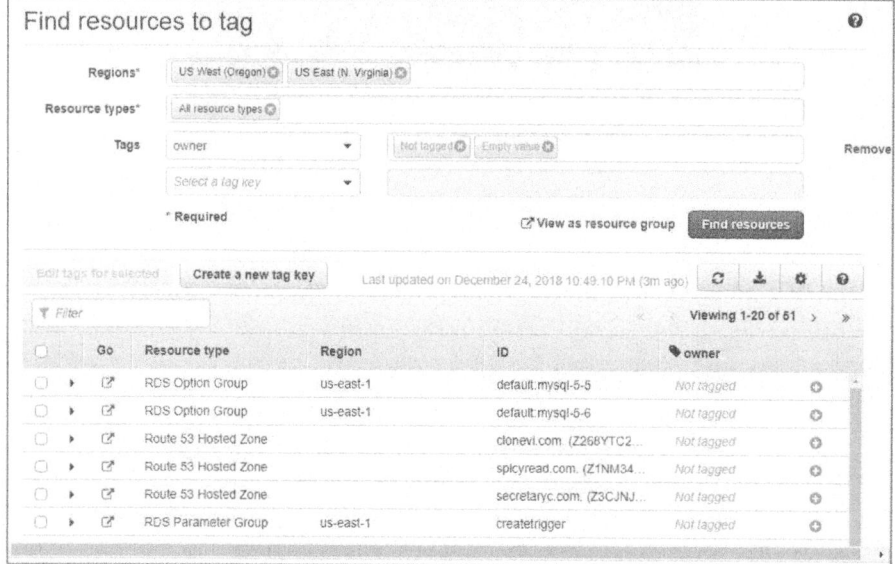

Figure 5.75: Tag Editor - Find resources to tag

Now you can click on the "+" in each row to add or edit the "owner" tag on a single page.

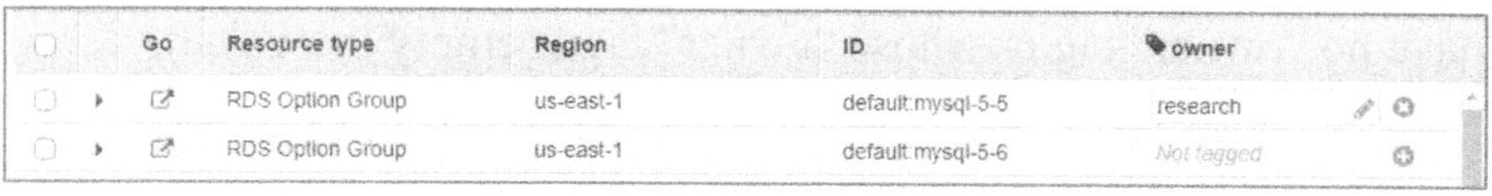

Figure 5.76: Tag Editor - add or edit tags

In addition, you can select the AWS resources by checking the checkbox at the beginning of the row; then click on "Edit tags for selected."

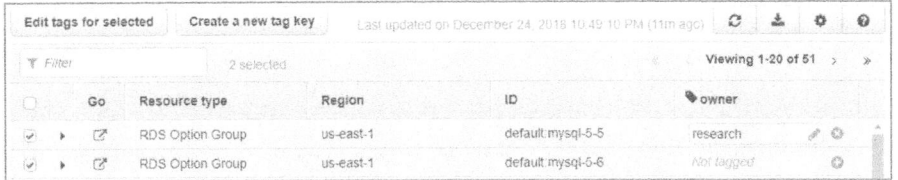

Figure 5.77: Tag Editor - select multiple resources to tag

On the popup screen, modify the "owner" tag and apply the changes.

Please note:

> If you click the first checkbox in the upper left corner to select all the rows, you are also selecting all the rows on the second and subsequent pages.
>
> You might think that you are selecting all the rows on the *current* page. But you are not; you are selecting all the rows on all the pages. This could be a huge mistake.

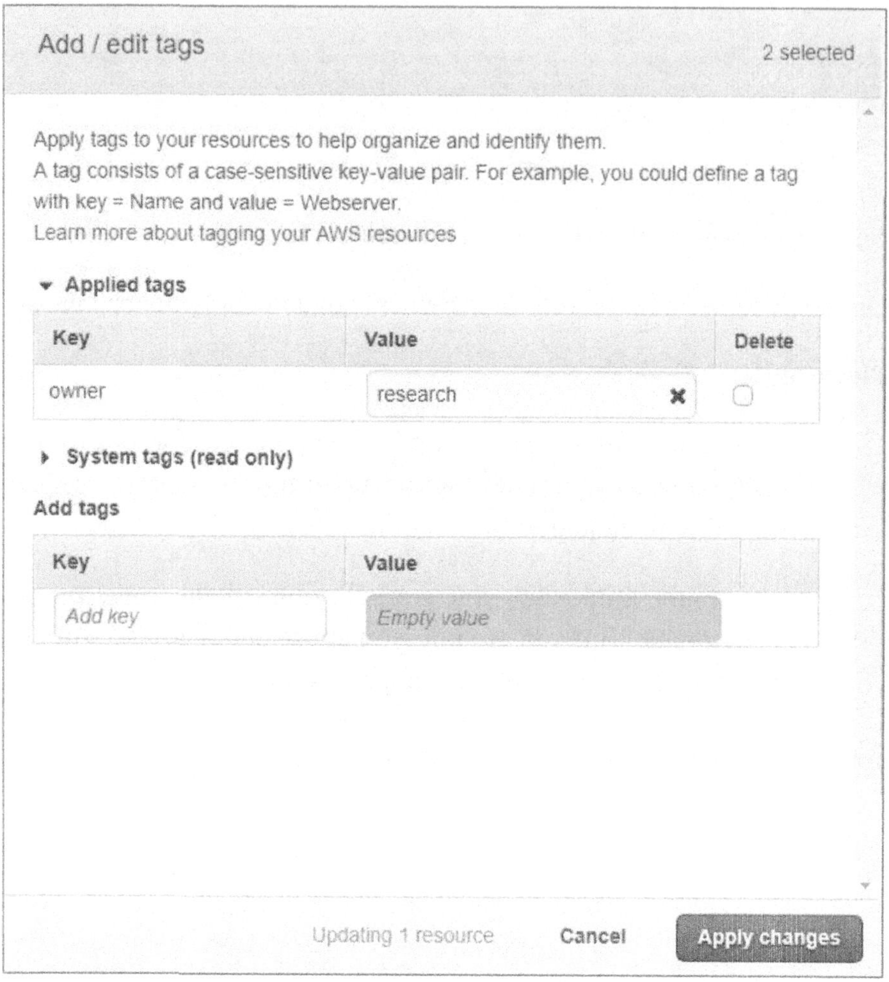

Figure 5.78: Tag Editor - Tag multiple resources at a time

When you click "Apply changes," the tags will be applied to all the selected resources. There is no way to undo.

5.7.5 Get Billing Data by Tags Using AWS Cost Explorer

...

Now you come to the page that allows you to "slice and dice" your billing data using "group by" above the chart plus the filters on the right.

You can do both: apply the filter then group the filtered results.

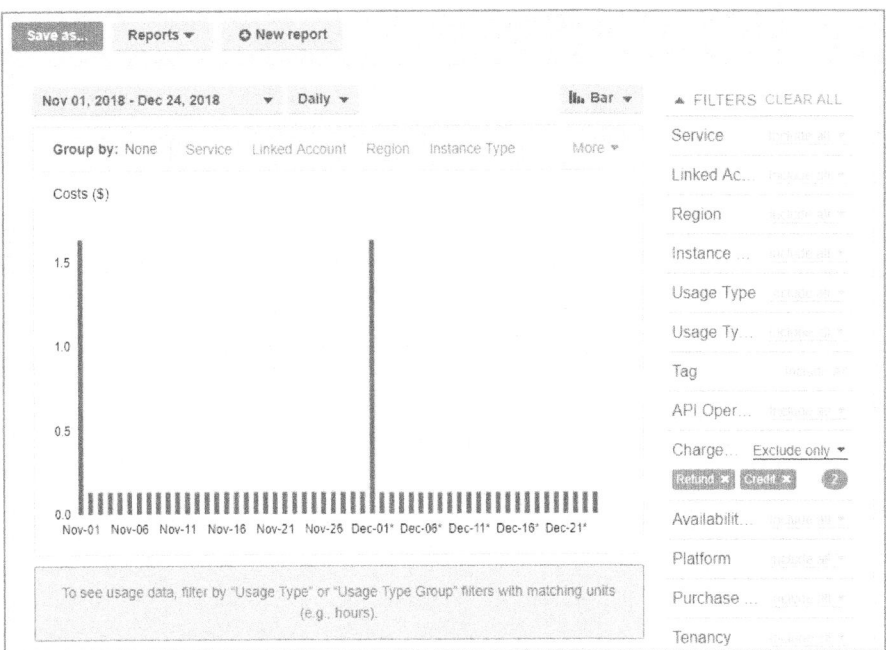

Figure 5.79: AWS Cost Explorer - Group By and Filter by tags

Let's try to group by the "owner" tag first. Click on "More" in the upper right corner of the chart, then "Tag," and select "owner."

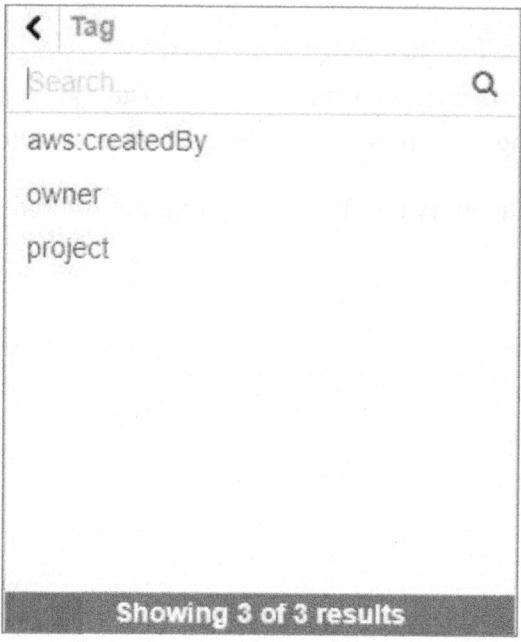

Figure 5.80: AWS Cost Explorer - Group by "owner" tag

Now you have the daily AWS expenditures group by "owner" tag. You can see the AWS expenditures by owner.

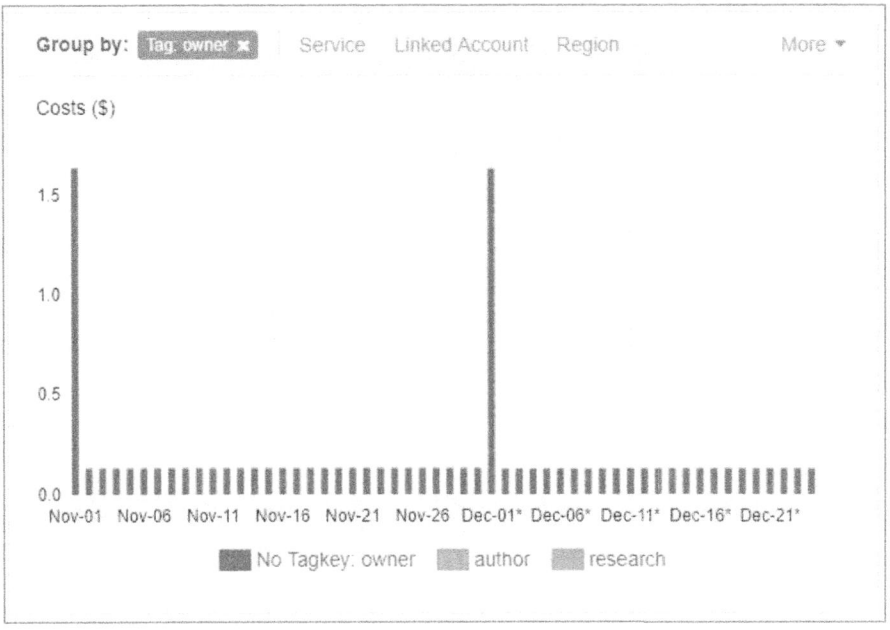

Figure 5.81: AWS Cost Explorer - Group by "owner" tag

You can further analyze the costs by using filters. For example, you can query the cost of each owner using the "machine learning" and "research" tags for projects.

On the right, click next to the "Tag" to see the popup screen below. Select "project," then check "machine learning" and "research," and then click on "Apply filters."

Now you have a report of the daily expenditures of these two projects, grouped by owner. You can also create a report of daily expenditure in addition to these two projects by changing "Include only" to "Exclude only" next to the "project" filter.

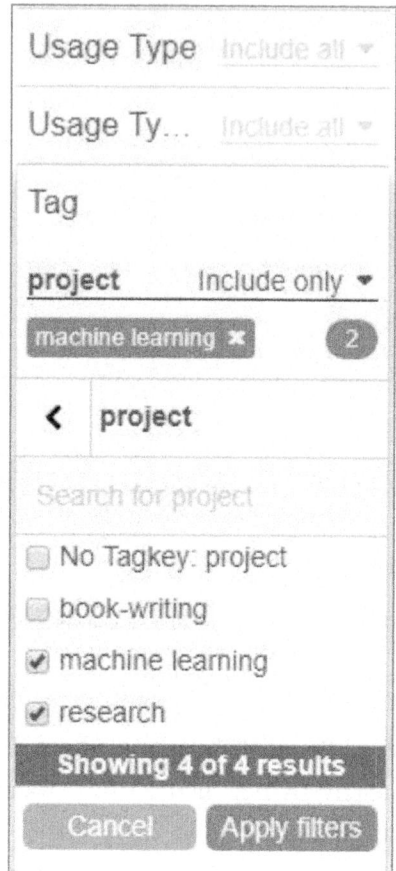

Figure 5.82: AWS Cost Explorer - Filter by "project" tag

Once you are satisfied with the report, you can save it by clicking "Save as…" in the upper left corner of the page.

Figure 5.83: AWS Cost Explorer - Save your report

On the popup screen, enter your report name.

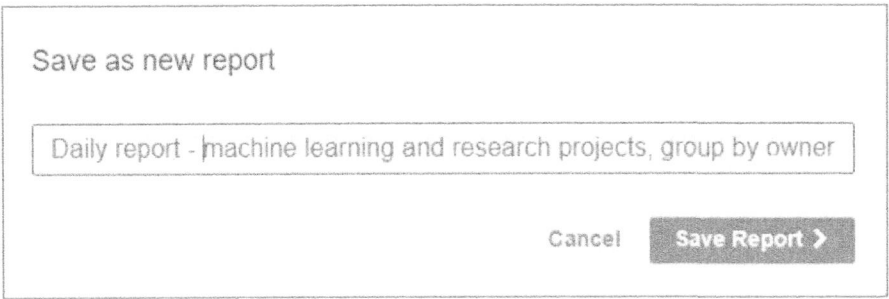

Figure 5.84: AWS cost Explorer - Save a new report

Now you have saved the cost allocation report saved. You can change the report name by clicking on the pen icon next to the report name.

Figure 5.85: AWS Cost Explorer - open the new report

Now you can click on the book icon on the left to go to the "Saved reports" page. There you can see the report you just saved.

Report name		Chart style	Time granularity	Group by
AWS Marketplace	🔒	ll.	Monthly	Service
Daily costs	🔒	ll.	Daily	
Daily report - machine learning ...		ll.	Daily	TagKeyValue:owner
Monthly costs by linked account	🔒	ll.	Monthly	LinkedAccount
Monthly costs by service	🔒	ll.	Monthly	Service
Monthly EC2 running hours costs ...	🔒	ll.	Monthly	
RI Coverage	🔒	∧∧	Daily	Not Applicable
RI Utilization	🔒	∧∧	Daily	Not Applicable

Figure 5.86: AWS Cost Explorer - All your saved reports

Now you can click on the name of the report to go to the report.

If you want to create similar reports filtered by tags, you can click the checkbox for that report, click on the button "Create Copy" to create a copy, modify it and save it. This is the easiest way to create a new report.

Once you have the reports filtered by project tag and grouped by owner tag, you can monitor the project costs and hold the owners accountable.

This works well only if all the AWS resources have been tagged properly.

One great feature of the Cost Explorer is in its "Advanced Options" which allows you to check "Show only untagged resources," as shown below. This option is located at the bottom of the filter section. Use this option to retrieve the costs of those untagged resources in your reports.

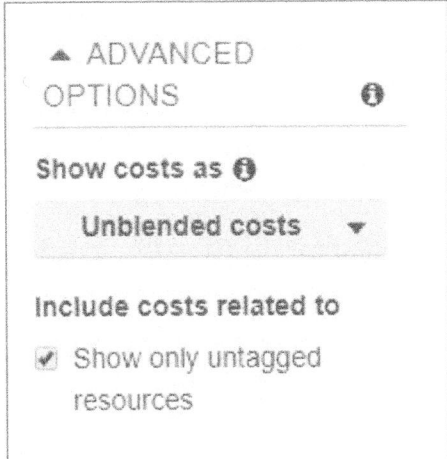

Figure 5.87: - AWS Cost Explorer - Show only untagged resources

Please note that you can download the report data to a CSV file and analyze the data in Excel. Click on the "Download CSV" button above the data table.

owner	Nov 1, 2018	Nov 2, 2018
Total cost ($)	1.63	0.13
No Tagkey: owner ($)	1.63	0.13

Figure 5.88: AWS Cost Explorer - Download report data

There are many ways to identify those untagged AWS resources.

Compared with AWS Tag Editor, there is a big advantage to using the Cost Explorer. It has the dollar values for those untagged resources. With the dollar values attached to your reports, the owners take the tagging more seriously.

5.7.6 Get Data Using AWS Cost Explorer API

AWS offers API for most of Cost Explorer's functionality. You can use it to retrieve data using AWS CLI commands.

There is only one end point for the CE API: https://ce.us-east-1.amazonaws.com.

Please note that this end point is in the region of us-east-1. If you are using AWS CLI, it may be easier for you to use us-east-1 as the region before you use the CE APIs.

5.7.7 Summary

This is a very short step-by-step guide to implementing tagging.

Tagging is the foundation of cost optimization, especially in an enterprise environment.

Once you have the high quality and consistent user-defined tags, you can visualize, analyze and control your AWS spending with more dimensions.

5.8 Implementation #7: How to Monitor RI Utilization and RI Coverage

5.8.1 Introduction

Reserved Instances, when implemented correctly, could save you a lot. However, the commitment also means that, if you are not using the resources you committed to using, you may not save as much as you can; you may even end up with wasting money on the resources you are not using.

The optimization of RIs has been covered previously. Below are the two reports to:

- help you identify more cost-saving opportunities with RIs
- measure how much of your RI commitment is actually being used

The reports are the RI Coverage report and the RI Utilization report.

Both of these reports are prebuilt by AWS. You can open each one or create a copy, modify it, and save it with a different name.

Go to Cost Explorer and click on the book icon for "Saved Reports," as shown below. The bottom two reports in this screen are "RI Coverage" and "RI Utilization."

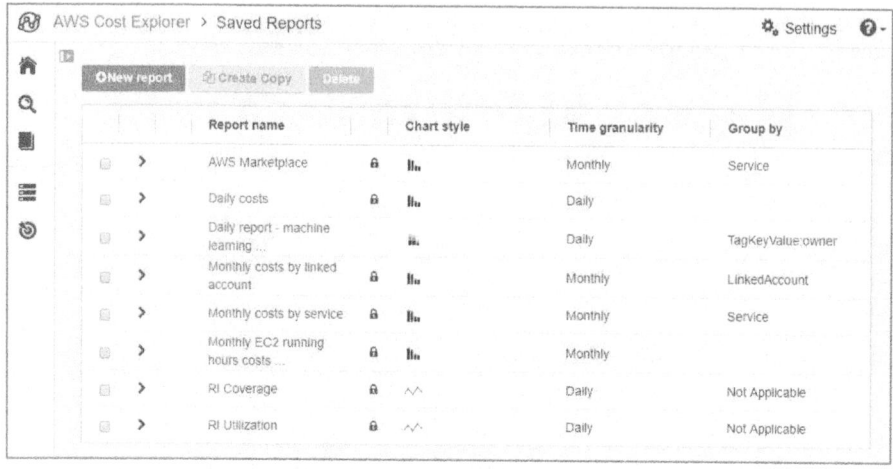

Figure 5.89: AWS Cost Explorer - Saved Reports

You can also create reservation budget to track the budget and set the alerts for your RI coverage and RI utilization.

LINK: Create a Reservation Budget and an Alert for RI Utilization of a Project

5.8.2 RI Coverage

RI Coverage report tells you how many of your On-Demand EC2 or RDS instances are covered by your RIs.

> The purpose of this report is to identify more cost-saving opportunities by purchasing more RIs.
>
> If your RI coverage for t2.xlarge is 20% yesterday, only 20% of your t2.xlarge On-Demand instances are covered by your RIs as of yesterday.
>
> This certainly does not mean that you should purchase RIs for the remaining 80%. There is no target of 100% RI Coverage

because you don't have to use all the resources for the length of your RIs.

Please use the optimization model to purchase the right number of RIs for the right type of instances.

Below is the RI Coverage report screen. You can use the filters on the right to narrow down the results. You can click on "View recommendations" to see what you can do to save more.

Figure 5.90: AWS Cost Explorer RI Coverage report

There is no data on the above screen. Here is a screen from the AWS with more data:

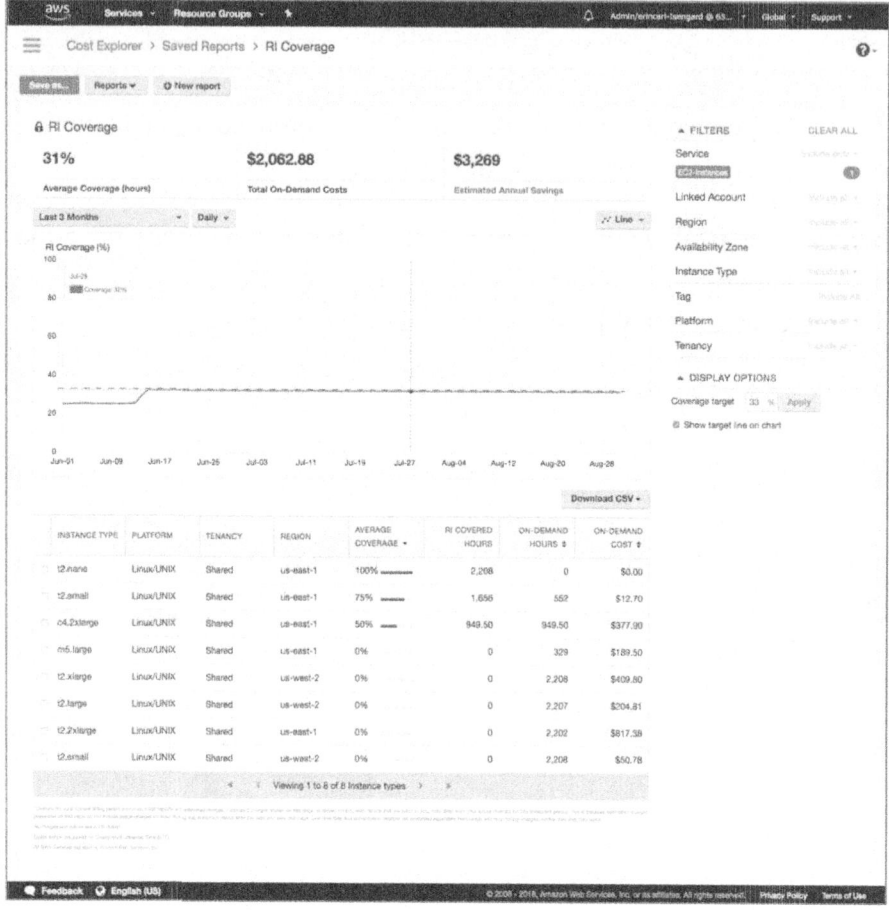

Figure 5.91: RI Coverage report - details

Source: https://aws.amazon.com/blogs/enterprise-strategy/accessing-your-ri-purchase-recommendations-and-identifying-opportunities-for-cost-optimization/

5.8.3 RI Utilization

An RI Utilization report tells you how much of your RI commitment is being used.

If you purchased 4 RIs for t2.xlarge instances and you had 2 t2.xlarge instances running as of yesterday, your RI utilization was 50% as of yesterday.

You were only using 50% of your RIs as of yesterday. You were not taking advantage of the other 50% of your RIs.

You should target your RI utilization at 100%.

Below is the RI Utilization report. You can use the filters on the right to narrow down the results.

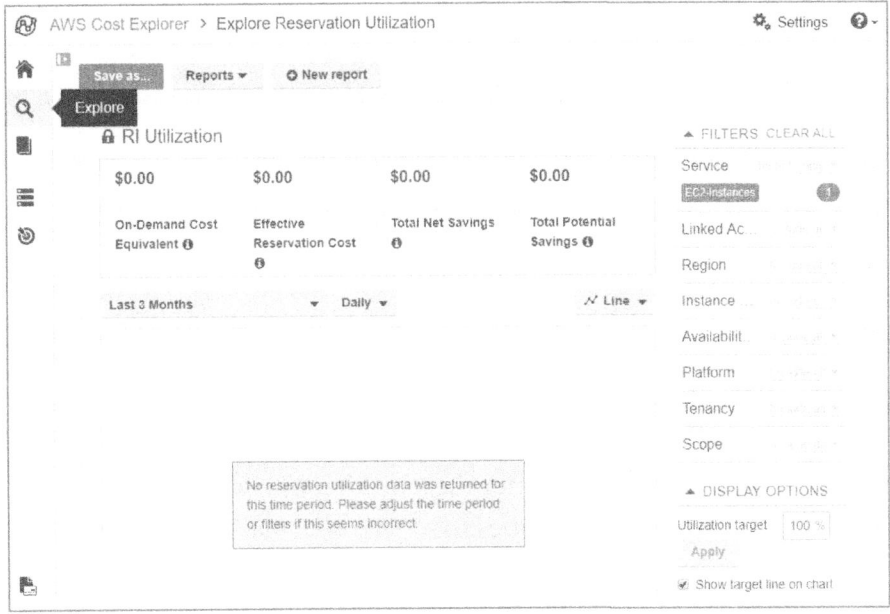

Figure 5.92: RI Utilization report

The above figure lacks data. Here is an example from AWS:

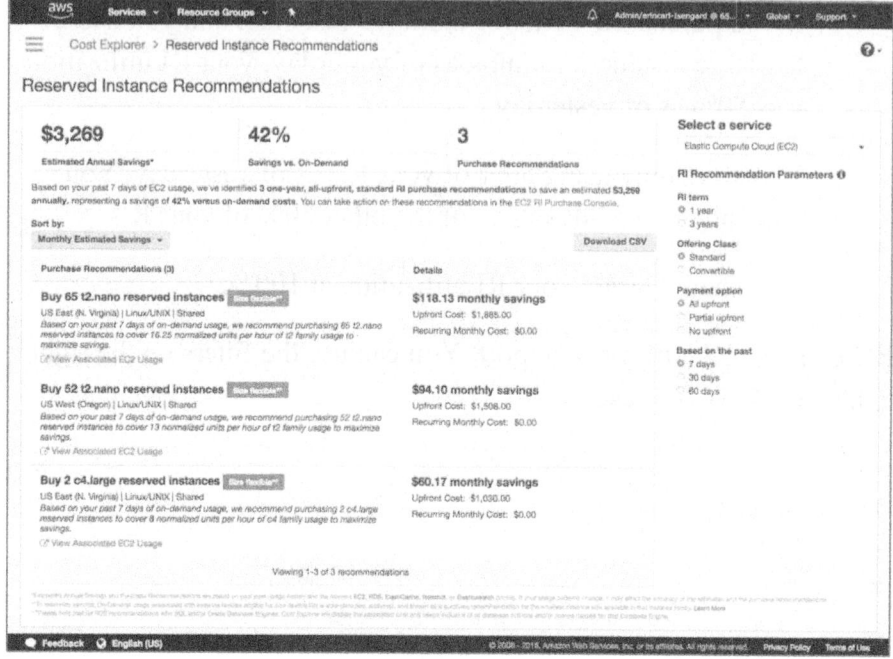

Figure 5.93: RI Utilization report - RI Recommendations

Source: https://aws.amazon.com/blogs/enterprise-strategy/accessing-your-ri-purchase-recommendations-and-identifying-opportunities-for-cost-optimization/

We recommend that you monitor these two reports once a week to identify cost-saving opportunities.

5.8.4 Reservation Summary

You should also check the following two pages periodically. They are accessible from the main navigation menu of Cost Explorer on the left, as shown below.

Figure 5.94: Cost Explorer Navigation Menu

The first report is a reservation summary.

Click on the second icon from the bottom on the left (as shown above).

On this "Reservation Summary" page, there is one very useful link: "Reservation expiring (next 30 days)." Click on this link.

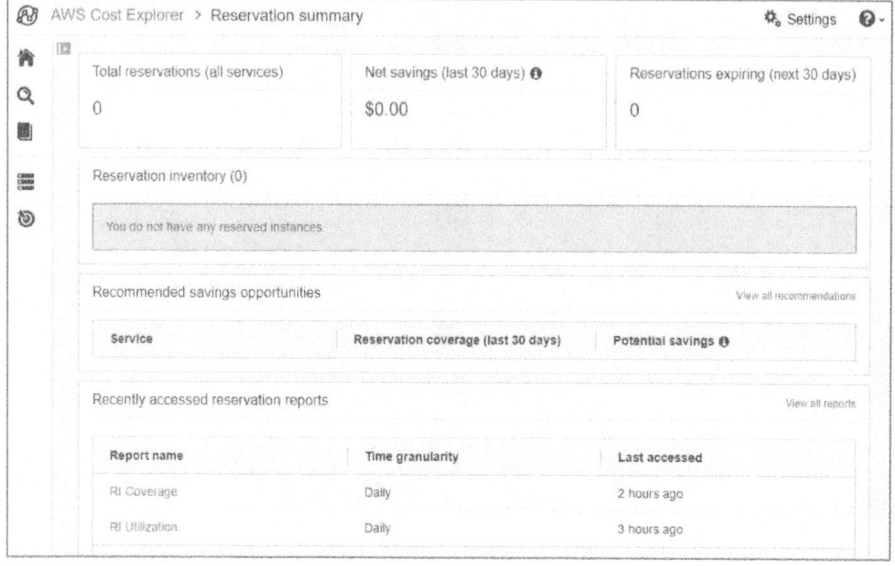

Figure 5.95: Reservation Summary

In this figure you can see the list of your reservations that will expire in the next 30 days. You should monitor this page and repurchase RIs if necessary.

Related links:

LINK: Reserved Instances

LINK: How to Maximize RI Utilization

5.8.5 Reserved Instance Recommendation

The second report is "Reserved Instance Recommendation."

Click on the last icon on the Cost Explorer navigation menu on the left. You will see the page as shown below.

Figure 5.96: RI Recommendations

You can examine this page to research on those "purchase recommendations." This page only gives you the recommendations. Whether to reserve them or not is up to you.

5.8.6 Summary

This step-by-step guide explained how to monitor RI Utilization and RI Coverage. You can use Cost Explorer to access the prebuilt reports on RI Utilization and RI Coverage.

You can use the "Reservation Summary" to find all the RIs that will be expiring in the next 30 days.

You can use the "Reserved Instance Recommendations" to identify the potential cost-saving opportunities.

5.9 Implementation #8: How to Set Up and Use AWS Athena for Cost Optimization

5.9.1 Introduction

You can analyze and visualize your raw billing data with many tools: Tableau, PowerBI, Amazon Quicksight, and AWS Cost Explorer.

For Amazon Quicksight:

> https://aws.amazon.com/blogs/big-data/query-and-visualize-aws-cost-and-usage-data-using-amazon-athena-and-amazon-quicksight/

AWS Athena is another option to gather billing data and analyze them for cost-saving opportunities. Athena allows you to query S3 files using the database query language SQL. If you know how to query a database with SQL, you know how to query data in S3 with Athena.

If you are not familiar with database language, you can skip this implementation. If you do know database language, it is very convenient to analyze the data in your own way, well worth the effort to set it up.

Setting up Athena queries for the billing data is not straight forward. This step-by-step guide makes it easy to set up and run Athena queries.

5.9.2 Data Gathering and Data Analysis with AWS Athena

There are several flavors of SQL language. AWS Athena uses Presto (https://prestodb.io/).

Here is an example of creating a database and table with Athena:

```
CREATE DATABASE handbook;

CREATE EXTERNAL TABLE handbook.mycost(
    identity_line_item_id STRING,

    identity_time_interval STRING,

    bill_invoice_id STRING,

    bill_billing_entity STRING,

    bill_bill_type STRING,

    bill_payer_account_id STRING,

    bill_billing_period_start_date STRING,

    bill_billing_period_end_date STRING,

    line_item_usage_account_id STRING,

    line_item_line_item_type STRING,

    line_item_usage_start_date STRING,

    line_item_usage_end_date STRING,

    line_item_product_code STRING,

    line_item_usage_type STRING,

    line_item_operation STRING,
```

```
line_item_availability_zone STRING,
line_item_resource_id STRING,
line_item_usage_amount STRING,
line_item_normalization_factor STRING,
line_item_normalized_usage_amount STRING,
line_item_currency_code STRING,
line_item_unblended_rate STRING,
line_item_unblended_cost STRING,
line_item_blended_rate STRING,
line_item_blended_cost STRING,
line_item_line_item_description STRING,
line_item_tax_type STRING,
line_item_legal_entity STRING,
product_product_name STRING,
product_alarm_type STRING,
product_availability STRING,
product_description STRING,
product_durability STRING,
product_free_tier STRING,
product_from_location STRING,
product_from_location_type STRING,
product_group STRING,
product_group_description STRING,
```

```
        product_location STRING,
        product_location_type STRING,
        product_mailbox_storage STRING,
        product_operation STRING,
        product_product_family STRING,
        product_region STRING,
        product_request_description STRING,
        product_request_type STRING,
        product_routing_target STRING,
        product_routing_type STRING,
        product_servicecode STRING,
        product_servicename STRING,
        product_sku STRING,
        product_storage_class STRING,
        product_storage_media STRING,
        product_to_location STRING,
        product_to_location_type STRING,
        product_transfer_type STRING,
        product_usagetype STRING,
        product_version STRING,
        product_volume_type STRING,
        pricing_rate_id STRING,
        pricing_public_on_demand_cost STRING,
```

pricing_public_on_demand_rate STRING,

pricing_term STRING,

pricing_unit STRING,

reservation_amortized_upfront_cost_for_usage STRING,

reservation_amortized_upfront_fee_for_billing_period STRING,

reservation_effective_cost STRING,

reservation_end_time STRING,

reservation_modification_status STRING,

reservation_normalized_units_per_reservation STRING,

reservation_recurring_fee_for_usage STRING,

reservation_start_time STRING,

reservation_subscription_id STRING,

reservation_total_reserved_normalized_units STRING,

reservation_total_reserved_units STRING,

reservation_units_per_reservation STRING,

reservation_unused_amortized_upfront_fee_for_billing_period STRING,

reservation_unused_normalized_unit_quantity STRING,

reservation_unused_quantity STRING,

reservation_unused_recurring_fee STRING,

reservation_upfront_value STRING,

resource_tags_aws_created_by STRING,

```
        resource_tags_user_owner STRING,
        resource_tags_user_project STRING
)

ROW FORMAT SERDE 'org.apache.hadoop.hive.serde2.OpenCSVSerde'

WITH SERDEPROPERTIES ("separatorChar" = ",", "escapeChar" = "\\")

STORED AS TEXTFILE

LOCATION 's3://handbook-billing-data/data-csv/raw-data/';
```

```
select
        line_item_usage_start_date as "start",
        line_item_usage_end_date as "end",
        line_item_usage_amount as amount,
        line_item_unblended_rate as unblended_rat,
        line_item_unblended_cost as unblended_cost,
        line_item_blended_rate as blended_rate,
        line_item_blended_cost as blended_cost,
        line_item_line_item_description as description
from handbook.mycost
```

```
where line_item_usage_amount is not null
limit 100;
```

5.9.3 AWS Athena as a Managed Service

AWS Athena is a managed service, which means you have nothing to manage on your own. You don't have to build a database and manage it.

AWS Athena is also inexpensive.

If you use Athena to analyze your billing data, your cost of using Athena will likely be quite small. You only pay for $5 per TB of data scanned. Your billing data could be a few GB. Most likely, you won't scan the entire S3 collection of files. If your billing data are partitioned, you only scan a portion of it for the selected years and months.

Best of all, if the query fails because of query timeout, you don't have to pay for that query.

5.9.4 Collect Billing Data in S3 Bucket

Here is how you will collect your billing data with two major steps:

- Create an S3 bucket to store the raw billing data.
- Create a billing report to send the billing data to the bucket.

5.9.4.1 Create S3 Bucket to Store the AWS Billing Report Data

Go to Amazon S3 Console, "Buckets." Click "Create bucket".

Enter the bucket name "handbook-billing-data," and select the region "US West (Oregon)."

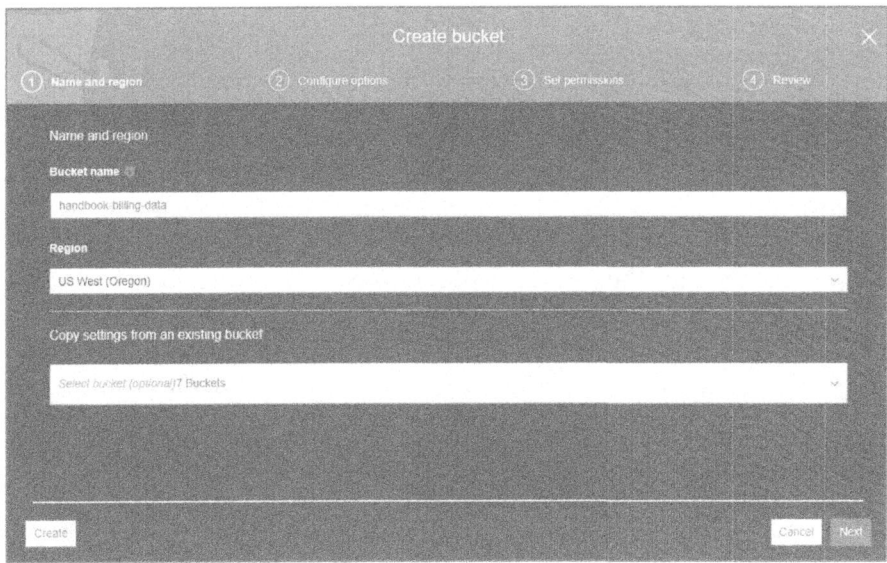

Figure 5.97: Create a bucket to store billing data

Configure options for the bucket. Don't enable the versioning. Specify the tags. Choose the encryption method.

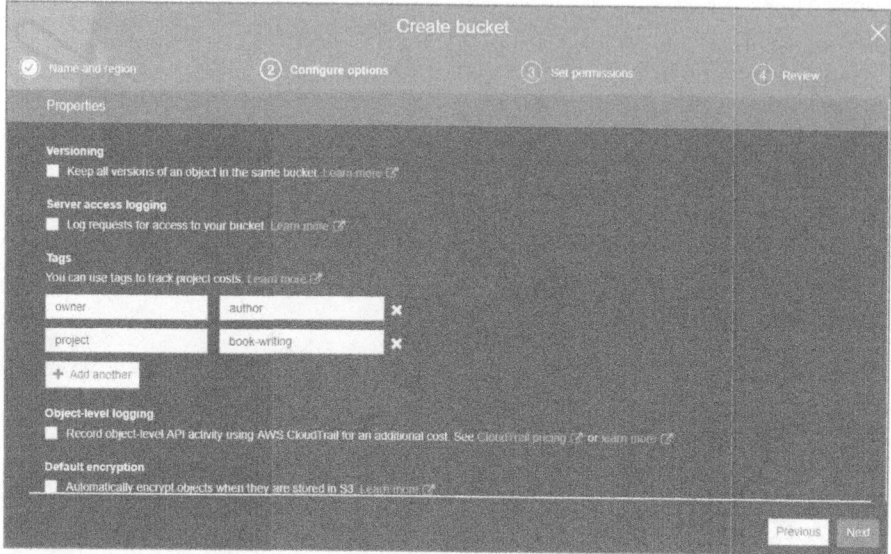

Figure 5.98: Create a bucket to store billing data - Configure options

Set permissions for the bucket. Do not allow any public access.

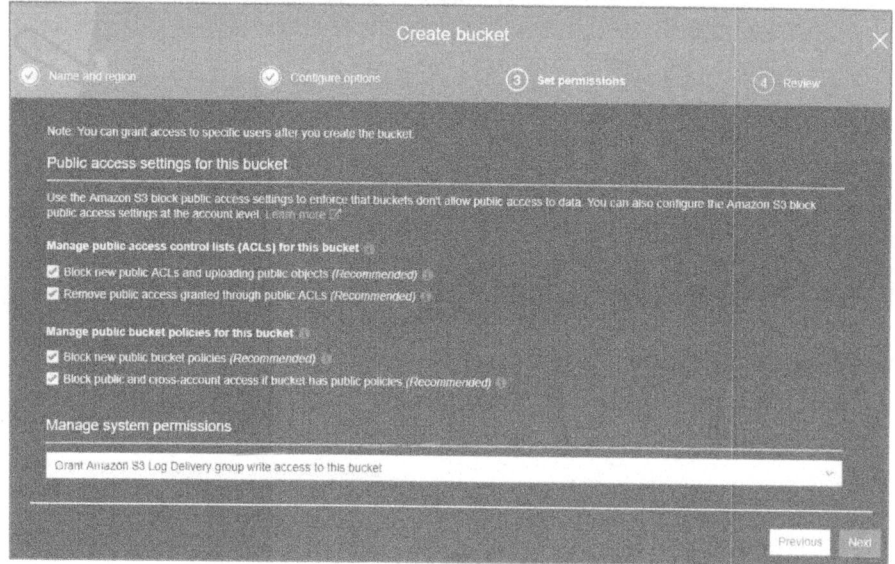

Figure 5.99: Create a bucket to store billing data - Set permissions

Review and create the bucket.

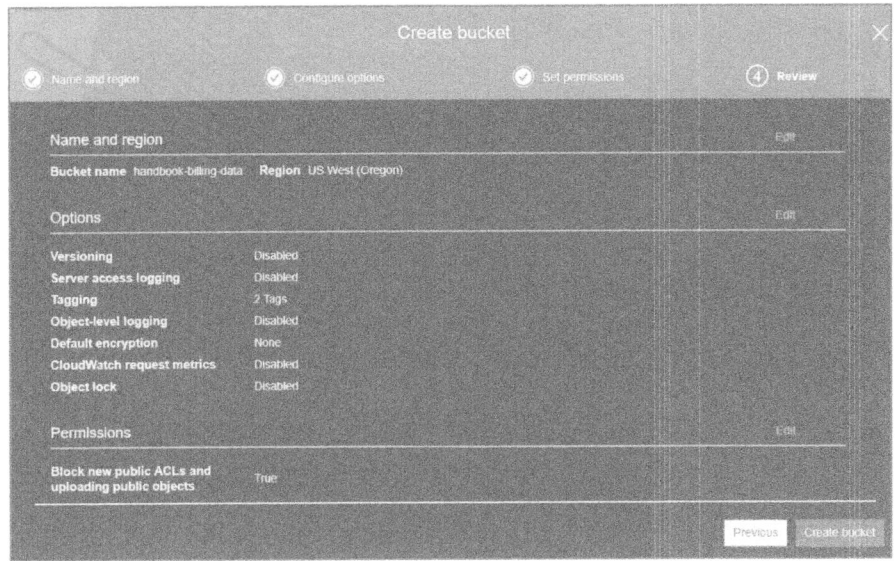

Figure 5.100: Create a bucket to store billing data - Review

5.9.4.2 Create an AWS Billing Report to Send Billing Data to an S3 Bucket.

Click your name in the top right corner of AWS Console, then click on "My Billing Dashboard," and then click on "Reports," as shown below.

Then click on "Create report."

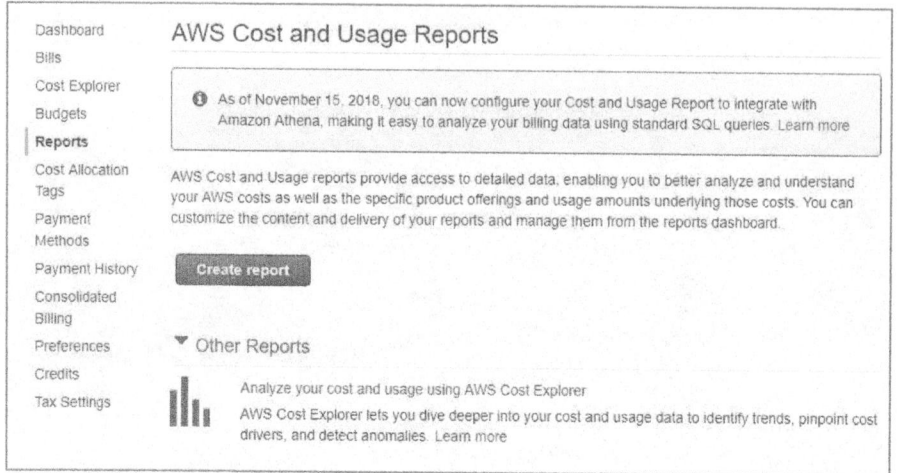

Figure 5.101: Create an AWS Cost and Usage Report

Follow these three steps to create the report.

Step 1 of 3: Report content. Specify the report name. The name will be validated so that the name is valid, meaning that it is not being used and the name does not contain spaces or certain special characters.

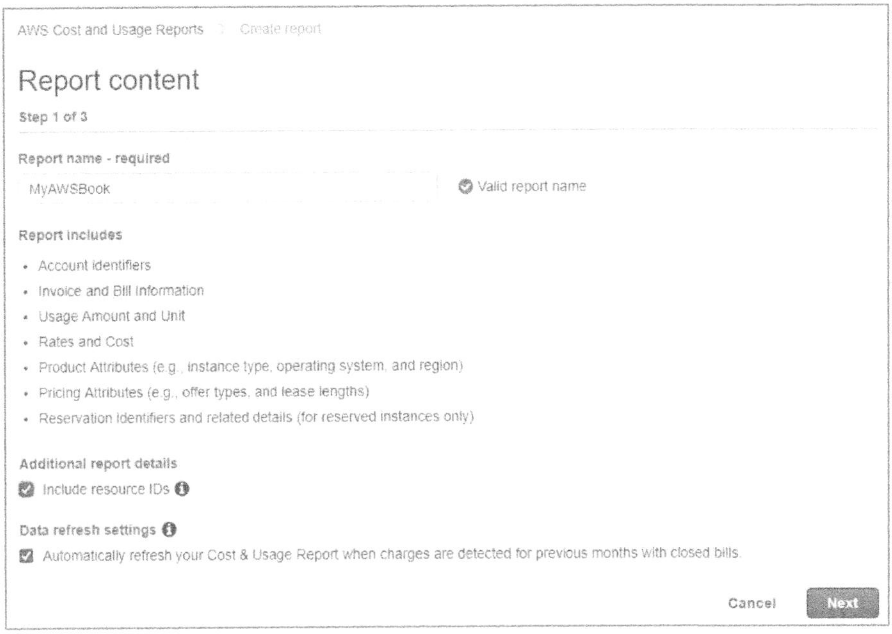

AWS Cost and Usage Reports > Create report

Report content
Step 1 of 3

Report name - required

MyAWSBook   ✓ Valid report name

Report includes
- Account identifiers
- Invoice and Bill Information
- Usage Amount and Unit
- Rates and Cost
- Product Attributes (e.g., instance type, operating system, and region)
- Pricing Attributes (e.g., offer types, and lease lengths)
- Reservation Identifiers and related details (for reserved instances only)

Additional report details
☑ Include resource IDs

Data refresh settings
☑ Automatically refresh your Cost & Usage Report when charges are detected for previous months with closed bills.

Cancel   **Next**

Figure 5.102: Create an AWS Cost and Usage Report - Step 1 - Report content

Step 2 of 3: Delivery options. Supply the S3 bucket that you want to save billing report data to.

Before you continue, you need to grant Athena access to the bucket "handbook-billing-data." Click on the link "sample policy" to open a new window with the sample policy for you.

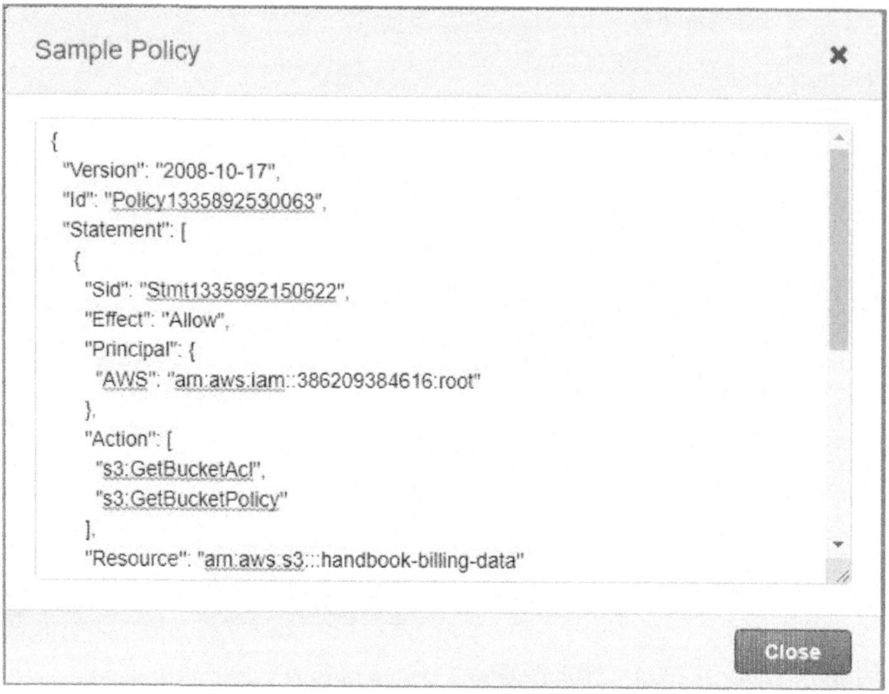

```
Sample Policy                                      ✕

{
  "Version": "2008-10-17",
  "Id": "Policy1335892530063",
  "Statement": [
    {
      "Sid": "Stmt1335892150622",
      "Effect": "Allow",
      "Principal": {
        "AWS": "arn:aws:iam::386209384616:root"
      },
      "Action": [
        "s3:GetBucketAcl",
        "s3:GetBucketPolicy"
      ],
      "Resource": "arn:aws:s3:::handbook-billing-data"
```

Figure 5.103: Create an AWS Cost and Usage Report - step 2 - Grant Athena access

Copy the text above.

Go to your S3 bucket "handbook-billing-data." Then go to "Permissions" and then to "Bucket Policy." Paste the text from above, and save it.

Figure 5.104: Create an AWS Cost and Usage Report - step 2 - The bucket policy

Now come back to the "Delivery options" page and enter the S3 bucket name "handbook-billing-data." Click "Verify." You should see "Valid Bucket."

Continue to select other options. For this learning experience, text/CSV with ZIP format is selected. Once you are comfortable with the billing data, you could try other options, such as Parquet format.

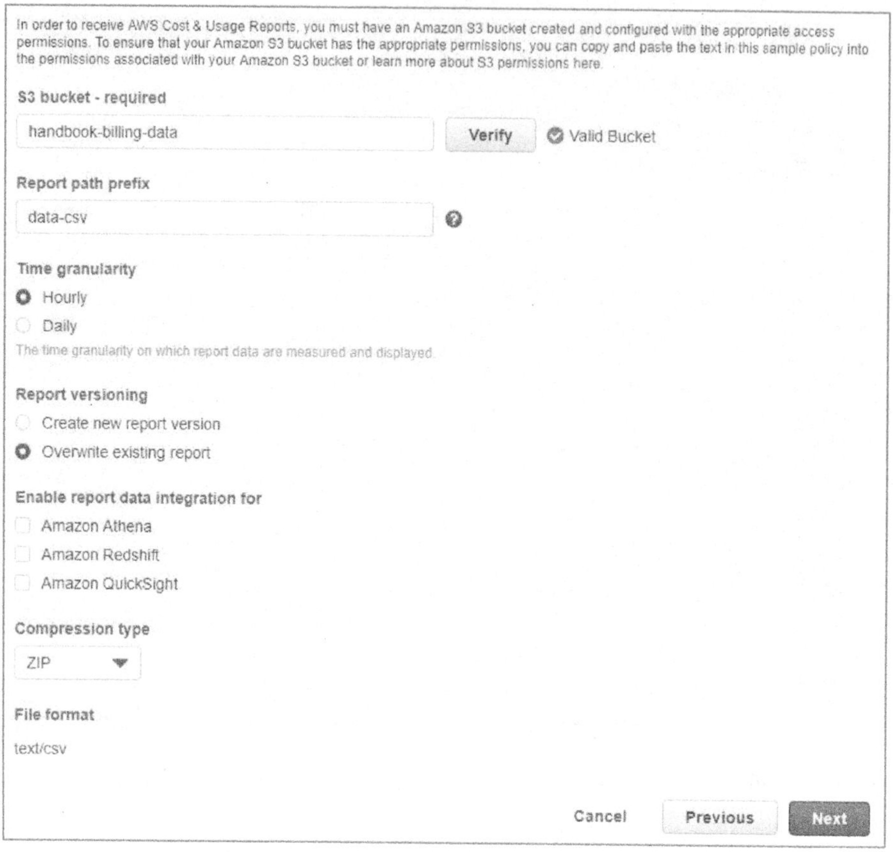

Figure 5.105: Create an AWS Cost and Usage Report - step 2 - Delivery options

The third step is to review your options and save.

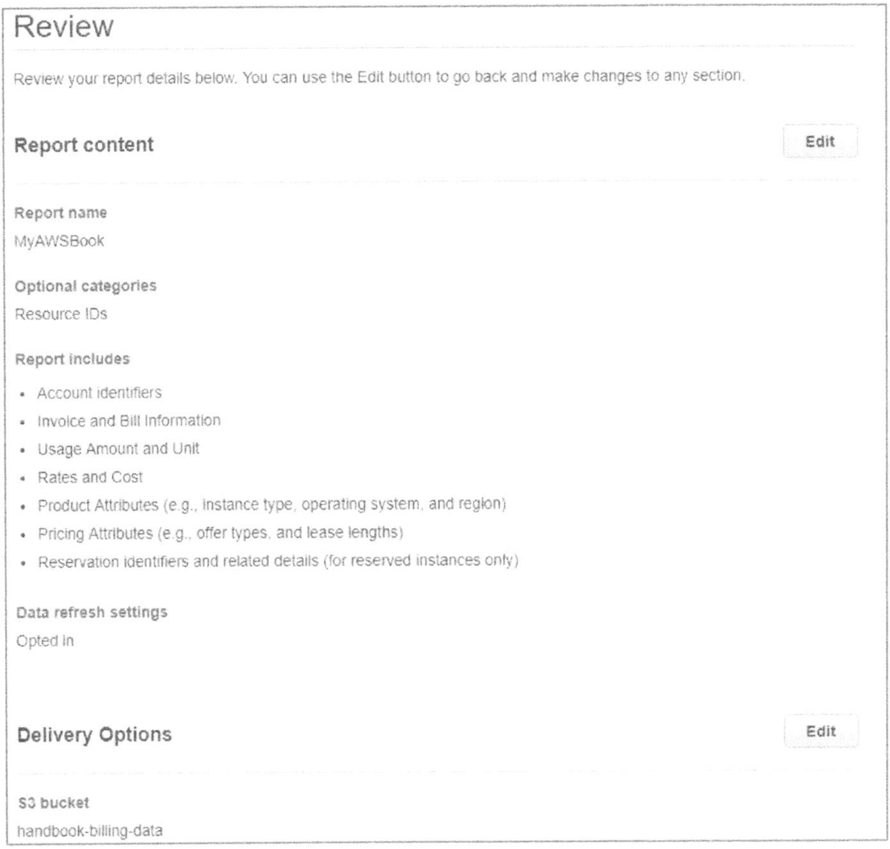

Review

Review your report details below. You can use the Edit button to go back and make changes to any section.

Report content — Edit

Report name
MyAWSBook

Optional categories
Resource IDs

Report includes
- Account identifiers
- Invoice and Bill Information
- Usage Amount and Unit
- Rates and Cost
- Product Attributes (e.g., instance type, operating system, and region)
- Pricing Attributes (e.g., offer types, and lease lengths)
- Reservation identifiers and related details (for reserved instances only)

Data refresh settings
Opted in

Delivery Options — Edit

S3 bucket
handbook-billing-data

Figure 5.106: Create an AWS Cost and Usage Report - step 3 - review and create

The billing report is now set up.

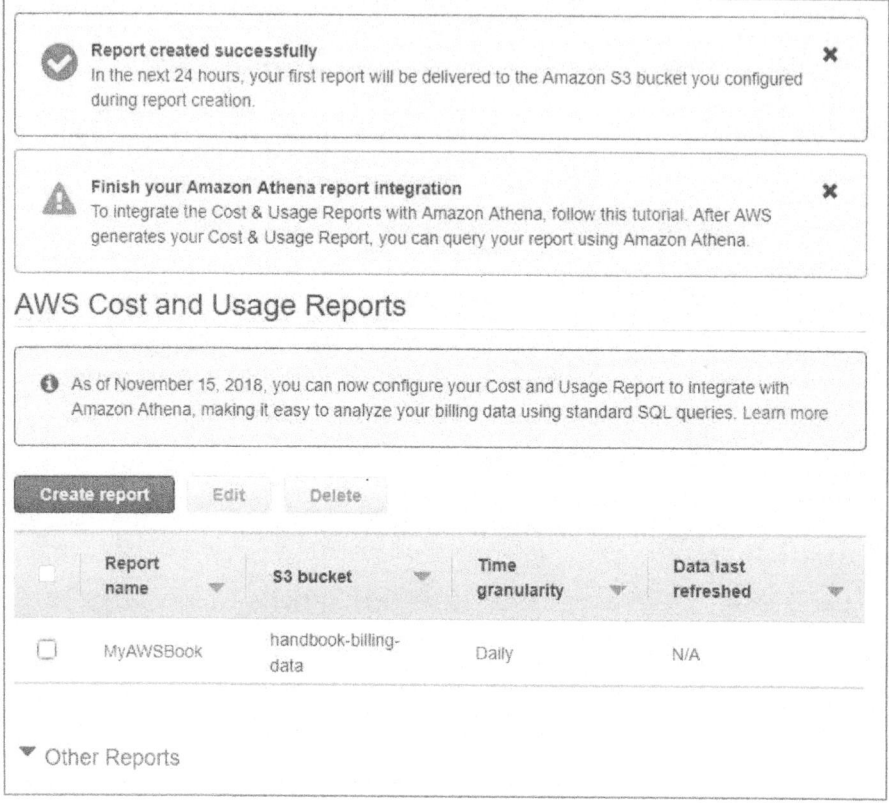

Figure 5.107: Create an AWS Cost and Usage Report - Result

5.9.4.3 Get to Know the Billing Data in the S3 Bucket

Now go to your S3 bucket, and you will see the billing data as shown below.

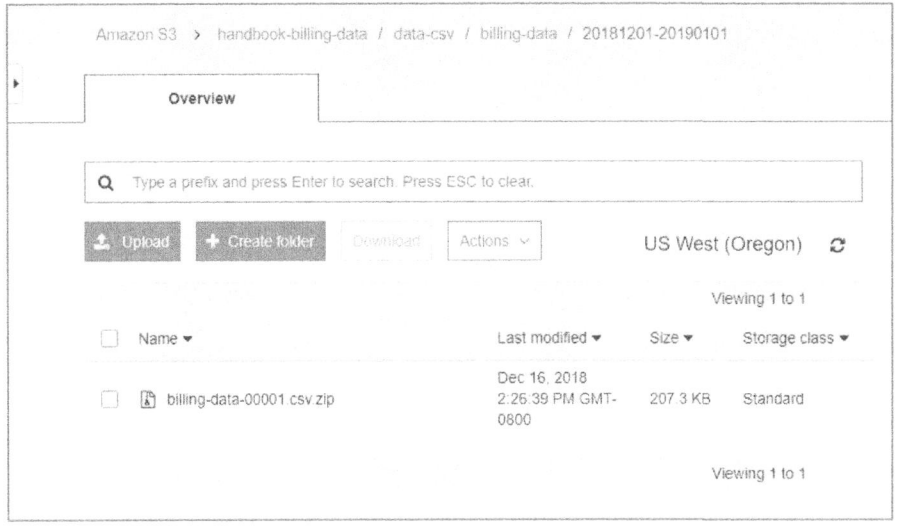

Figure 5.108: AWS Cost and Usage data in the billing data bucket

Download the zip file, unzip it, and open it to see the content.

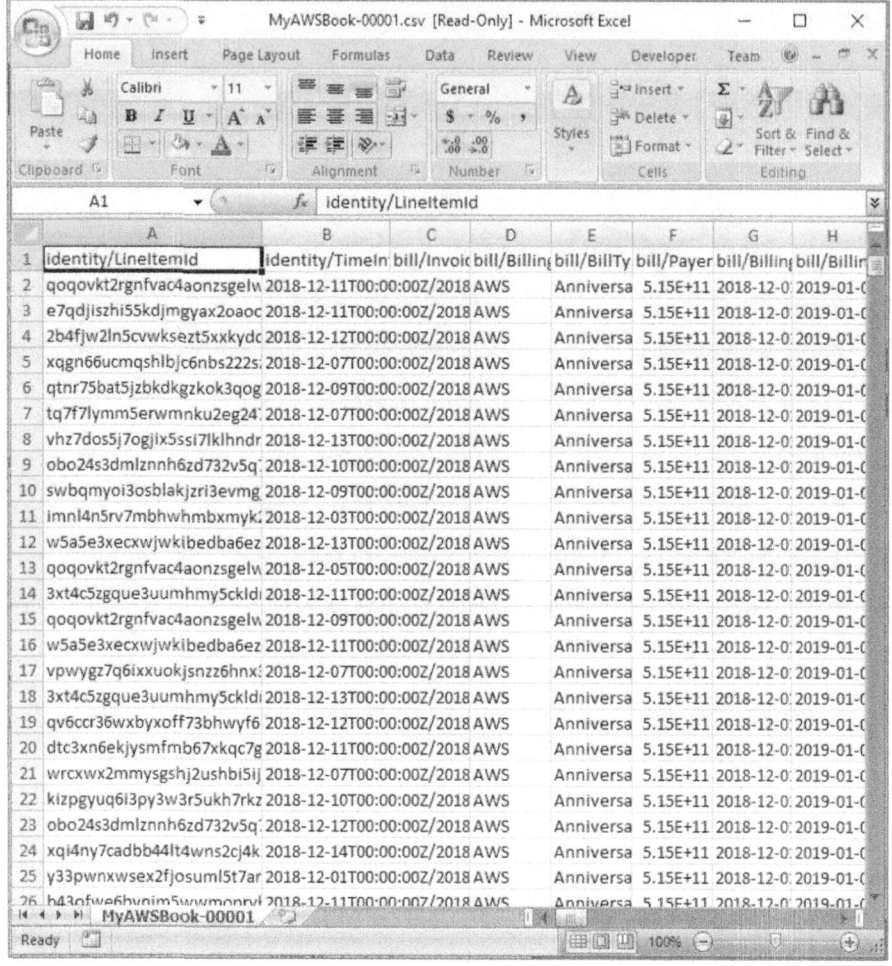

Figure 5.109: Sample billing data in the CSV file

5.9.4.4 Set Up for Athena Query

Create a prefix for Athena query: "s3://handbook-billing-data/data-csv/raw-data/".

Upload the unzipped file to this folder. Athena supports parquet, GZIP and other formats; ZIP, however, is not supported. Thus, you need to unzip it and upload it. This step is for your learning purposes. Once you have learned how to use Athena to query data, you can choose Parquet, GZIP, and other formats. You can also create a Lambda function to replace your manual copying process and schedule it to run.

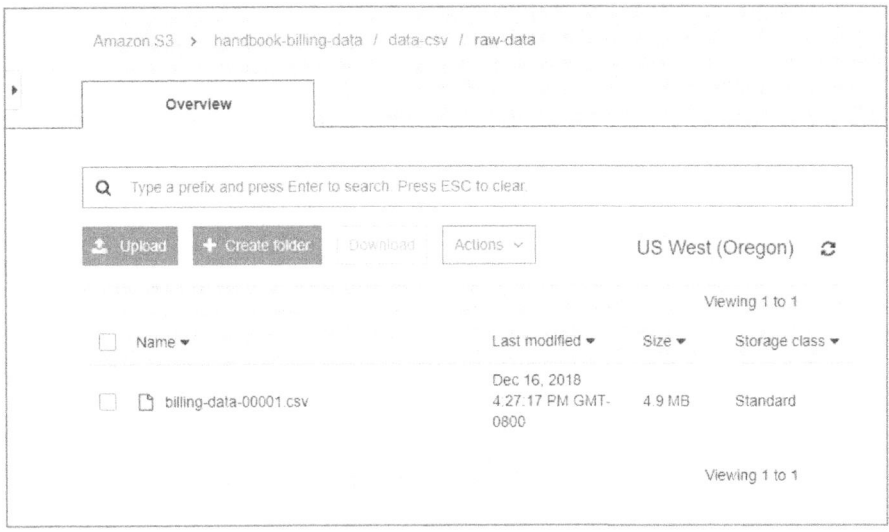

Figure 5.110: Copy the billing data file to its own prefix for query

5.9.4.5 Use Athena to Analyze Billing Data

Once you have set up the billing report, you will see a "manifest.json" file and a "create_table.sql" file.

The "manifest.json" file tells you what billing data has been saved to this bucket. You can modify the "create_table.sql" file to create a table in Athena.

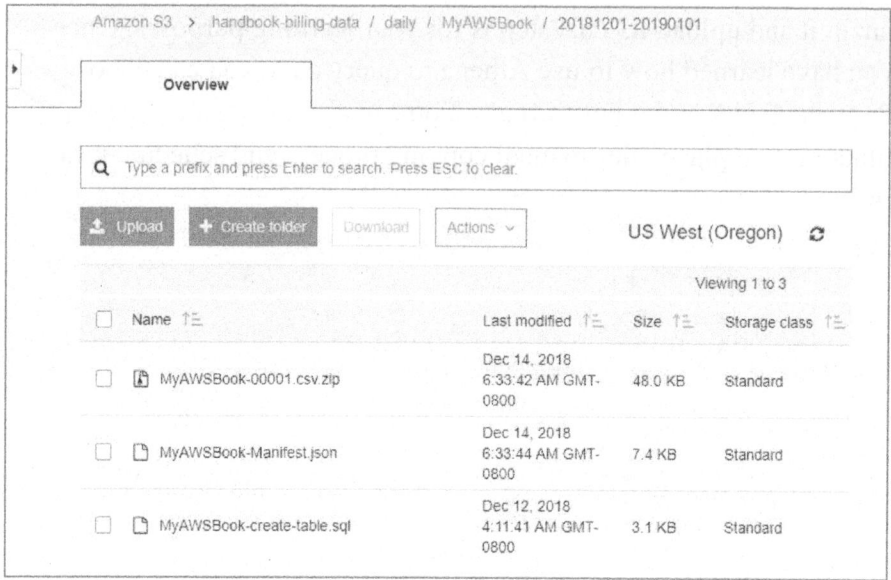

Figure 5.111: Other files related to the billing data: create_table.sql.

Create Athena database and table.

Figure 5.112: Create an Athena database and table for the billing data.

Query the data.

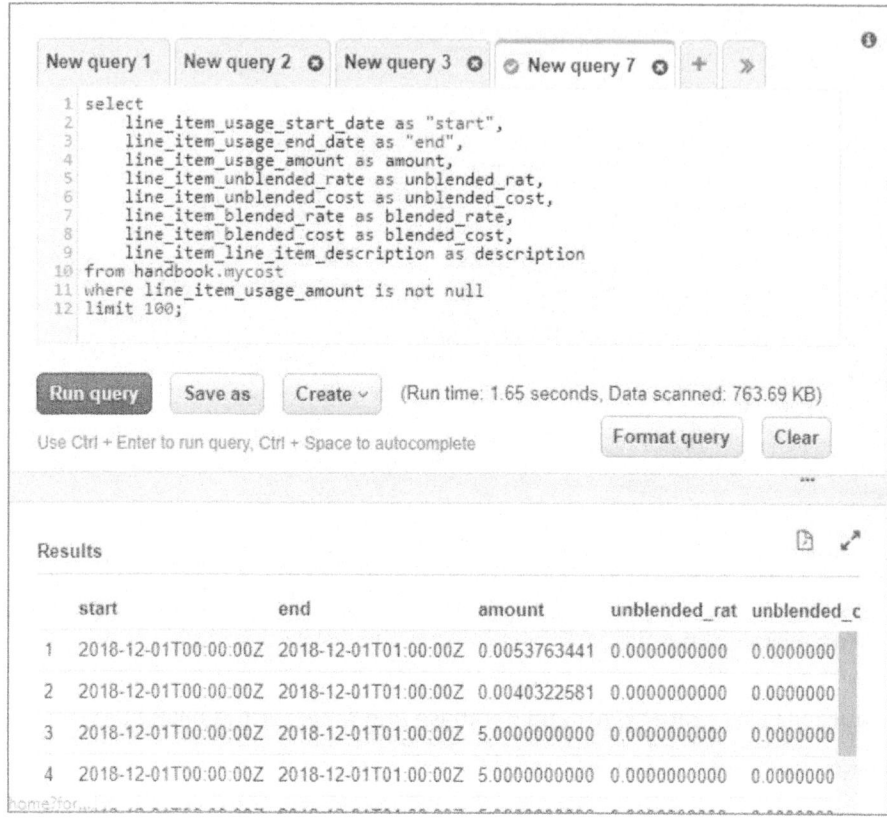

Figure 5.113: Athena query to get the billing data.

Download the results.

All your queries, including the failed ones, are available in the "History" as shown below. You can click on the "Download results" in the last column to download your query results.

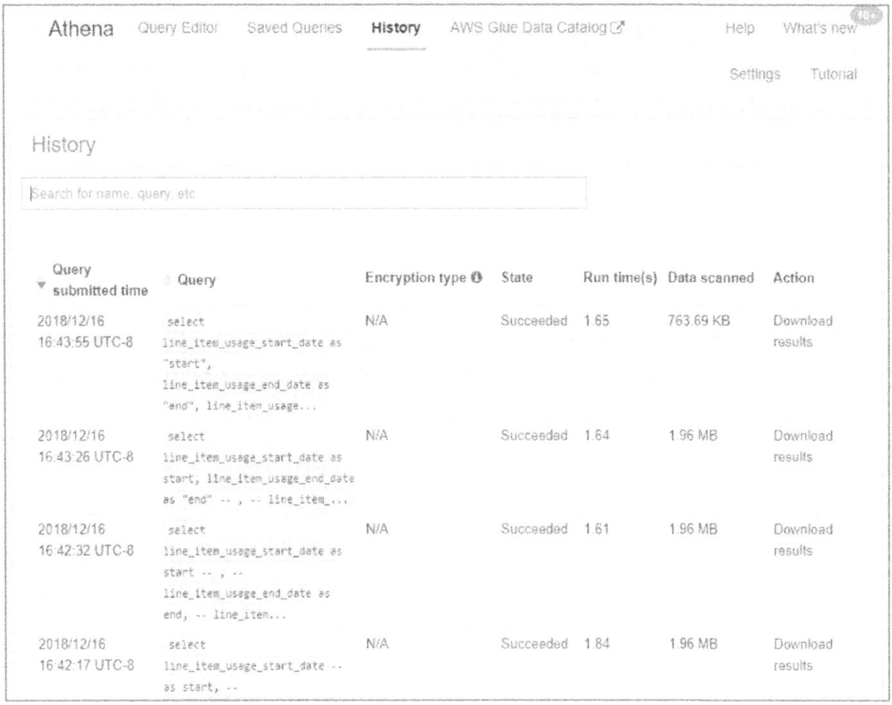

Figure 5.114: Download Athena query results from History

5.9.5 Identify Cost-Saving Opportunities with AWS Athena

When using AWS Athena for the billing report data, you can analyze your billing data however you want to. Such flexibility is attractive to engineers and business analysts who know how to query the data.

You can use Cost Explorer or Cost Explorer API to obtain most of the data you need. However, for complex queries such as the following, using AWS Athena is much easier.

- Give me all the EC2 instances (instance ID) that are running between 8:00 p.m. and 6:00.a.m. Give me the total cost during this period.
- Tell me what happened on July 16, 2018, when the cost spiked 150% compared to June 16, 2018.
- Give me all the EC2 instances whose total cost in the last quarter is over $1,000.
- Give me the top 10 owners (based on "owner" tag values) who have the highest ratio, by billing amount, of On-Demand Instances over Spot Instances.
- Give me the average spending for all projects ("project" tag values) for the year 2018.

5.9.6 Areas of Improvement

The above demonstration is a working example of how to set up and use AWS Athena to query billing data and identify opportunities for cost savings.

This is the starting point. You can improve the process further.

- You can explore further with a partition of the billing table by year and month to speed up the queries and save the cost of queries.
- You can create a Lambda function to move or archive the billing data.
- You can explore other, better formats, such as Parquet, for the billing data.
- You can create a python module to send queries to Athena, to generate the reports, to save the reports to an S3 bucket, and to deliver the reports to your list of emails.
- You can join your billing table to other Athena tables.

- You can use AWS Quicksight with Athena to visualize the billing data.
- You can use Terraform to implement nearly every step in codes instead of using the Web Console.

There are also a few things to pay attention to.

- If your billing data are cumulative, make sure your query only works on a copy of the data; otherwise, you may count the same billing item several times. To avoid this mistake, you can overwrite the historical data.
- Make sure the billing data prefix in your "CREATE TABLE" statement does not contain non-billing data. Remove the manifest and other files from the prefix.
- The first row of the CSV file contains the field names. Instead of removing the first row, you may want to treat each field in your "CREATE TABLE" statement as a "string," even though the data type may be "timestamp," "double," or something else. In your query, convert the string back to datetime or double. Add criteria such as this to filter out the header row and the noise. This is not ideal at all, but it works:

> WHERE line_item_usage_amount IS NOT NULL
>
> AND CAST(line_item_usage_amount AS DOUBLE)>0

Don't lose sight of your goal to use AWS Athena to analyze the billing data and cut costs.

5.9.7 Summary

You may be overwhelmed by this implementation - use AWS Athena to analyze billing data, but you may not have to use AWS Athena.

If you want to analyze the billing data in your own way, this option is better than some of the alternatives, such as importing the raw billing data into a database to run the queries.

With direct access to the billing data, you can identify numerous cost optimization opportunities that you might not otherwise know about.

5.10 Implementation #9: How to Set Up and Use AWS S3 Inventory for AWS Cost Optimization

5.10.1 Introduction

AWS S3 Inventory provides you a CSV, ORC, or Parquet output file with the metadata of objects in the S3 buckets.

You can configure each bucket to generate S3 inventory data daily or weekly.

You specify the source bucket and the destination bucket. The output file will be stored in the destination file.

Then you can download the file. You can also use Athena to query the file.

The following screen captures the fields in the output file: bucket name, object key, version ID (if the bucket's versioning is enabled), object size, storage class, last modified date, and similar.

Bucket	Key	VersionId	IsLatest	IsDeleteMaker	Size	LastModifiedDate	Etag	StorageClass	MultipartUploaded	ReplicationStatus
example-bucket	object1			FALSE	2.4E+08	2016-08-11T01:19	e80d8eda4	STANDARD	TRUE	
example-bucket	object2			FALSE	0	2016-08-10T22:23	d41d8cd98	STANDARD	FALSE	
example-bucket	object3			FALSE	9	2016-08-10T20:18	9090441e4	STANDARD_IA	FALSE	
example-bucket	object4			FALSE	9	2016-08-10T20:36	9090441e4	STANDARD_IA	FALSE	
example-bucket	object1			FALSE	22	2016-08-10T20:35	9090441e4	STANDARD	FALSE	
example-bucket	object1			FALSE		2016-08-10T20:34	9090441e4	REDUCED_RED	FALSE	
example-bucket	object1			FALSE		2016-08-10T21:13	9090441e4	GLACIER	FALSE	

Figure 5.115: AWS S3 Inventory - sample data

Source: https://docs.aws.amazon.com/AmazonS3/latest/dev/storage-inventory.html

5.10.2 AWS S3 Inventory and Cost Optimization

S3 Inventory data was among the most used metadata during our AWS cost optimization efforts.

When you have petabytes of data to operate, every second counts. If it takes 0.7 seconds to delete an object from a bucket, it takes more than 8 days to delete 1,000,000 objects.

It was not unusual to operate on over 1,000,000 objects. We have had a few operations over 25,000,000 objects.

We launched 10 EC2 instances. Each instance ran 10 screens (batches). The big job was distributed to 100 smaller jobs. The operation could finish in hours, not days.

S3 Inventory data makes it easier to divide such a big job into smaller jobs and is less expensive as well. After all, GetObjects or ListObjects becomes costly when the number of objects reaches tens of millions.

For example, you may want to delete 1,000,000 objects (let's count each version as one object) from Bucket A in the region us-west-2. However, before you delete an object, you want to make sure that the object exists in backup Bucket B in the region us-east-1.

It is much slower and much more expensive to rely on GetObjects or ListObjects.

With S3 Inventory data, you can query the data of both buckets, and compare the data using Python, or import the data into your database and compare them with database queries.

You can then generate a list of objects to delete. You can divide the list and create several smaller batches of delete commands.

Even though the S3 inventory does not have up-to-date data, in this case and in many other cases, the inventory data are good enough for the operation.

5.10.3 Set Up S3 Inventory for an S3 Bucket

You need to create a bucket to store the S3 Inventory output file "handbook-s3-inventory."

This bucket is called a destination bucket - the inventory data will end up in this bucket. The region of this destination bucket, US West (Oregon), must match the region of the source buckets. The source buckets are those buckets whose metadata will be extracted by S3 Inventory.

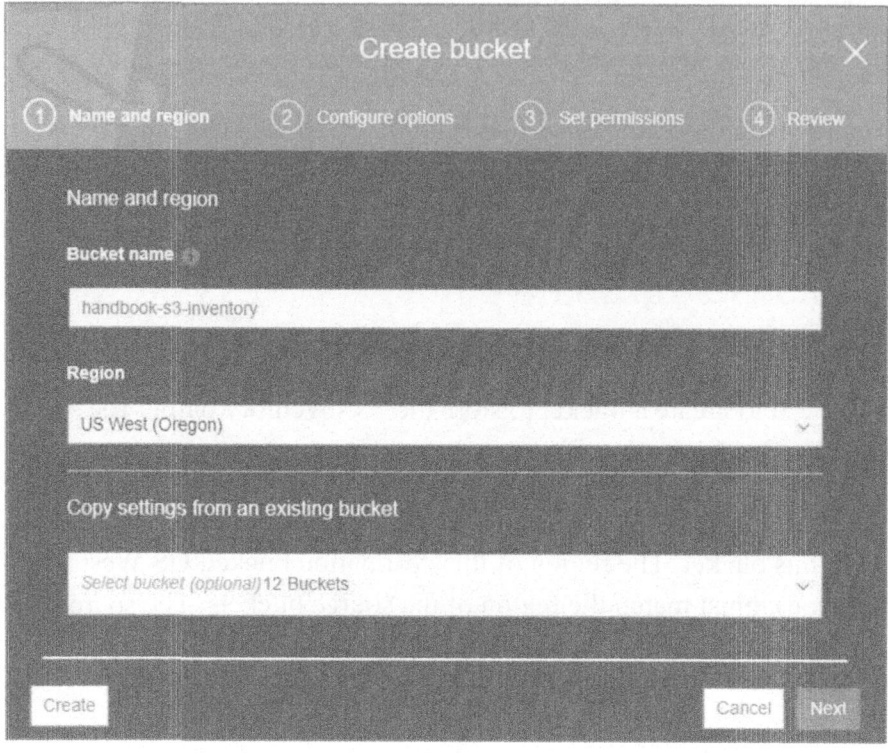

Figure 5.116: Set up S3 Inventory - Create bucket

5.10.4 Grant Permissions

You need to add policy to the destination bucket to allow AWS to put objects (output files and manifest files) in the destination bucket.

Go to the destination buckct, then "Permissions," then "Bucket Policy." Add the following policy and save it.

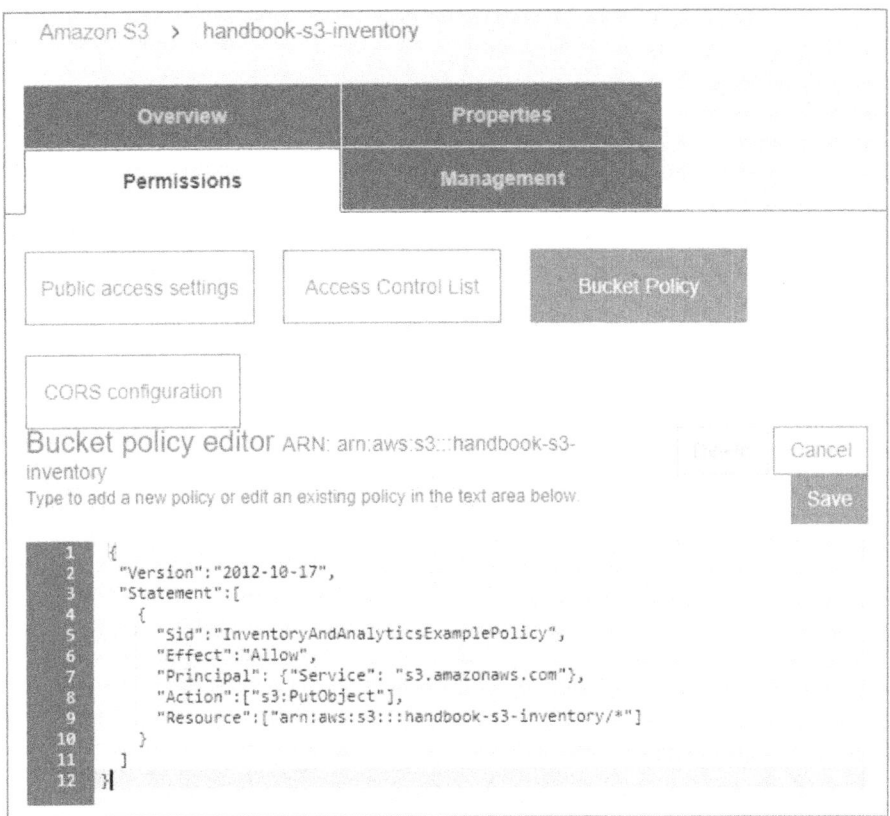

Figure 5.117: Set up S3 Inventory - Bucket policy

5.10.5 Configure S3 Inventory

Now configure S3 Inventory for each source bucket. Let's start with the bucket "handbook-medical-image."

Go to the bucket "handbook-medical-image," click on "Management," then "Inventory." Click on "Add new" at the bottom of the screen:

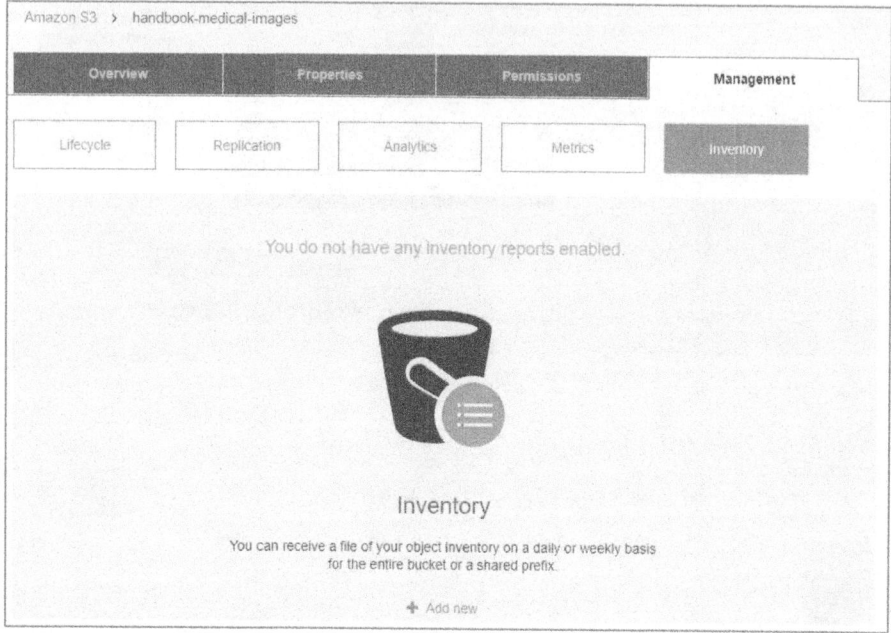

Figure 5.118: Set up S3 Inventory - Add new

Now you can configure the S3 Inventory settings.

Use the bucket name as the inventory name. Select the destination bucket. Select "Daily" for the frequency.

Inventory name	Filters	Destination bucket	Destination prefix	Frequency	Last export
handbook-medical-	Filt	handbook-s3-inventory	Type pre	Daily	

Figure 5.119: Set up S3 Inventory - Add new - options

In the advanced settings, choose CSV as the output file format. Choose "Current version only" for the object versions if you only need to track the latest version. Let's choose "Include all versions" because we need information on all versions.

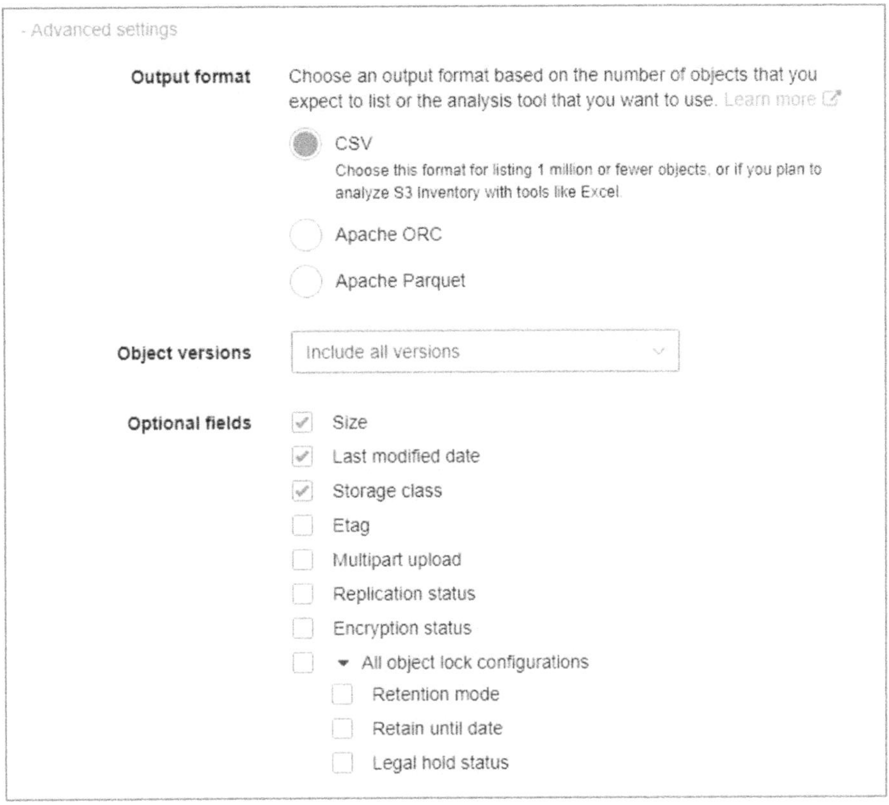

Figure 5.120: Set up S3 Inventory - Advanced settings

Select "None" for encryption; then save it.

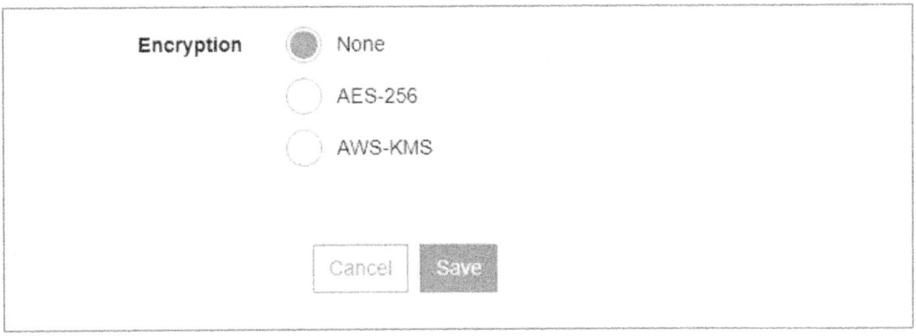

Figure 5.121: Set up S3 Inventory - Encryption

AWS will check whether the destination bucket has the appropriate policy to allow AWS to save output files to the destination bucket. AWS will recommend a valid policy. Because our policy is valid, we can ignore the recommendation.

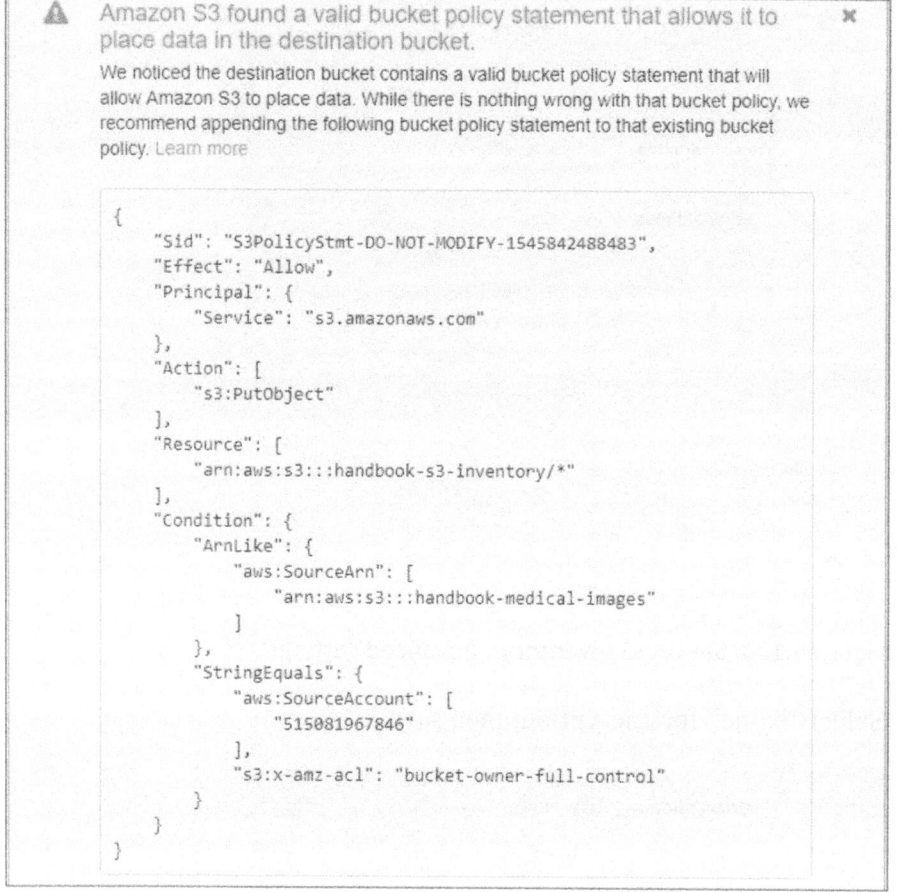

Figure 5.122: Set up S3 Inventory - Destination bucket policy

You now have the S3 Inventory configured for the bucket "handbook-medical-images."

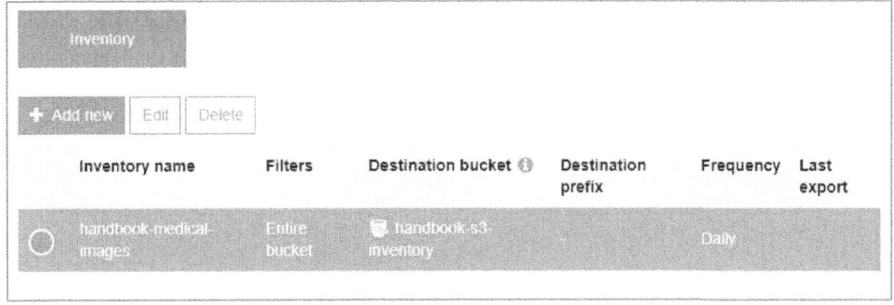

Figure 5.123: Set up S3 Inventory - result

Please do the same for the other buckets.

Note that how you configure this S3 Inventory affects your output data schema which will be used in the "CREATE TABLE" statement in Athena, which will be covered later.

It is important to configure all the buckets in exactly the same way so that it is easier to aggregate and analyze your data.

It may take up to 24 hours to see the inventory data in your destination bucket.

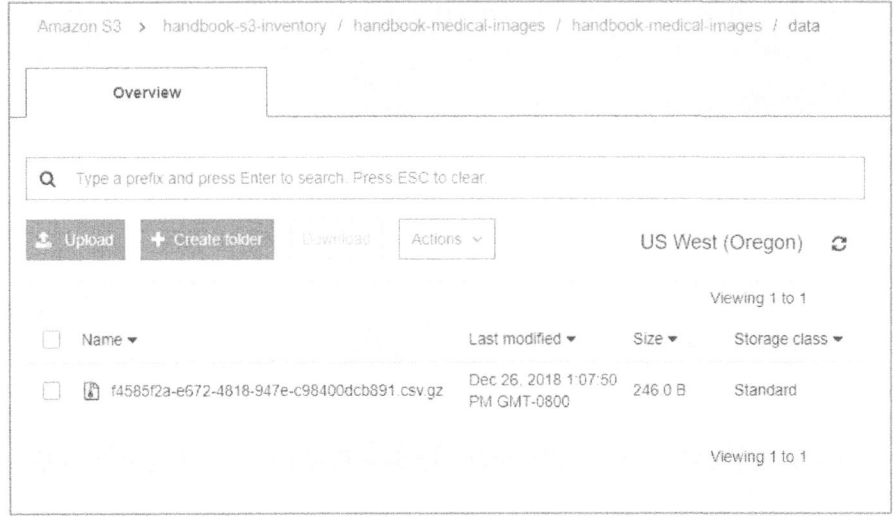

Figure 5.124: Set up S3 Inventory - Inventory file

Now you can download the .csv.gz file, unzip it, and open it for examination.

Please note that AWS Athena works with the .gz file. You do not have to decompress it before you run the queries.

5.10.6 Use Athena to Query S3 Inventory Data

Now that you have the S3 Inventory data, you can analyze the data in many ways to help optimize your AWS storage costs.

5.10.6.1 Obtain Permissions to Run Athena Queries on S3 Inventory Data

Before you get started, please make sure you have the necessary permission to run Athena actions, in addition to the permission to access the underlying data behind Athena queries. In this case, you need permission to access S3 Inventory destination bucket "handbook-s3-inventory."

Permission to run Athena actions:

> Request AmazonAthenaFullAccess (or a customized one in your organization) to be attached to your user account.
>
> For more granular access, please check the Athena documentation.

Permission to access the Athena query location (S3 bucket), which is the underlying bucket:

Request access to the bucket "handbook-s3-inventory." If the access is granted through bucket policy, you can use the following:

```
{
    "Version": "2012-10-17",
    "Statement": [
        {
            "Sid": "forAthenaQuery",
            "Effect": "Allow",
            "Principal": {
                "AWS": "arn:aws:iam::AccountA-ID:user/username"
            },
            "Action": [
                "s3:GetBucketLocation",
                "s3:ListBucket",
                "s3:GetObject"
            ],
            "Resource": [
                "arn:aws:s3:::handbook-s3-inventory",
                "arn:aws:s3:::handbook-s3-inventory/*"
            ]
        }
    ]
}
```

If the permission is granted through roles or policies, you can add the following statement to your role or policy:

```
{
    "Effect": "Allow",
    "Action": [
        "s3:GetObject",
        "s3:ListBucket"
    ],
    "Resource": [
        "arn:aws:s3:::handbook-s3-inventory"
    ]
}
```

5.10.6.2 Create S3 Inventory Reports Using Athena Queries

For demonstration purposes, let's work on the first of five reports mentioned in the section "Identify candidate objects for Standard IA and One Zone IA":

Report #1: Summary reports of all buckets: storage size group by storage class.

Having all the permission you need, now go to AWS Athena Console.

LINK: Implementation #8: How to Set Up and Use AWS Athena for Cost Optimization

Create an Athena table, and comment out those fields that were not selected in the S3 Inventory configuration:

Figure 5.125: Create an S3 Inventory table in Athena

```
CREATE EXTERNAL TABLE handbook.s3_inventory(

    bucket string,

    key string,

    version_id string,

    is_latest string,

    is_delete_marker string,

    size string,

    last_modified_date string,

    -- e_tag string,
```

```
    storage_class string -- ,
    -- is_multipart_uploaded string,
    -- replication_status string,
    -- encryption_status string,
    -- object_lock_retain_until_date string,
    -- object_lock_mode string,
    -- object_lock_legal_hold_status string
)
ROW FORMAT SERDE
'org.apache.hadoop.hive.serde2.OpenCSVSerde'
WITH SERDEPROPERTIES ("separatorChar" = ",", "escapeChar" = "\\")
STORED AS TEXTFILE
LOCATION 's3://handbook-s3-inventory/'
```

Now you can run the query:

```
select * from handbook.s3_inventory
where bucket='handbook-medical-images'
limit 1000;
```

Here is the query output:

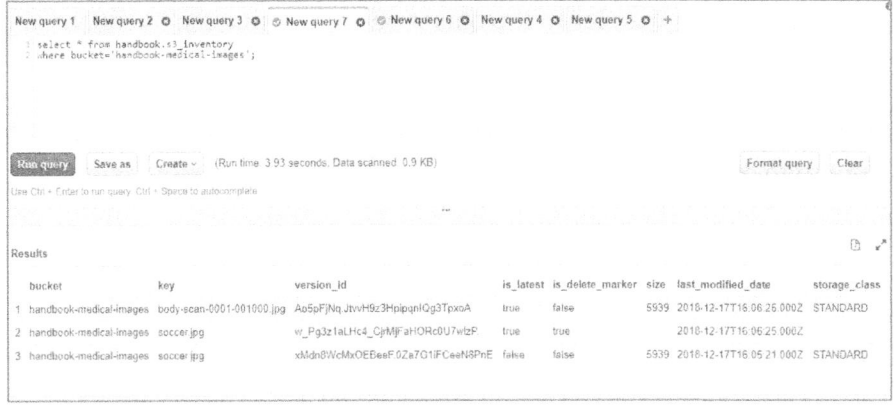

Figure 5.126: S3 Inventory -Athena query output

Now you can click on the download icon on the right, above the header row, to download the output to a CSV file. You can also go to "History" in the menu to access all the queries you have run, and download the output file from there.

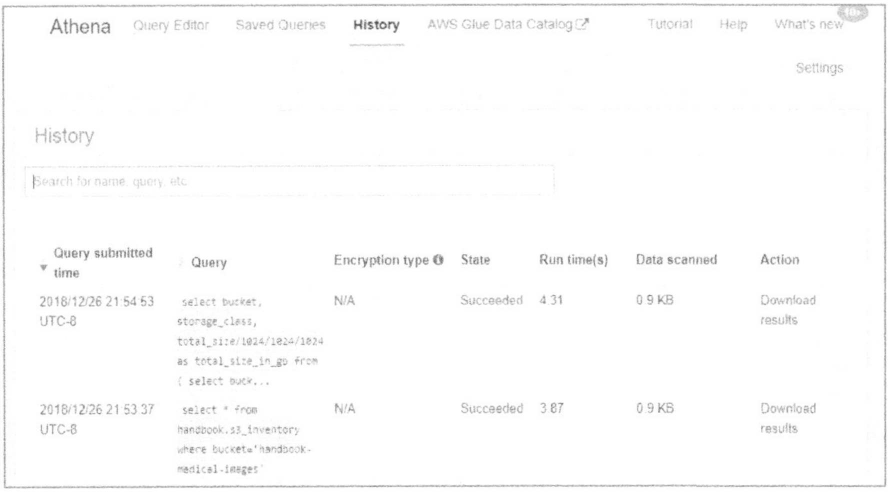

Figure 5.127: S3 Inventory - Download Athena query output from History

With the CSV output file, you can write a Python script to process the CSV file.

For example, you can delete the object versions using the "version_id" in this file.

Let's get back to Report #1 - Summary reports of all buckets: storage size group by storage class.

```
select bucket, storage_class, total_size/1024/1024/1024 as total_size_in_gb

from (

    select bucket, storage_class, sum(CAST(size as bigint)) as total_size

    from handbook.s3_inventory

    where size != '' and CAST(size as bigint)>0

    group by bucket, storage_class

)

order by bucket, storage_class, total_size_in_gb

;
```

Here is the query output for Report #1. In this case, there is not much data to illustrate.

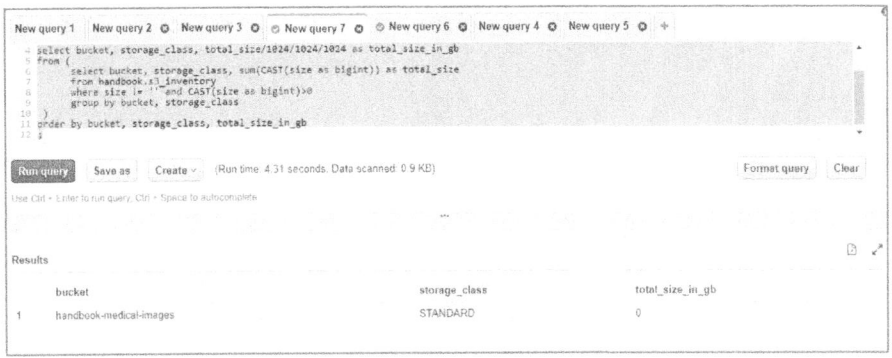

Figure 5.128: S3 Inventory - Athena query for report #1

5.10.6.3 Verify Athena Output Data with AWS S3 Metrics

Your Athena output data may not be accurate. The inventory data may not be up to date.

If you use the size and object count, you can cross-reference the data with S3 Metrics.

Go to the S3 bucket, then "Management," then "Metrics."

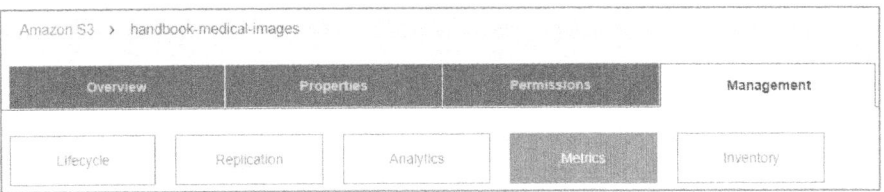

Figure 5.129: S3 Inventory - Verify Athena query output with S3 Metrics

Now you have the "Total size" report.

Figure 5.130: S3 Metrics - Total size

You have the object count as well.

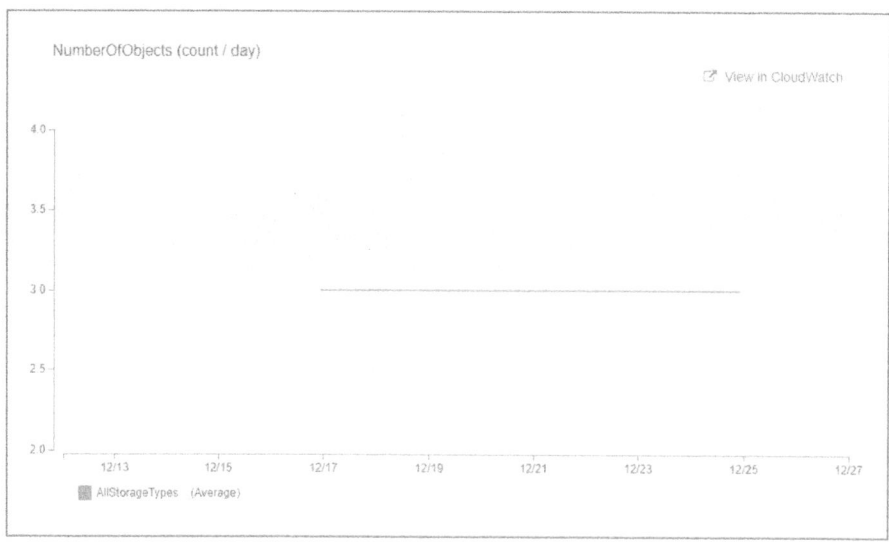

Figure 5.131: S3 Metrics - Total objects

Compare your Athena output data with the above data in Metrics. Neither the data in your S3 Inventory nor the data in Metrics are up to date. However, the numbers should be very close.

Cross-referencing prevents you from making simple mistakes such as counting an object multiple times because the old inventory data have not been archived and removed from the current bucket.

5.10.7 Archive Inventory Data

One common issue with S3 inventory data is that it has a snapshot of metadata every day or every week. The frequency of the update depends on your configuration.

When you run Athena queries, you may get duplicated data. For example, you have 6 daily inventory data. If an object has not been modified in those 6 days, you are counting this object 6 times, or inflating the total size as much as 6 times.

One remedy is to only keep the last snapshot of the inventory data.

You can implement this easily by adding a lifecycle rule to the destination bucket "handbook-s3-inventory."

Go to the bucket, then "Management," then "Lifecycle." Click on "Add lifecycle rule."

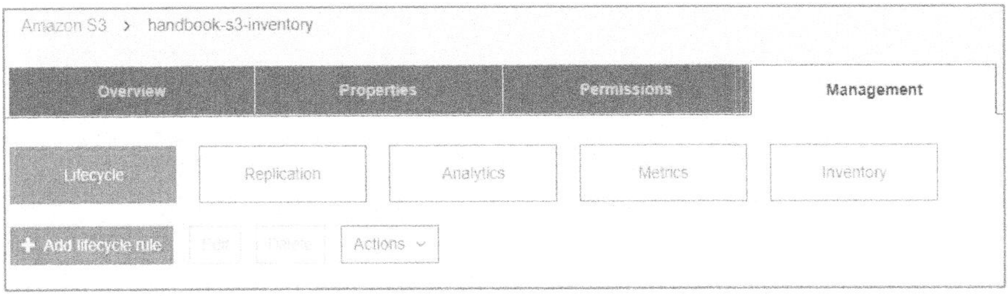

Figure 5.132: Use S3 Lifecycle policy to delete old Inventory data

Then enter the name of the rule: Delete old copy of S3 Inventory data.

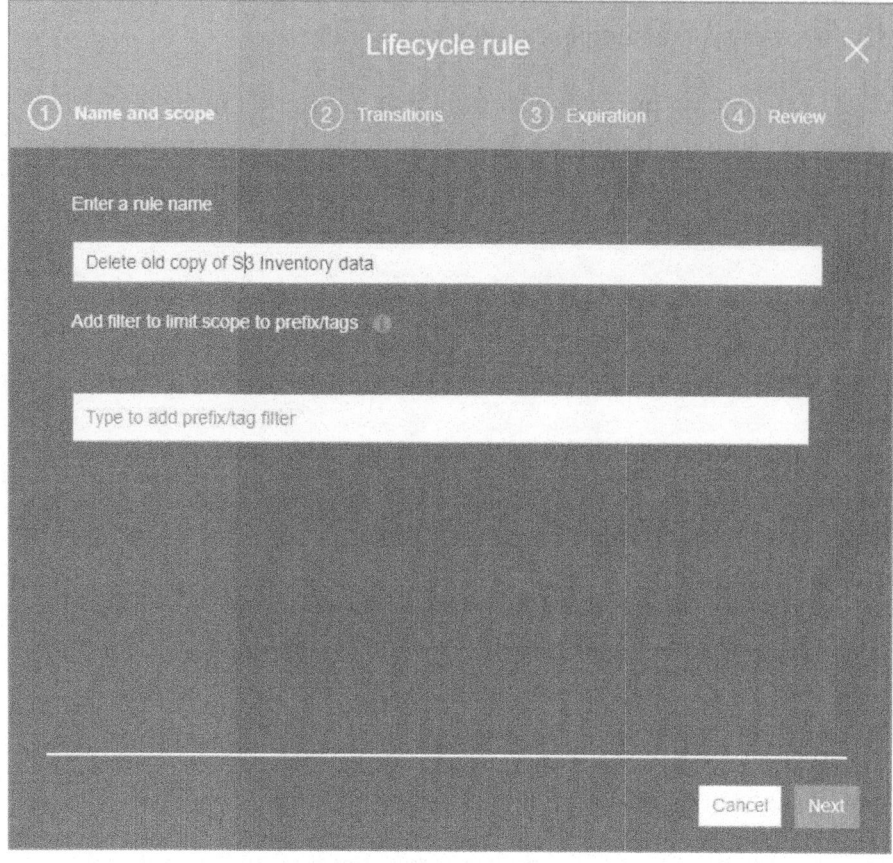

Figure 5.133: S3 Inventory - Destination bucket - Lifecycle rule name

Don't do anything on "Transitions." Just click "Next."

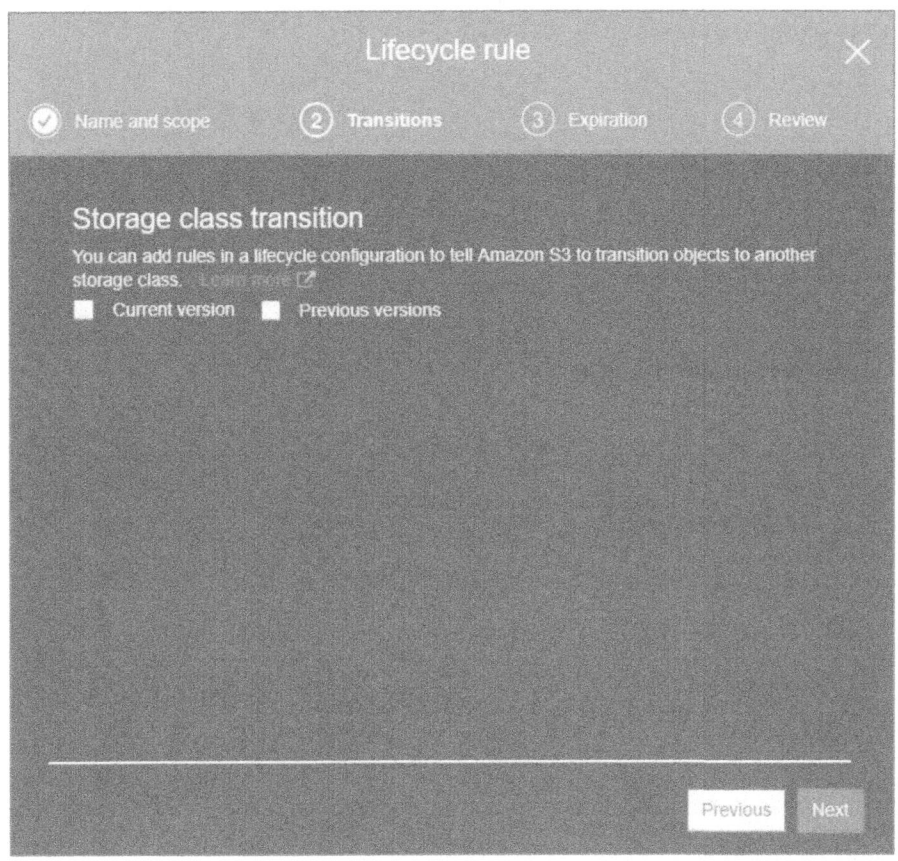

Figure 5.134: S3 Inventory - Destination bucket - Lifecycle rule- transitions

Now set expiration for 1 day since our inventory is configured to run daily. You may choose weekly if your buckets do not change much daily.

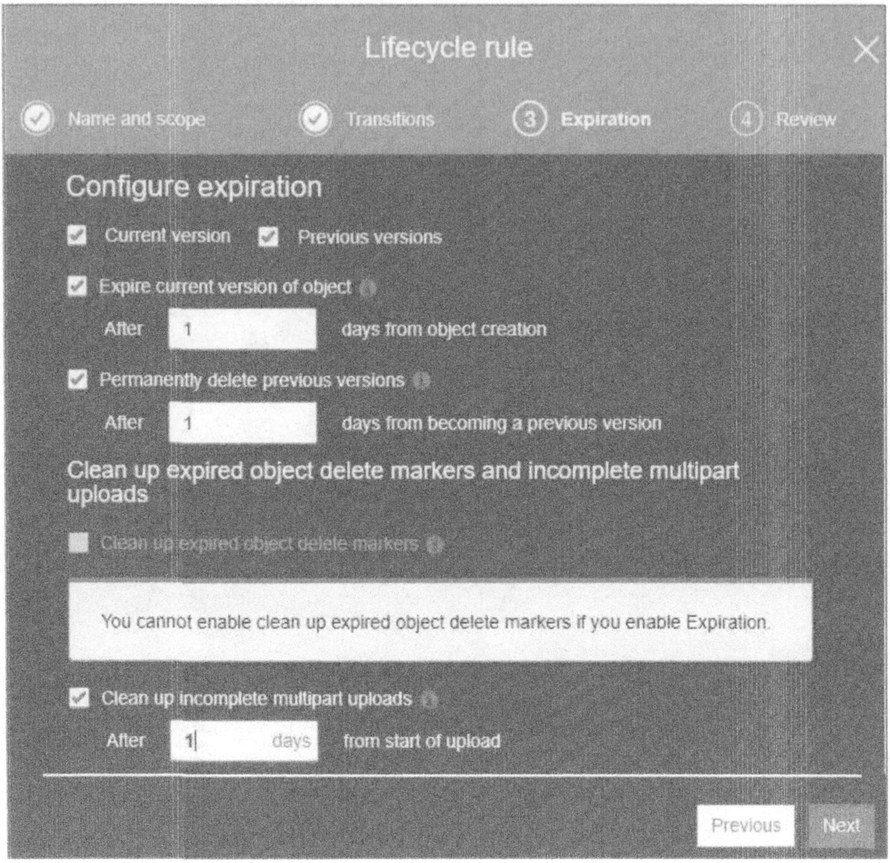

Figure 5.135: S3 Inventory - Destination bucket - Lifecycle rule - Expiration

Now review and save.

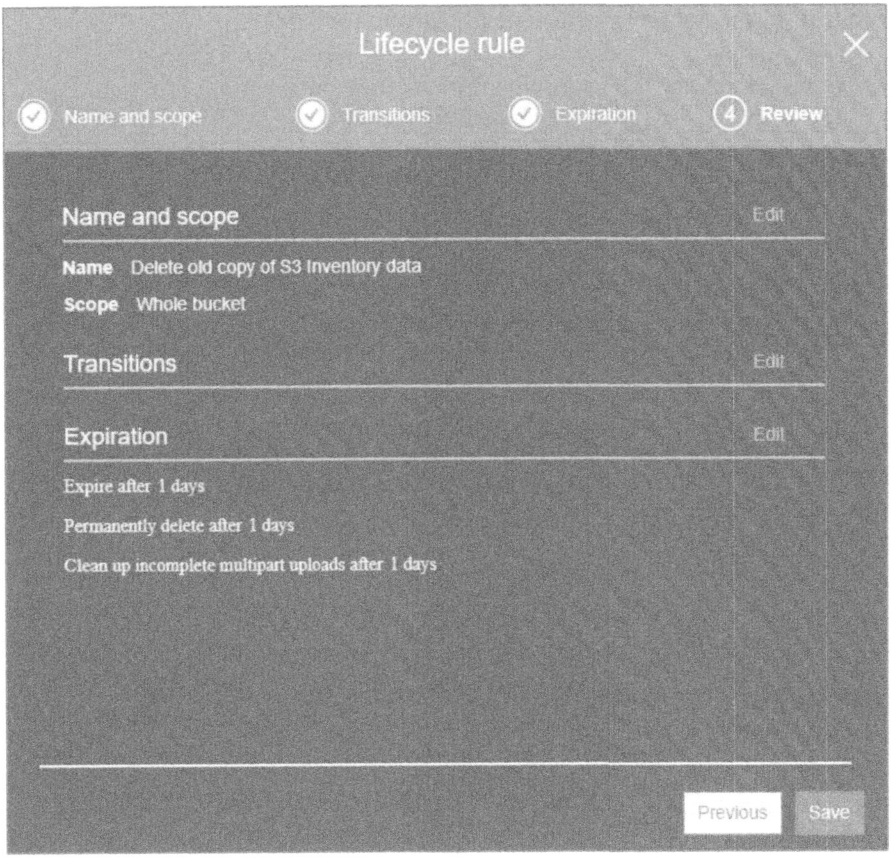

Figure 5.136: S3 Inventory - Destination bucket - Lifecycle rule - Review

You now have the lifecycle rule that tells AWS to delete everything that is older than 1 day in the bucket "handbook-s3-inventory."

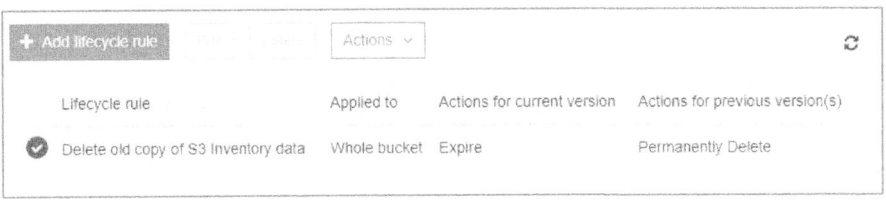

Figure 5.137: S3 Inventory - Destination bucket - Lifecycle rule - result

This way, when you run Athena queries, you only query the data from the last generated inventory data. There will be no double counting.

What if you want to keep the old S3 inventory data?

There are two ways to archive S3 inventory data.

One is to schedule a lambda function to copy everything in the bucket "handbook-s3-inventory" to another bucket, maybe "handbook-s3-inventory-archive." Schedule the lambda function to run once a day. All the new inventory data will be copied from "handbook-s3-inventory" to "handbook-s3-inventory-archive."

The other way is to configure a new S3 inventory to save the inventory data to "handbook-s3-inventory-archive." Now you have two S3 Inventory configurations for each bucket: one saves inventory data to "handbook-s3-inventory," another saves to ""handbook-s3-inventory-archive." This may be a huge effort if you have a lot of buckets and you do it manually. If you use AWS CLI or Terraform to configure S3 Inventory, this may not be a big deal at all.

Now you have historical inventory data in "handbook-s3-inventory-archive," and the latest inventory data in "handbook-s3-inventory."

5.10.8 Summary

If you are serious about cost optimization for your S3 storage, S3 inventory data is very useful.

The benefits are fully elaborated in this section:

LINK: Top Five S3 Inventory Reports for AWS S3 Cost Optimization

This step-by-step guide, in addition to the step-by-step guide for using Athena in the previous chapter, keeps the raw metadata of your buckets at your disposal.

This is especially useful when you know how to run database queries.

You can now optimize your storage costs in your own way.

5.11 Implementation #10: How to Set Up and Use AWS S3 Server Access Logging for AWS Cost Optimization

5.11.1 Introduction

AWS S3 Server Access Logging is a feature that enables you to log all the access to a bucket. You can analyze the logs for security auditing or many other purposes.

We are using the S3 access logs here to optimize AWS costs.

More often than not, when a project is completed or when an employee leaves the company, the S3 buckets or prefixes are left behind. These are expensive to maintain, but no one is willing to take the risk of deleting them.

When we asked our teams to clean up their buckets or prefixes, one of the most frequently asked questions was:

Can you tell me who last accessed the objects in this bucket or prefix, when they accessed them, and how they accessed them?

AWS S3 inventory should include some data like "last-accessed-date." Unfortunately, this is not an option at the time of writing. However, you will learn how to answer this question here.

Once teams have such information about their buckets or prefixes, they can move much faster and with more confidence with regard to whether they should delete or archive the objects in the buckets or prefixes.

5.11.2 Enable S3 Server Access Logging

AWS S3 Server Access Logging is not enabled by default when you create a bucket.

Before you enable server access logging, please note that the collection of log files becomes increasingly large over time. We have had a collection of 5 TB of log files just for one bucket. It is extremely difficult to analyze such a big collection of log files.

5.11.2.1 Create a Bucket to Store S3 Access Logs

Let's create a bucket to store S3 access logs: handbook-s3-logs.

Please note that the region of this bucket must be the same as the region of the buckets for which you want to enable the server access logs. If you have multiple regions, you have to create one bucket for each region.

In the "Name and region," enter the bucket name "handbook-s3-logs" and select a region "US West (Oregon)."

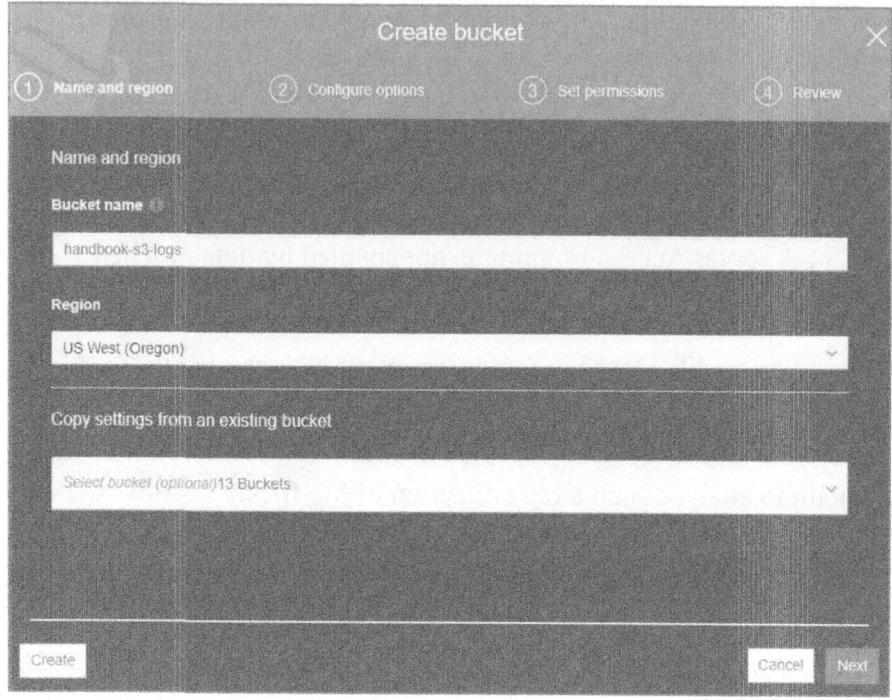

Figure 5.138: Enable S3 server access log - create destination bucket

In the "Configure options," take the default and click "Next."

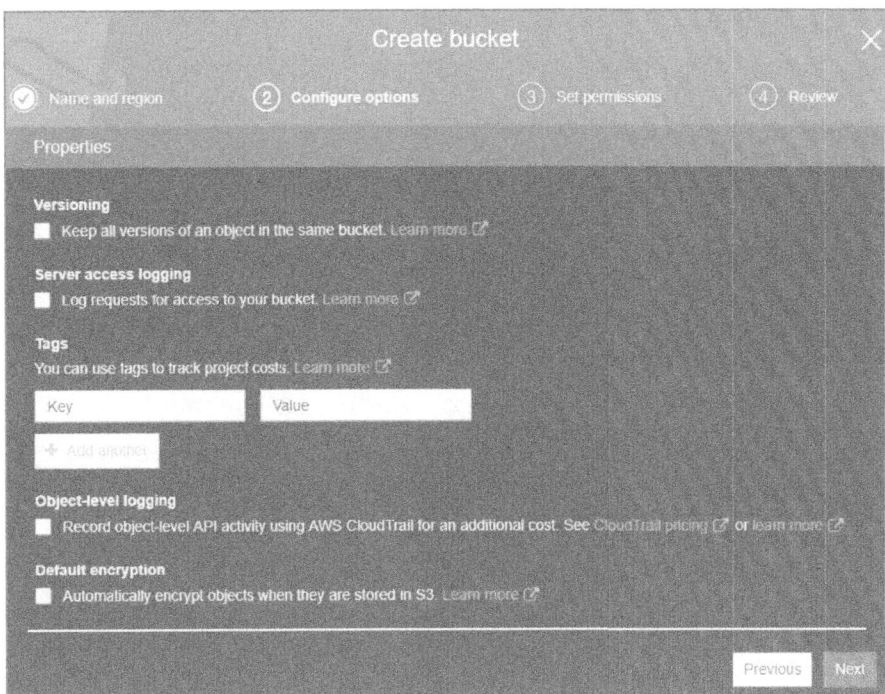

Figure 5.139: Enable S3 server access log - destination bucket - configuration options

In "Set permissions," take the default settings and click "Next."

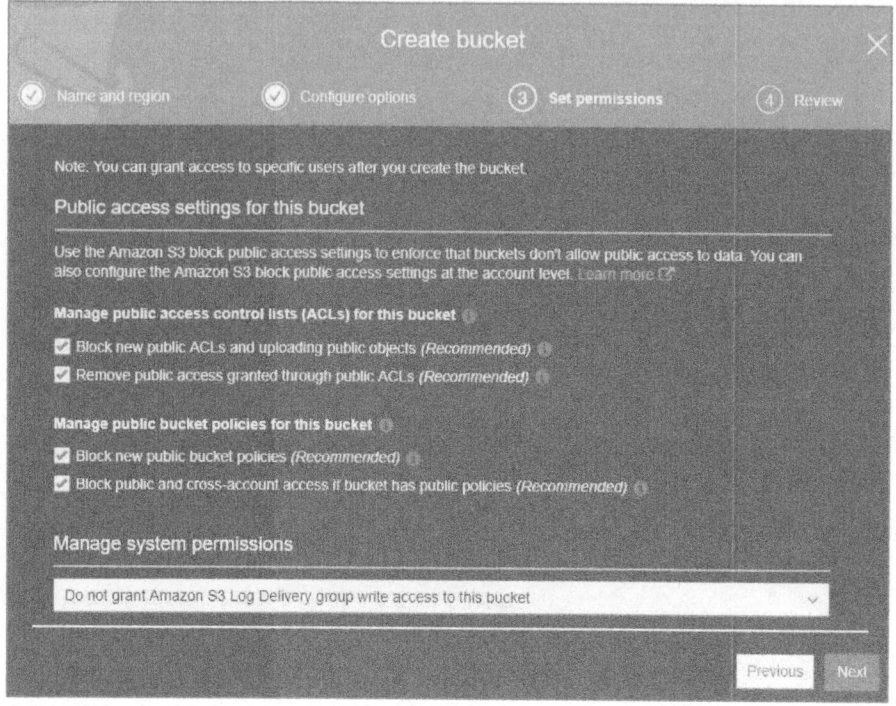

Figure 5.140: Enable S3 server access log - destination bucket - set permissions

Review the settings and click "Create bucket."

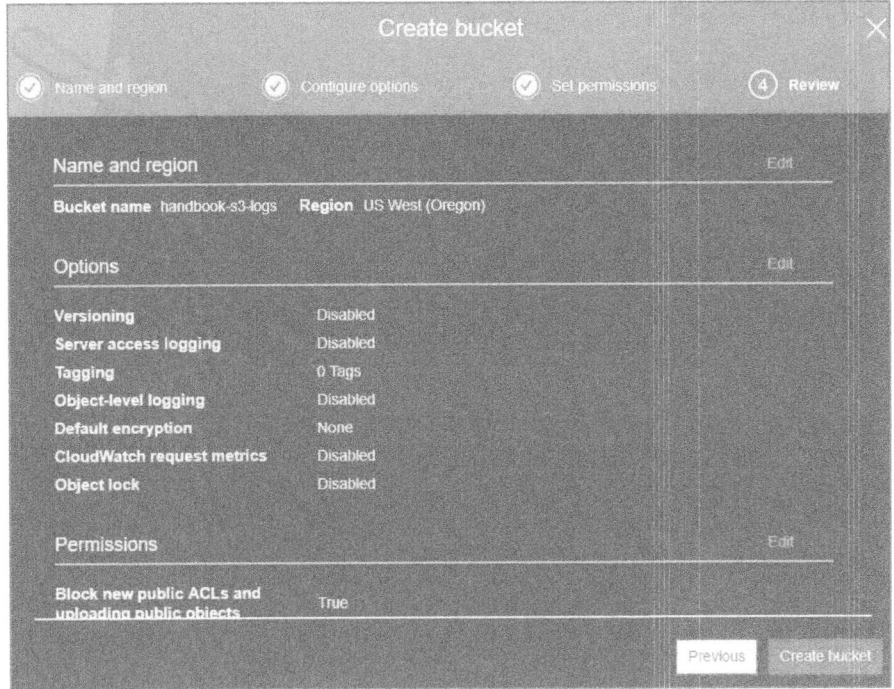

Figure 5.141: Destination bucket - Review

Now you have a new bucket, "handbook-s3-logs", in the region "US West (Oregon)."

5.11.2.2 Enable Server Access Logging

Now go to the bucket "handbook-medical-images" and enable server access logs to log all the access to the objects in this bucket.

Go to the bucket, then "Properties." Click on the box "Server access logging."

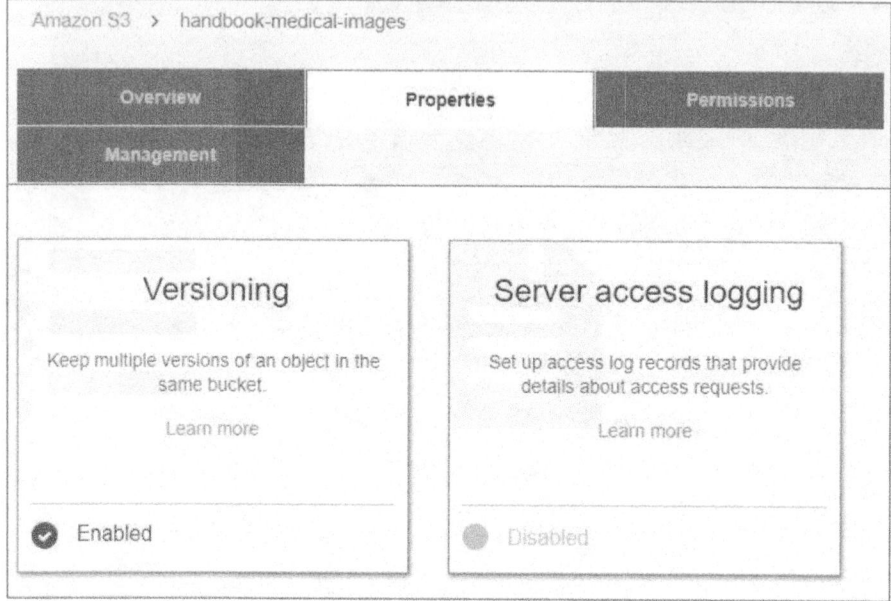

Figure 5.142: Enable server access logging - Source bucket

On the popup screen, select "Enable logging," then select the target bucket "handbook-s3-logs."

You will only see buckets in the same region as the current bucket, "handbook-medical-images." If you don't see your bucket in the dropdown list, please check to see if your bucket is in another region.

Enter the bucket name as the target prefix and click "Save."

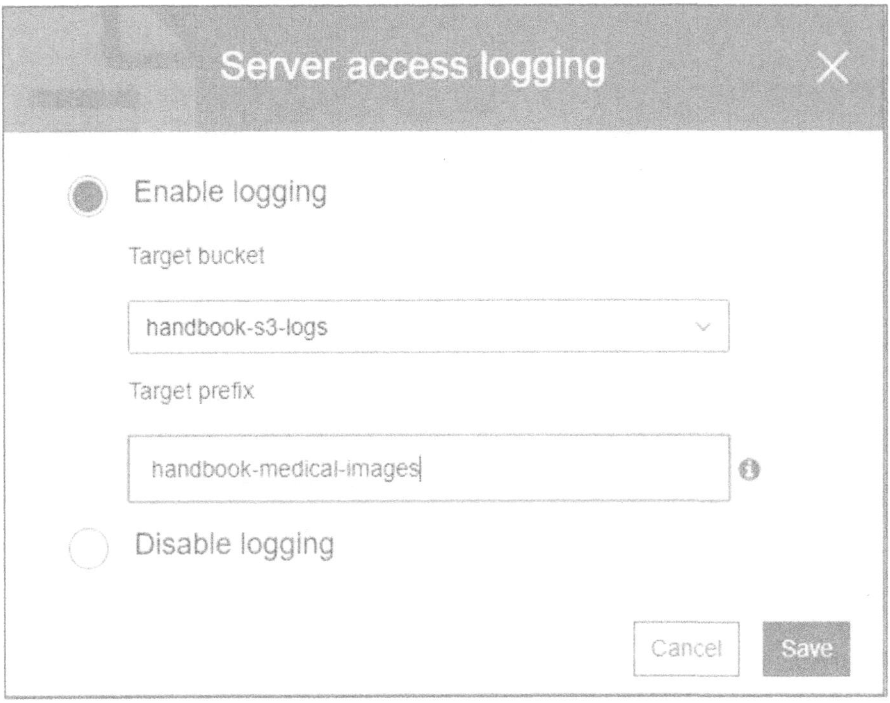

Figure 5.143: Enable server access logging - source bucket - Enable logging

Now you see that server access logging has been enabled.

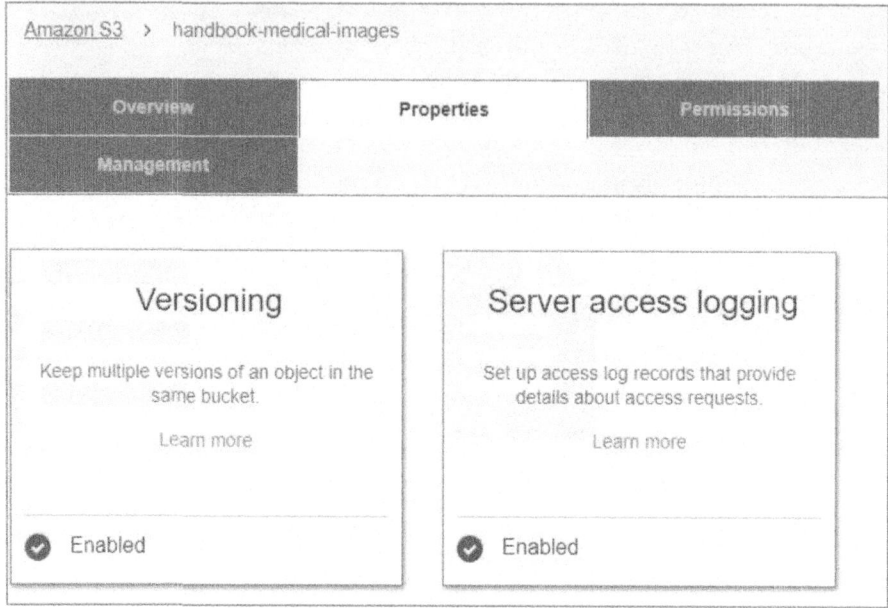

Figure 5.144: Enable server access logging - enabled

Repeat this process to enable server access logging for the other buckets.

After a few minutes, go to your bucket "handbook-s3-logs." You will see the access log files (.txt files) as shown below. As you can see, it is important to specify the prefix using the bucket name while you enable server access logging. This way, the log file has the bucket name in the file name.

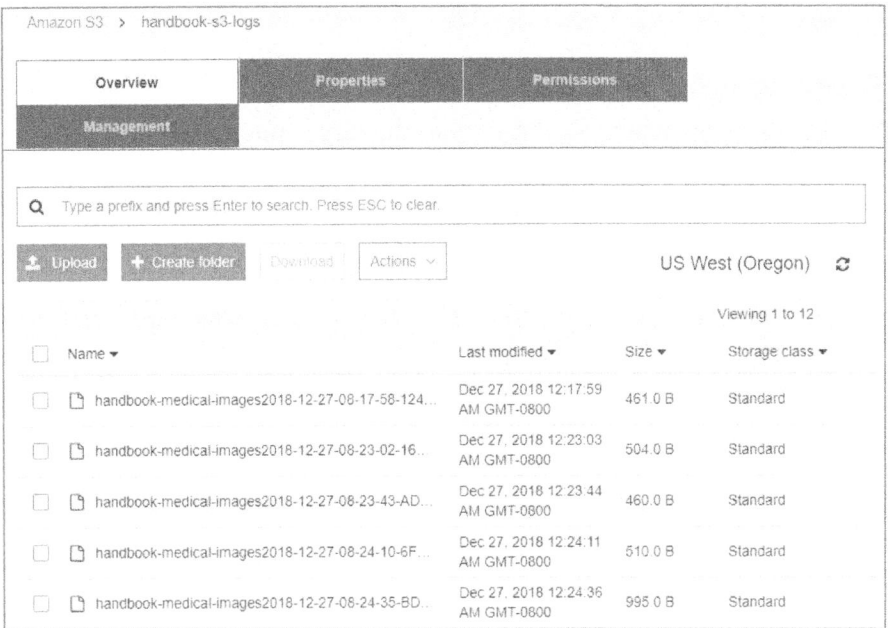

Figure 5.145: S3 server access log files

5.11.2.3 Content of the Access Log File

If you download one of the files and open it, you will see log data such as these (the IP# xx.xx.x.31 has been masked):

> c94c6680840adfbef904539929e860dd7f0489c42d8c107c6afc57601
> b2f1ffc handbook-medical-images [27/Dec/2018:07:39:16 +0000]
> xx.xx.x.31
> c94c6680840adfbef904539929e860dd7f0489c42d8c107c6afc57601
> b2f1ffc 214FB153095935D3 REST.GET.LOGGING_STATUS -
> "GET /handbook-medical-images?logging= HTTP/1.1" 200 - 237 -
> 446 - "-" "S3Console/0.4, aws-internal/3 aws-sdk-java/1.11.467
> Linux/4.9.124-0.1.ac.198.71.329.metal1.x86_64 OpenJDK_64-
> Bit_Server_VM/25.192-b12 java/1.8.0_192" -

Please keep in mind that it may take a few hours or even longer for AWS to deliver the access log files to the target bucket, in this case, "handbook-s3-logs." You may not see your latest access logs.

5.11.3 Use Athena to Query Data in the Server Access Logs

Now let's use Athena to query the logs. Remember, you can create the access reports for many purposes. Here we would like to create reports to help us optimize AWS costs.

Please follow this link to set up AWS Athena:

LINK: Implementation #8: How to Set Up and Use AWS Athena for Cost Optimization

Please note that if your bucket contains many objects and these objects are accessed frequently by your applications or users, your S3 log bucket could grow very quickly. After a year or two, it could grow into several terabytes. In that case, you should archive the log files and save the files into prefixes such as "/year/month/." This process makes retrieving log data faster.

5.11.3.1 Obtain Permission to Run Athena Queries on S3 Access Logs

Similar to how you grant permission to allow Athena to query S3 inventory data, use this link for permission:

LINK: Obtain Permissions to Run Athena Queries on S3 Inventory Data

You need to grant permission to allow Athena to query S3 access log files.

Permission to run Athena actions:

Request AmazonAthenaFullAccess (or a customized one in your organization) to be attached to your user account.

For more granular access, please check the Athena documentation.

Permission to access the Athena query location (S3 bucket), which is the underlying bucket:

Request access to the bucket "handbook-s3-logs." If access is granted by using bucket policy, you can use the following:

```
{
    "Version": "2012-10-17",
    "Statement": [
        {
            "Sid": "forAthenaQuery",
            "Effect": "Allow",
            "Principal": {
                "AWS": "arn:aws:iam::AccountA-ID:user/username"
            },
            "Action": [
                "s3:GetBucketLocation",
                "s3:ListBucket",
                "s3:GetObject"
            ],
            "Resource": [
                "arn:aws:s3:::handbook-s3-logs",
                "arn:aws:s3:::handbook-s3-logs/*"
            ]
        }
    ]
}
```

If permission is granted by using roles or policies, you can add the following statement to your role or policy:

```
{
    "Effect": "Allow",
    "Action": [
        "s3:GetObject",
        "s3:ListBucket"
    ],
    "Resource": [
        "arn:aws:s3:::handbook-s3-logs*"
    ]
}
```

5.11.3.2 Create S3 Access Reports Using Athena Queries

Now that you have all the permission you need, let's query the logs.

Create an Athena table. Copy the following text into Athena Query Editor and modify the table name and bucket location to fit your needs. Run the query to create the table.

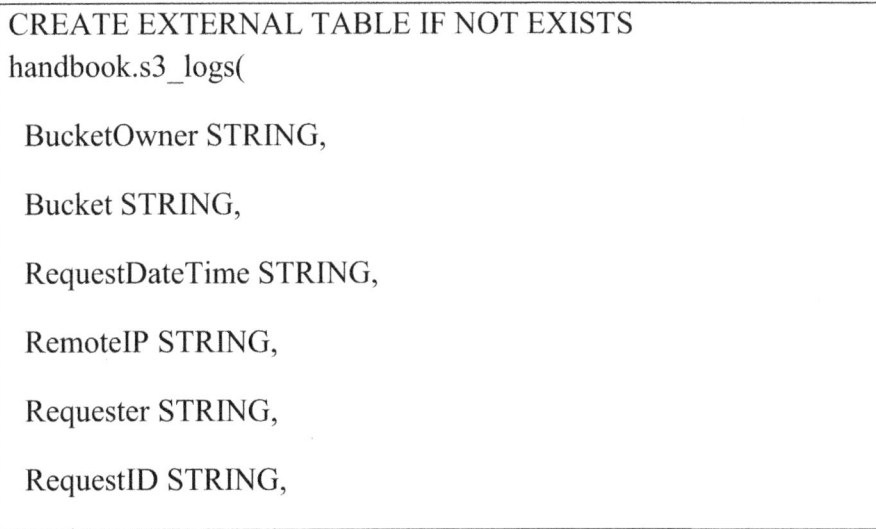

Figure 5.146: Create an Athena table for S3 server access logs

CREATE EXTERNAL TABLE IF NOT EXISTS handbook.s3_logs(

  BucketOwner STRING,

  Bucket STRING,

  RequestDateTime STRING,

  RemoteIP STRING,

  Requester STRING,

  RequestID STRING,

```
Operation STRING,

Key STRING,

RequestURI_operation STRING,

RequestURI_key STRING,

RequestURI_httpProtoversion STRING,

HTTPstatus STRING,

ErrorCode STRING,

BytesSent BIGINT,

ObjectSize BIGINT,

TotalTime STRING,

TurnAroundTime STRING,

Referrer STRING,

UserAgent STRING,

VersionId STRING)
ROW FORMAT SERDE
'org.apache.hadoop.hive.serde2.RegexSerDe'

WITH SERDEPROPERTIES (

'serialization.format' = '1',

 'input.regex' = '([^ ]*) ([^ ]*) \\[(.*?)\\] ([^ ]*) ([^ ]*) ([^ ]*) ([^ ]*)
([^ ]*) \\\"([^ ]*) ([^ ]*) (- |[^ ]*)\\\" (-|[0-9]*) ([^ ]*) ([^ ]*) ([^ ]*)
([^ ]*) ([^ ]*) ([^ ]*) (\"[^\"]*\") ([^ ]*)$'

)LOCATION 's3://handbook-s3-logs/'
```

Open another tab in the Query Editor; run the following query:

```
select *

from handbook.s3_logs

where bucket='handbook-medical-images'

limit 100;
```

You now see a sample of log data:

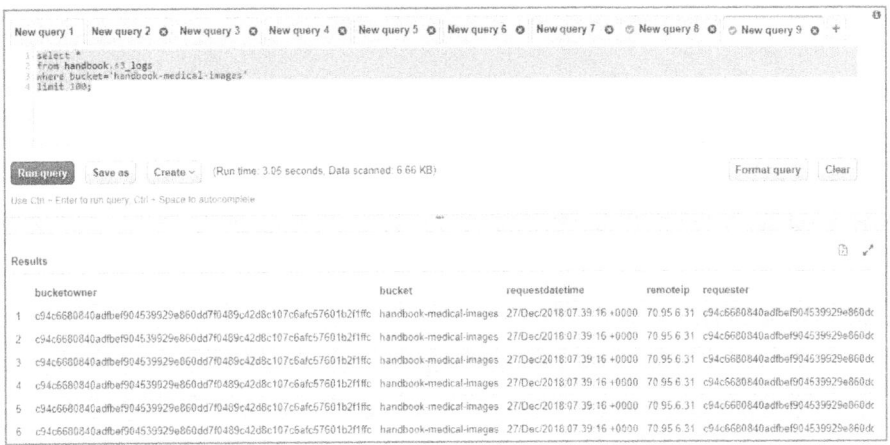

Figure 5.147: Athena query for S3 Access Logs

With the sample data, you can revise your query to obtain the answer to this question: Who has accessed this bucket most recently?

Your query could look like this one:

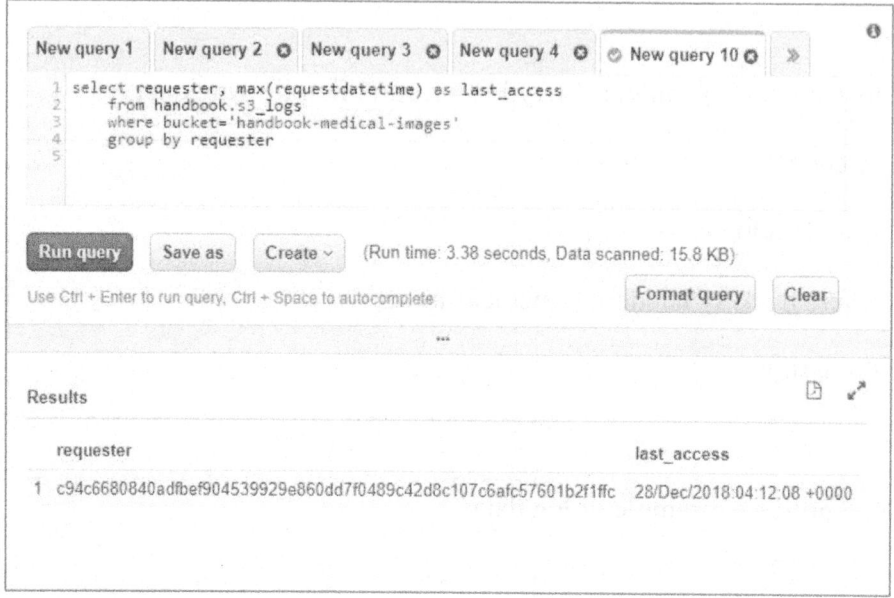

Figure 5.148: Athena query - get last access info for a bucket

The text of the query is as follows:

```
select requester, max(requestdatetime) as last_access

from handbook.s3_logs

where bucket='handbook-medical-images'

group by requester
```

The query results will give you a list of requesters (users or applications) and their last access date.

Figure 5.149: Athena query result - last accessed by user and last accessed date

Now you can dig into further: what were those requesters doing during their last access?

You can run the following query:

```
with
  b as (
    select requester, max(requestdatetime) as last_access_date
    from handbook.s3_logs
    where bucket='handbook-medical-images'
    group by requester
  ),
  a as (
    select *
    from handbook.s3_logs
    where bucket='handbook-medical-images'
  )
select a.*
from a
join b
  on (a.requester=b.requester and a.requestdatetime = b.last_access_date)
where a.bucket='handbook-medical-images'
order by a.requester, a.requestdatetime DESC
limit 100;
```

And the results are as follows:

Figure 5.150: S3 Access Logs with Athena - last access details

The results tell you what those requesters were doing in their last access: what the operation was, what the remote IP# was, what the object key was, the request status, and similar.

With such information, you can decide whether the bucket can be archived or deleted.

5.11.4 Summary

You do not generally rely on S3 access logs to make decisions on cost optimization. Unfortunately, this seems to be the only way to determine who last accessed a bucket or a prefix.

You have many other tools to analyze the log files, such as Suma Logic and other data mining and log file analysis tools.

You can also launch your own EMR cluster to analyze the access logs.

Using AWS Athena gives you another option, especially when you also use Athena for other purposes.

It is not easy to find last access information for S3 buckets and prefixes. The last-access information is critical in the decision-making process to clean up S3 objects. This step-by-step guide suggests one way to move forward.

5.12 Chapter Summary

This chapter presented the total of 10 step-by-step implementation guides. Seven of them could help you reduce your AWS Cloud costs right now.

1. Implementation #1: How to Estimate the Monthly AWS Cost, Save It and Share It
2. Implementation #2: How to Set Up AWS Budget Alerts
3. Implementation #3: How to Implement a Schedule to Start and Stop an EC2 or RDS Instance
4. Implementation #4: How to Implement S3 Lifecycle Policies for AWS Cost Optimization
5. Implementation #5: How to Implement Data Lifecycle Management
6. Implementation #6: How to Tag AWS Resources for Cost Optimization
7. Implementation #7: How to Monitor RI Utilization and RI Coverage

You were also given three bonus step-by-step implementation guides. They are for advanced users who can mine the raw billing data and identify cost-saving opportunities in their own way.

1. Implementation #8: How to Set Up and Use AWS Athena for Cost Optimization
2. Implementation #9: How to Set Up and Use AWS S3 Inventory for AWS Cost Optimization
3. Implementation #10: How to Set Up and Use AWS S3 Server Access Logging for AWS Cost Optimization

The previous three chapters have given you the tools, data and methods to execute your cost optimization strategies.

These step-by-step guides can help you get started. You can dig deeper on your own. You can iterate and improve the process to make it more consistent and more efficient. You can automate the repetitive processes.

Cost optimization is an on-going effort. It is also a team effort. It is everyone's responsibility.

Table of Figures

Figure 2.1: AWS Total Cost of Ownership - TCO Calculator - Inputs............. 23
Figure 2.2 AWS TCO Calculator - Results 24
Figure 2.3 AWS TCO Calculator - Results - Cost Breakdown........................ 25
Figure 2.4: AWS Trusted Advisor Dashboard 33
Figure 2.5: AWS Trusted Advisor - Checklist and recommendations 34
Figure 2.6 AWS bill details by service 38
Figure 2.7 AWS bill details by account.. 39
Figure 2.8 AWS bill details by service - EC2 40
Figure 2.9 AWS bill details by service - S3.. 41
Figure 2.10 AWS bill details by service - DynamoDB 42
Figure 2.11 AWS Cost Explorer - Exploring Cost and Usage 43
Figure 2.12: Launch "My Billing Dashboard." 50
Figure 2.13: Launch Cost Explorer 51
Figure 2.14: AWS Cost Explorer - Main... 52
Figure 2.15: AWS Cost Explorer - Explore Cost & Usage............................... 53
Figure 2.16: AWS Cost Explorer - Filter by Service.. 54
Figure 2.17: AWS Cost Explorer - EC2 Cost 55
Figure 2.18: AWS Cost Explorer - Save as - report name 55
Figure 2.19: AWS Cost Explorer - Saved report 56
Figure 2.20: AWS Cost Explorer - Saved reports.. 57
Figure 5.1: AWS Simple Monthly Calculator - Main..................................... 142
Figure 5.2: AWS Simple Monthly Calculator - EC2 and EBS 143
Figure 5.3: AWS Simple Monthly Calculator - S3 144
Figure 5.4: AWS Simple Monthly Calculator - RDS...................................... 144
Figure 5.5: AWS Simple Monthly Calculator - DynamoDB.......................... 145
Figure 5.6: AWS Simple Monthly Calculator - Portfolio.............................. 147
Figure 5.7: AWS Simple Monthly Calculator - Save and Share Configuration
 148
Figure 5.8: AWS Simple Monthly Calculator - Save and Share Link 148
Figure 5.9: AWS Budget - main 153
Figure 5.10: AWS Budget - Select budget type 153

Figure 5.11: AWS Budget - Cost Budget - Set your budget - name and amount 154
Figure 5.12: AWS Budget - Cost Budget - Set your budget - filter by tag.... 156
Figure 5.13: AWS Budget - Cost Budget - Set your budget - filter by service 157
Figure 5.14: AWS Budget - Cost Budget - Set your budget - amount change after filtering 157
Figure 5.15: AWS Budget - Cost Budget - Set your budget - cost explorer. 158
Figure 5.16: AWS Budget - Cost Budget - Configure alerts 159
Figure 5.17: AWS Budget - Cost Budget - Confirm budget - 1 160
Figure 5.18: AWS Budget - Cost Budget - Confirm budget - 2 160
Figure 5.19: AWS Budge - main - with new budget 161
Figure 5.20: AWS Budget - Detail View 162
Figure 5.21: Usage Budget - select budget type 164
Figure 5.22: Usage Budget - Set your budget - name and amount............. 165
Figure 5.23: Usage Budget - Set your budget - filter by tag 166
Figure 5.24: Usage Budget - Cost Explorer chart 167
Figure 5.25: Usage Budget - Configure alerts.. 168
Figure 5.26: Usage Budget - Confirm budget - part 1 169
Figure 5.27: Usage Budget - Confirm budget - part 2 169
Figure 5.28: AWS Budget - Main 170
Figure 5.29: AWS Budget - Reservation Budget - select budget type 171
Figure 5.30: AWS Budget - Reservation Budget - budget name and threshold 172
Figure 5.31: AWS Budget - Reservation Budget - filter by tag 173
Figure 5.32: AWS Budget - Reservation Budget - configure alerts 174
Figure 5.33: AWS Budget - Reservation Budget - confirm 175
Figure 5.34: AWS Budget - Reservation Budget - main............................... 176
Figure 5.35: Schedule to start and stop an EC2 instance - AWS Instance Scheduler... 179
Figure 5.36: - S3 Lifecycle Policy - Add lifecycle rule................................... 184
Figure 5.37: S3 Lifecycle Policy - Add lifecycle rule - step 1: Name and scope 185
Figure 5.38: S3 Lifecycle Policy - Add lifecycle rule - step 2: Transition...... 186
Figure 5.39: S3 Lifecycle Policy - Add lifecycle rule - step 3: Expiration...... 187

Figure 5.40: S3 Lifecycle Policy - Add lifecycle rule - step 4: Review and Save 188
Figure 5.41: S3 Lifecycle Policy - Add lifecycle rule - result 189
Figure 5.42: S3 Lifecycle Policy - with lifecycle rule - Storage class 190
Figure 5.43: S3 Lifecycle Policy - Add lifecycle rule - Transition to Glacier. 191
Figure 5.44: S3 Lifecycle Policy - Add lifecycle rule - Delete objects after 90 days 192
Figure 5.45: S3 Lifecycle Policy - Add lifecycle rule - all rules 193
Figure 5.46: S3 Cross Region Replication - Create a bucket 194
Figure 5.47: S3 Cross Region Replication - Add rule 195
Figure 5.48: S3 Cross Region Replication - Set source 196
Figure 5.49: S3 Cross Region Replication - Set source 2 197
Figure 5.50: S3 Cross Region Replication - Set destination 198
Figure 5.51: S3 Cross Region Replication - Configure options 199
Figure 5.52: S3 Cross Region Replication - Review and Save 200
Figure 5.53: S3 Cross Region Replication - Rule added 201
Figure 5.54: AWS Bill - EBS costs 204
Figure 5.55: Add target tags to volumes for snapshot lifecycle policy 206
Figure 5.56: Add target tags to volumes 207
Figure 5.57: Lifecycle Manager 208
Figure 5.58: Create a snapshot lifecycle policy - description and target tags 209
Figure 5.59: Create a snapshot lifecycle policy - schedule 209
Figure 5.60: Create a snapshot lifecycle policy - copying tags to snapshots 210
Figure 5.61: Create a snapshot lifecycle policy - IAM role 211
Figure 5.62: Create a snapshot lifecycle policy - success 211
Figure 5.63: List of snapshot lifecycle policies 212
Figure 5.64: Snapshots before snapshot lifecycle policy 214
Figure 5.65: Snapshots created by snapshot lifecycle policy 214
Figure 5.66: New tags in the snapshots created by snapshot lifecycle policy 215
Figure 5.67: AWS Cost Allocation Tags - Activate 220
Figure 5.68: Cost Allocation Tags - Activate "project" and "owner" tags... 221
Figure 5.69: Cost Allocation Tags - Activate - Confirm 221

Figure 5.70: Cost Allocation Tags - results 222
Figure 5.71: Tagging S3 Objects 223
Figure 5.72: Tag EC2 instance during the launch process 223
Figure 5.73: Tagging EC2 instance - Add/Edit tags 224
Figure 5.74: Tagging with Tag Editor - Launch Tag Editor 225
Figure 5.75: Tag Editor - Find resources to tag 226
Figure 5.76: Tag Editor - add or edit tags 226
Figure 5.77: Tag Editor - select multiple resources to tag 227
Figure 5.78: Tag Editor - Tag multiple resources at a time 228
Figure 5.79: AWS Cost Explorer - Group By and Filter by tags 229
Figure 5.80: AWS Cost Explorer - Group by "owner" tag 230
Figure 5.81: AWS Cost Explorer - Group by "owner" tag 231
Figure 5.82: AWS Cost Explorer - Filter by "project" tag 232
Figure 5.83: AWS Cost Explorer - Save your report 232
Figure 5.84: AWS cost Explorer - Save a new report 233
Figure 5.85: AWS Cost Explorer - open the new report 233
Figure 5.86: AWS Cost Explorer - All your saved reports 234
Figure 5.87: - AWS Cost Explorer - Show only untagged resources 235
Figure 5.88: AWS Cost Explorer - Download report data 235
Figure 5.89: AWS Cost Explorer - Saved Reports 238
Figure 5.90: AWS Cost Explorer RI Coverage report 239
Figure 5.91: RI Coverage report - details 240
Figure 5.92: RI Utilization report 241
Figure 5.93: RI Utilization report - RI Recommendations 242
Figure 5.94: Cost Explorer Navigation Menu 243
Figure 5.95: Reservation Summary 244
Figure 5.96: RI Recommendations 245
Figure 5.97: Create a bucket to store billing data 253
Figure 5.98: Create a bucket to store billing data - Configure options 254
Figure 5.99: Create a bucket to store billing data - Set permissions 254
Figure 5.100: Create a bucket to store billing data - Review 255
Figure 5.101: Create an AWS Cost and Usage Report 256
Figure 5.102: Create an AWS Cost and Usage Report - Step 1 - Report content 257

Figure 5.103: Create an AWS Cost and Usage Report - step 2 - Grant Athena access 258
Figure 5.104: Create an AWS Cost and Usage Report - step 2 - The bucket policy 259
Figure 5.105: Create an AWS Cost and Usage Report - step 2 - Delivery options 260
Figure 5.106: Create an AWS Cost and Usage Report - step 3 - review and create 261
Figure 5.107: Create an AWS Cost and Usage Report - Result 262
Figure 5.108: AWS Cost and Usage data in the billing data bucket 263
Figure 5.109: Sample billing data in the CSV file 264
Figure 5.110: Copy the billing data file to its own prefix for query 265
Figure 5.111: Other files related to the billing data: create_table.sql. 266
Figure 5.112: Create an Athena database and table for the billing data.... 267
Figure 5.113: Athena query to get the billing data. 268
Figure 5.114: Download Athena query results from History 269
Figure 5.115: AWS S3 Inventory - sample data 273
Figure 5.116: Set up S3 Inventory - Create bucket 276
Figure 5.117: Set up S3 Inventory - Bucket policy 277
Figure 5.118: Set up S3 Inventory - Add new 278
Figure 5.119: Set up S3 Inventory - Add new - options 278
Figure 5.120: Set up S3 Inventory - Advanced settings 279
Figure 5.121: Set up S3 Inventory - Encryption 279
Figure 5.122: Set up S3 Inventory - Destination bucket policy 280
Figure 5.123: Set up S3 Inventory - result 281
Figure 5.124: Set up S3 Inventory - Inventory file 281
Figure 5.125: Create an S3 Inventory table in Athena 285
Figure 5.126: S3 Inventory -Athena query output 287
Figure 5.127: S3 Inventory - Download Athena query output from History 287
Figure 5.128: S3 Inventory - Athena query for report #1 289
Figure 5.129: S3 Inventory - Verify Athena query output with S3 Metrics. 289
Figure 5.130: S3 Metrics - Total size 290
Figure 5.131: S3 Metrics - Total objects 290
Figure 5.132: Use S3 Lifecycle policy to delete old Inventory data 291

Figure 5.133: S3 Inventory - Destination bucket - Lifecycle rule name 292
Figure 5.134: S3 Inventory - Destination bucket - Lifecycle rule- transitions 293
Figure 5.135: S3 Inventory - Destination bucket - Lifecycle rule - Expiration 294
Figure 5.136: S3 Inventory - Destination bucket - Lifecycle rule - Review.. 295
Figure 5.137: S3 Inventory - Destination bucket - Lifecycle rule - result 295
Figure 5.138: Enable S3 server access log - create destination bucket 300
Figure 5.139: Enable S3 server access log - destination bucket - configuration options 301
Figure 5.140: Enable S3 server access log - destination bucket - set permissions 302
Figure 5.141: Destination bucket - Review 303
Figure 5.142: Enable server access logging - Source bucket 304
Figure 5.143: Enable server access logging - source bucket - Enable logging 305
Figure 5.144: Enable server access logging - enabled 306
Figure 5.145: S3 server access log files 307
Figure 5.146: Create an Athena table for S3 server access logs 311
Figure 5.147: Athena query for S3 Access Logs 313
Figure 5.148: Athena query - get last access info for a bucket 314
Figure 5.149: Athena query result - last accessed by user and last accessed date 314
Figure 5.150: S3 Access Logs with Athena - last access details 316

Index

abnormal spending . 159, 163, 176
Accelerated Computing............. 99
accountabilities 35
administrative costs......... 110, 112
aggregate 57, 281
Agile..................................... 63, 68
alerts 17, 36, 65, 87, 150, 152, 158, 159, 162, 167, 168, 172, 174, 176, 238
Amazon Glacier 28
analyze . 17, 18, 20, 43, 44, 47, 49, 58, 61, 64, 76, 123, 128, 130, 231, 235, 236, 246, 252, 269, 271, 272, 281, 282, 298, 299, 316
Architect for cost...................... 32
Athena .. 18, 58, 59, 115, 116, 123, 246, 247, 252, 257, 258, 264, 265, 266, 267, 268, 269, 270, 271, 272, 273, 281, 282, 284, 285, 287, 289, 291, 295, 296, 308, 309, 310, 311, 313, 314, 316, 317, 318
Aurora 41, 119, 120, 141, 144, 180
automation................. 70, 116, 218
auto-start . 177, 178, 180, 181, 218
auto-stop .. 177, 178, 180, 181, 218
Availability Zone 104, 107, 109
AWS accounts............... 15, 16, 18
AWS bill 26, 32, 37, 38, 39, 40, 41, 42, 49, 81, 109, 134, 204
AWS Organizations 14, 15, 16, 18, 30, 76
AWS pricing 26, 76, 142
AWS TCO Calculator 24, 25
AWS Trusted Advisor 32, 33, 34
backup 65, 66, 70, 79, 182, 193, 197, 200, 205, 274

barriers 37
baseline 36, 46, 48, 62, 95, 96, 135, 136, 149
best practices ... 12, 30, 31, 44, 45, 66, 67, 73, 93, 103
bid 101
Billing and Cost Management console 151, 219
Billing dashboard 152
billing data . 43, 49, 50, 57, 58, 64, 73, 229, 246, 252, 253, 254, 255, 259, 262, 263, 264, 265, 266, 267, 268, 269, 270, 271, 272, 318
billing reports 36
blockers 71
Boto3 .... 22, 57
Bucket Policy 258, 276
Budget 17, 36, 150, 151, 152, 153, 154, 156, 157, 158, 159, 160, 161, 162, 163, 164, 165, 166, 167, 168, 169, 170, 171, 172, 173, 174, 175, 176, 238, 318
budget alert 162, 163, 170
business intelligence tool 49
business outcome 47
business processes 65, 67
Business risk 69
by the progress 47
calculator 22, 25, 141
Calculator. 23, 141, 142, 143, 144, 145, 147, 148, 149
Capacity Multiplier 78, 91, 92
capacity pools 104
CE API 236
change process 37
Change process 37
child account 16

CI/CD pipeline 202
CLI 57, 236, 296
Cloud cost multipliers ... 80, 92, 95
Cloud economics 20, 76
CloudFront 29
CloudWatch alarms 151
Collaboration risk 69
colocation 22, 66, 197
Communication ... 70, 72, 179, 203
compliance 130, 197
Compliance risk 69
Compute Optimized 99
computing ... 26, 39, 48, 64, 65, 73, 77, 100, 116, 135, 204, 217
computing costs 39
Consolidated Billing 15, 16, 107
consolidation 31
Continuous Deployment 21, 66
Continuous Integration 21, 66
Convertible Reserved Instance 98, 99
Convertible RIs 107, 108, 110
corporate policies 66, 72
cost allocation report 220, 233
cost allocation tags 16, 17, 220, 221, 222
cost awareness 31, 65, 67, 82
cost breakdown 24
cost budgets 150
cost components 27, 76
cost estimates 82, 149
Cost Explorer 15, 16, 36, 43, 49, 50, 51, 52, 53, 54, 55, 56, 57, 58, 60, 65, 98, 110, 111, 157, 167, 228, 229, 230, 231, 232, 233, 234, 235, 236, 237, 238, 239, 242, 243, 244, 245, 246, 269
cost optimization 20, 27, 32, 35, 36, 37, 42, 45, 46, 47, 48, 62, 63, 67, 68, 69, 70, 72, 74, 114, 139, 149, 178, 203, 205, 218, 236, 272, 274, 296, 316, 318, 333
Cost optimization .. 37, 70, 72, 319
Cost Optimization Checks 33
Cost Optimization pillar 45, 103
cost optimization strategies 20, 27, 62, 318
Cost Optimization Strategies 30
cost-saving potential 37
create a table 265
Create budget 153, 163, 171
creating a database 247
cron jobs 116
cross-account access 16
cross-functional 63, 68, 82
Cross-Region Replication 193, 195, 196
CRR See Cross-Region Replication
culture 35, 82
Current vs. budgeted 163, 170
Data Lifecycle Management .... 42, 204, See Data Lifecycle Management
Data Management Lifecycle ... 205
Database costs 41
database queries 58, 123, 274, 296
decentralized 35, 120
Dedicated Hosts 97
Deep Archive .. 121, 122, 127, 136
derivative data 65, 70
detached EBS volume 34
development environment 35, 36, 82, 86, 177
disaster recovery 66, 79, 193, 197, 202, 203
DynamoDB .. 29, 41, 42, 106, 115, 141, 142, 144, 145, 147, 178

EBS volumes 28, 32, 42, 141, 143, 217
ebs-snapshot-schedule ..206, 207, 208, 214
efficiency 36, 48
Elastic Load Balancer 104
Elasticsearch Service 115
employee exiting 67
employee on-boarding 67
EMR 115, 116, 316
Enable logging 304, 305
Enterprise Support .112, 134, 135, 331, 332
Environment Multiplier. 78, 89, 90
file types 60
FILTERS 53
finance manager 49
financial commitment 105
Financial risk 70
five pillars 44
Forecast usage 167
forecasted costs 36
forecasted expenditures 17
Forecasted vs. budgeted . 163, 170
frugality 36
General Purpose 99, 100, 204
Github 67
Glacier 28, 58, 61, 62, 121, 122, 127, 128, 136, 165, 182, 183, 190, 191, 197, 198, 200
Glue 115
granular 47, 57, 282, 309
granularity 18, 47
hour multiplier 83
idle 32, 34, 84
in bulk 224
infrastructure code 202
Infrastructure-as-Code 202
Innovation risk 69
IOPS 205

iterate 72, 318
JIRA 68, 71
Kanban 63, 68
Lambda 22, 28, 72, 115, 116, 117, 265, 270
lambda function 177, 178, 181, 296
lessons learned 32, 69, 71, 72
Lifecycle Policy184, 185, 186, 187, 188, 189, 190, 191, 192, 193, 205, 207
load balancers 32, 79
manage costs proactively 67
managed service 252
managed services 41, 96, 114, 115, 116, 136
manifest.json 265
master 30, 68, 71
maximize RI utilization 113
MD5 Checksum 130
measure 20, 46, 47, 48, 62, 76, 218, 237
Memory Optimized 99
metrics 47, 48, 49, 62, 63
milestone 69, 71
mistake 70, 71, 150, 227, 271
month multiplier 85
Multi-AZ 79, 180
Multipart Upload 183
Multiple accounts 31
My Billing Dashboard 50, 220, 255
MySQL 41, 119, 120, 141, 144
NAT instances 16
net present value 127
New employee orientation 31
nonproduction environments ... 66, 90
On-Demand Instances . 32, 66, 96, 97, 100, 101, 102, 104, 105,

106, 108, 109, 110, 113, 114, 136, 141, 270
One Zone IA...121, 122, 123, 124, 284
on-premises 22, 23, 25
open source 22, 67, 119, 120
Oracle 41, 119
owner 17, 34, 70, 214, 219, 221, 222, 225, 226, 227, 229, 230, 231, 234, 251, 270
ownership 21, 35, 85
Parquet 259, 265, 270, 273
pay-as-you-go 21
PostgreSQL 41, 119, 120
price reductions 108, 110
primary AWS account 15, 16
priorities 72
project kickoff 31
proper tagging 178, 205, 224
purchase recommendations 245
Python 22, 274, 287
Quicksight 246, 271
QuickSight 49
RDS 28, 35, 41, 79, 80, 82, 83, 85, 86, 87, 95, 96, 106, 111, 112, 113, 115, 119, 120, 136, 141, 142, 144, 177, 178, 180, 181, 218, 238, 318
RDS instance 82, 87, 95, 178, 180, 181
RDS instances 41, 96, 111, 112, 113, 119, 120, 136, 177, 178, 180, 218, 238
Redundancy Multiplier 79
regular business hours 83, 177
Relational Data Services 41
replicate 182, 195, 196
reservation attributes 99
reservation budget 171, 238
Reservation expiring 243

Reservation Summary 110, 242, 243, 244, 245
Reserved Instance Recommendation 244
Reserved Instances 97, 98, 99, 104, 105, 106, 109, 110, 237
responsibility 37, 319
retention ... 65, 66, 69, 79, 89, 121, 136, 202, 203, 216, 217
RI Coverage ... 111, 112, 113, 171, 174, 237, 238, 239, 240, 245
RI coverage budgets 150
RI instances 73
RI Utilization . 111, 112, 113, 114, 170, 237, 238, 240, 241, 242, 245, 318
RI utilization budgets 150
RI Utilization Report 111
risk mitigations 70
ROI 25, 64, 90, 109
roles and responsibilities 68, 73
S3 Inventory 58, 59, 123, 273, 274, 275, 276, 277, 278, 279, 280, 281, 282, 284, 285, 287, 289, 291, 292, 293, 294, 295, 296, 308, 318
S3 Metrics 289, 290
S3 Select 96, 132, 133, 136
saved report 56
Scheduled Instances 109
Scheduled RIs 107, 109
scope and tenancy 99
SCRUM 63, 68, 71
security auditing 298
Server Access Logging 58, 298, 299, 303, 318
Server Access Logs 58, 308
serverless architecture 96, 114, 116, 136
Simple Email Service 116

Simple Notification Service....115
Simple Queue Service..............115
snapshot lifecycle policy..42, 206, 207, 209, 210, 211, 213, 214, 215, 216, 217
Snowball 129
SNS notifications 104, 151
software 22, 27, 31, 66, 72, 90, 96, 119, 120, 130, 136
Spot Instance Advisor..............104
Spot Instances..32, 45, 66, 96, 97, 98, 100, 101, 102, 103, 104, 114, 136, 270
Spot prices................................101
SQL Server............22, 41, 119, 120
SSD 73, 141, 204
stakeholders..70, 73, 88, 110, 113, 180, 181, 202
stand up meeting 71
Standard IA.....58, 60, 61, 62, 121, 122, 123, 124, 125, 126, 127, 183, 184, 185, 189, 284
Standard Reserved Instance 98
Standard RIs............107, 108, 110
step-by-step guides............45, 318
storage..22, 26, 27, 29, 39, 40, 53, 58, 59, 60, 61, 62, 64, 65, 73, 79, 80, 84, 95, 96, 100, 116, 121, 122, 123, 124, 125, 130, 135, 136, 141, 182, 183, 186, 189, 190, 197, 198, 200, 204, 205, 217, 249, 273, 282, 284, 286, 288, 296, 297
storage class......27, 59, 60, 61, 62, 121, 125, 136, 182, 189, 190, 197, 198, 273, 284, 288
Storage Optimized 99
stories 69, 71

Tableau 49, 246
Tag Editor....... 224, 225, 226, 227, 228, 235
Tagging..... 37, 218, 219, 223, 224, 225, 236
tags 37, 47, 57, 65, 154, 177, 178, 181, 195, 196, 205, 206, 207, 208, 209, 210, 214, 215, 216, 217, 218, 219, 220, 221, 222, 223, 224, 226, 228, 229, 231, 234, 236, 250, 251, 253
target.... 36, 63, 64, 68, 69, 71, 73, 206, 207, 209, 216, 238, 241, 249, 304, 308
TCO 20, 22, 23, 24, 25, 90
third-party tools 67, 104
threshold 159, 162, 163, 167, 171, 172
Time Multiplier 78, 80, 81, 85, 86, 88, 181
time zones 87
top-level prefixes 59, 60
training modules 66
transparency...................... 65, 218
unblended costs........................ 51
underutilized....................... 34, 89
under-utilized............................ 32
under-utilized............................ 64
unnecessary spending 36
usage budgets........................ 150
usage policy 72, 73
User Guide.............................. 139
visibility 31, 35
visualize 16, 49, 236, 246, 271
volume discounts..................... 31
Well-Architected Framework .. 44, 45, 103

The authors and publisher make no representations or warranties of any kind and assume no liability of any kind with regard to the accuracy or completeness of the contents and specifically disclaim any implied warranties of merchantability or fitness of use for a particular purpose. Neither the author nor the publisher shall be held liable or responsible to any person or entity with respect to any loss or incidental or consequential damages caused, or alleged to have been caused, directly or indirectly, by the information or programs contained herein.

Acknowledgments

To our friends Sammy, James, Xiaoxi Wang, and many others who have provided us invaluable feedback and who have helped us in editing of this book.

To Sistemas TMake S.A. de C.V. for providing AWS credits to run the labs and providing the AWS infrastructure for publishing and marketing this handbook.

To the different members of the AWS Enterprise Support team who have helped us learn more about the inner workings of their services and who listened to our needs and incorporated our feedback into AWS Cloud products over time.

Trademarks

"AWS," or Amazon Web Services, is a trademark of Amazon, Inc.

All other trademarks in this book belong to their respective owners.

Some of the contents in this book are in part based on our working experiences with AWS Enterprise Support teams. However, this book is not endorsed by and has no relationship with Amazon, Inc., and its affiliates.

Website for corrections, updates, and complementary materials

The website for this book is:

https://CloudCostOptimizationHandbook.com

Please visit this website for corrections of and updates to this book.

This website also hosts additional resources you may need, such as complementary materials and tips on cost optimization.

Please subscribe to the newsletter for the latest updates.

You can also see how to reach out to the authors on the website.

Ordering Information:

Bulk orders and special discounts are available for quantity purchases by corporations, associations, and others. For details, please visit the website above.

The purpose of this handbook is to share our experiences and knowledge in optimizing and controlling AWS Cloud expenses so that you can do the same.

What is inside:

Cost optimization strategies based on real world experiences and use cases.

Step-by-step implementation guides of cost reduction tactics.

Audience:

AWS Cloud Users: Cloud Practitioners, Software Developers, Solutions Architects, DevOps Engineers, Database Administrators and SysAdmins that use AWS resources.

AWS Billing Managers: Controllers, Accountants and Financial Managers who want to learn how to analyze and control the AWS expenses.

About the authors:

Qinlin Luo: Entrepreneur, Database Administrator, Data Engineer, Financial Analyst with experience in medical devices, biotech, healthcare and financial services industries.

Ernesto Ruy Sanchez: AWS Software Developer, Solutions Architect and DevOps Engineer with experience in automation, development operations and continuous delivery of commercial enterprise software in highly regulated environments.

Made in the USA
Monee, IL
21 April 2023